THE FOUR SEASONS OF
ITALIAN COOKING

*The Four Seasons of Italian Cooking is dedicated
to the many devoted cooks, chefs, farmers, and gardeners
who generously assisted us with their knowledge
and patience. Their devotion to cooking and the fine art of
living in Italy was the inspiration for this project.*

Recipes and text by A. J. Battifarano
Photography and design by Alan Richardson
Design consulting by Nora Negron
Production by Plentyworks, Inc.
Illustrations by Rodica Prato

Time-Life Books is a division of Time Life Inc.

TIME LIFE INC.
President and CEO: George Artandi

TIME-LIFE BOOKS
President: Stephen R. Frary

TIME-LIFE CUSTOM PUBLISHING
Vice President and Publisher: Terry Newell

Vice President of Sales and Marketing: Neil Levin
Director of New Product Development: Teresa Graham
Director of Design: Christopher M. Register
Production Manager: Carolyn Bounds
Quality Assurance Manager: James D. King
Prepress services by the Time-Life Imaging Center.

Special thanks to Susan Derecskey and Susan Stuck.

Library of Congress Cataloging-in-Publication Data
Battifarano, A.J. 1948-
     The four seasons of Italian cooking : harvest recipes from
the farms and vineyards of the Italian countryside / A.J. Battifarano
and Alan Richardson.
            p.   cm.
     Includes index.
     ISBN 0-7835-5328-5
     1. Cookery, Italian. 2. Food habits—Italy.   I. Richardson,
Alan 1956-   . II. Title.
TX723.B335   1998   98-2731
641.5945—dc21   CIP

Books produced by Time-Life Custom Publishing are available at a special
bulk discount for promotional and premium use. Custom adaptations can
also be created to meet your specific marketing goals. Call 1-800-323-5255.

THE FOUR SEASONS OF

ITALIAN COOKING

Harvest Recipes from the Farms and Vineyards
of the Italian Countryside

A. J. BATTIFARANO *and* ALAN RICHARDSON

ABOVE, Gianluca and Claudio Viberti on the front porch with the Sunday morning crowd at Al Buon Padre (see page 25). *RIGHT*, cherries in the Asti market. *BELOW*, Osso Buco con Funghi Porcini *(page 71)*. *BELOW RIGHT*, a sheep used for producing pecorino toscano *(see page 112)*. *FAR RIGHT*, Tajarin al Coltello *(page 28)*.

INTRODUCTION

My love affair with Italian food began long before my first trip to Italy. Once there, however, all that I had eaten previously seemed lackluster in contrast. The first encounter was brief, but my affections for the food grew deeper. I was captivated by the lively, pure, and natural flavors, and how they melded together in perfect harmony; and charmed by a wealth of culinary traditions. From that day forward the Italian kitchen influenced my manner of cooking and eating and my expectations about food. Returning home, my attention focused on re-creating those high-spirited flavors. Many culinary expeditions were to follow as I journeyed to faraway places to sample foods at their place of birth. With each subsequent visit, I grew more familiar with the country. As my own understanding and appreciation increased, the rest of the world developed an infatuation with Italian food as well. The food of Italy has become one of the best loved cuisines in the world, but sadly it appears to be the most misunderstood.

The broad diversity of foods throughout the country and the wide variety of ingredients and cooking techniques, which change from region to region and frequently from one part of a region to another, create a lavish repertoire of dishes. As elsewhere, history, climate, geography, and the politics of the land have influenced the food. Though we Americans refer to the food of Italy as Italian food, Italians themselves identify their food by region, province, or even by small villages. A Neapolitan would tell you his food was *napolitano* and a Tuscan would call his cooking *toscano*. Italian food in reality is made up of many individual cuisines.

In spite of countless differences in ingredients and flavors, a common bond unites the kitchens of Italy's twenty regions. Italians pay careful attention to the selection of ingredients, which they handle in a pure and simple manner. The flavors that result are natural yet powerful. This is what sets Italian cooking apart from all others and is often overlooked when re-creating it outside of Italy. Mediocre ingredients merely produce a disappointing facsimile.

Italians are passionate about their food. They devote a good deal of time to conferring about it, marketing, preparing, and sincerely enjoying it. Many even care enough to nurture and produce it. Eating is a simple pleasure, which, most Italians agree, contributes to a fine quality of life—important enough to cease business for three hours each day to allow for a leisurely lunch.

Over the years I have amassed a treasure trove of information and advice collected throughout Italy from seasoned cooks and culinary artisans, all eager to share their experience and acquired knowledge. I have been instructed on local cooking techniques, the selection of ingredients, and rewarded with heirloom recipes. Those haunting Italian flavors, aromas, and textures are now re-created daily in my own kitchen.

Techniques required practice and repetition, and

learning exactly how to evaluate quality when selecting ingredients took careful study. I followed the cycle of the seasons in Italy and traveled back roads to farms, vineyards, orchards, and kitchen gardens. I sampled foods prepared by those who grew and produced it—the food they have proudly nurtured and use in traditional dishes just as their mothers and grandmothers before them, making slight variations at times to take advantage of modern conveniences but never compromising the results. They rely solely on the generosity of mother nature, using what she provides and when she provides it.

In the pages that follow I will introduce you to many of those generous individuals and offer their advice and recipes. Alan Richardson has brilliantly captured the flavor of each place on film and provides exciting images of cooking techniques, recipes in progress, and local dishes just as they are about to be served. He has visited Italy's markets each season to record the abundance of quality ingredients. I will provide you with basic information on the fruits and vegetables harvested each season as well as the essential ingredients needed for a well-stocked Italian kitchen.

Join us on our journey to uncover the finest Italy has to offer. The seasons have provided the road map as we travel to Piedmont's wine country in autumn for the *vendemmia*, or the wine harvest, arriving in time for the appearance of the highly acclaimed white truffles of Alba. We were introduced to the mystique behind the subterranean fungi and sampled the foods that best complement the grand wines of Piedmont—Barolo, Barbaresco, Dolcetto, Barbera, and Moscato d'Asti—prepared on and near the vineyards by their producers. Later in the season we moved on to the "green heart" of Italy, Umbria, the region landlocked in the center of the country where the mushrooms that grow prolifically find their way into many of its robust dishes.

The home-baked country breads of Tuscany that were prepared for us provide winter kitchens with warmth and a comforting aroma. The fragrance of just-pressed Tuscan olive oil adds character to the boldness of regional winter fare. Traveling on to the northernmost region of Italy, Lombardy, near the border of Switzerland, we sampled the rustic foods of Valtellina. Lush pastures ensure many flavorful cheeses and rich dairy products, and the buckwheat grown at high elevations is used in pasta and polenta.

In spring we explored the merits of Tuscany's famous cheese, *pecorino toscano*, and were offered a taste of the season Tuscan style. We then headed back to Piedmont—this time farther north in the Basso Monferrato region—visiting two farms in the village of Vignale Monferrato in time for the arrival of the season's bounty of artichokes, asparagus, carrots, and strawberries, handled in the traditional Monferrina fashion.

We visited Italy's south in summer and were awed by the massive water buffalo that roam in the provinces of Salerno and Caserta in the region of Campania. They supply milk mainly for the production of *mozzarella di bufala* and for other milk products as well. We looked in on the kitchen of a buffalo farm to learn just how mozzarella should be served. We traveled on to see the breathtaking gardens and orchards clinging to a cliff in the small seaside city of Amalfi. The abundant supply of fruit and vegetables they bring forth are paired with the fruits of the sea to create a lavish summer feast. Finally we toured Italy's lush kitchen garden, the region of Apulia, conferring with a mastermind of the kitchen as she magically transformed the flavorful vegetables of the region into tantalizing summer nourishment in the old-fashioned Apulian style.

For those who have already savored their way through Italy, I hope to help you recapture many memorable moments. For those of you who have not yet eaten Italian food in its native land, I hope to offer you its true flavor, the flavor that for nearly thirty years has continued to charm and delight me.

Buon viaggio e buon appetito!
A. J. BATTIFARANO

MARKETING IN ITALY

The seasons provide the table with variety and excitement. Newly harvested fruits and vegetables ripened to perfection and eaten in their proper season close to their source yield the finest flavor and texture. As an added bonus they offer greater nutritional value and are usually obtained at the lowest price. Quality of this sort is essential to the Italian kitchen. Italians adhere to the rhythms of nature just as we all once did.

Most Italians shop daily, assuring that the ingredients they use are the freshest. They rarely store perishable foods for extended periods. Refrigerators, which are usually small, are used for milk, cheese, yogurt, and eggs. Meat and fish are purchased the day they will be cooked. Produce is eaten the day it is obtained or the next.

Small specialty shops located in cities, towns, and village centers are convenient shopping sources. They present superb quality products and extend professional, courteous service. Meat is purchased from a butcher shop, or a *macelleria*, local-style breads are baked daily at a bread shop, or *panetteria*, and fruit and vegetables, displayed and handled like rare jewels, are sold at a vegetable store, or *frutta e verdura*, where the vendor will handpick for your needs—no touching allowed. After all, they are the experts and their intention is to furnish you with only the best.

Open-air markets are a deep-rooted tradition. Cities and villages have designated market days when a troupe of traveling vendors set up shop in a piazza or city street. The smaller markets may be made up of a dozen or so food and houseware stands while larger ones could include clothing, linens, and antiques. The umbrella-covered stalls sometimes wind through several city blocks. The market is a place to meet neighbors and friends and catch up on local gossip, but more importantly it is where family meals are planned on the basis of the finest ingredients available that day.

There are always several vendors selling fresh fruits and vegetables. Cheese and other dairy products are sold from refrigerated trucks as are both raw and cooked meats. There are vendors who sell cured meats and at least one stall for pickled and preserved condiments—olives, capers, anchovies, pickled peppers and the like—as well as dried herbs, nuts, and dried beans. Markets in rural locations could provide an opportunity for a beekeeper to display his honey or an artisanal cheesemaker to sell his handmade products.

MARKETING AT HOME

Quality does not equate with extravagance. The best ingredients are available to all of us often at prices equal to or less than inferior products. Discerning quality and finding it requires a small investment in time, but the rewards are gratifying.

Shopping for the best quality raw materials requires a skill that must be developed. Employ all of your senses. Use your eyes to conduct a visual inspection: observe the color, size, shape, texture, and finish. Feel for tenderness, crispness, or flexibility. Smell the aroma. It should be pleasing: sweet, flowery, herbaceous, or pungent. Taste whenever possible and ask questions. Well-trained, experienced professionals are eager to offer advice and information.

Specialty shops, such as butcher shops, fish markets, cheese shops, and ethnic markets, often carry products of a higher quality and render more personalized service than large chain supermarkets and are likely to cater to your special needs—provide a particular cut of meat you request, order a certain imported cheese, or fillet the fish you have selected.

The freshest possible produce would of course be that which is home-grown, snipped from the garden and brought directly into the kitchen, but a stunning array of just-harvested vegetables and fruit from small local farms can be obtained at old-fashioned farmers' markets, which are fast sprouting up throughout the country. An increasing demand for better quality, more flavorful vegetables and fruit has inspired many farmers to grow heirloom varieties that are reminiscent of the earthier flavors of the past. Roadside farmstands in rural locations and pick-your-own farms are other options.

Avoid the temptation of both in-season and out-of-season produce that has been shipped long distances, particularly those that are more fragile: tomatoes, apricots, and pears, for instance. Perishable produce must be shipped immature and underripe to withstand the long journey and possible rough handling. They will never develop to their full expectation.

On the following pages entitled, Essential Ingredients, advice is offered to assist you in purchasing the necessary staple ingredients required for a well-stocked Italian kitchen. Included is a directory on Italian cheeses. Consult the beginning pages of each seasonal chapter entitled "In the Seasonal Market" for information that will guide you in your selection of produce. Each vegetable and fruit is listed in the season of its peak availability.

ESSENTIAL INGREDIENTS

MILK PRODUCTS AND EGGS
latticini e uova

The grassy cattle pastures of northern Italy produce richly flavored dairy products—cow's milk, cream, butter, and cheese; the central and southern regions use products made from sheep's and goat's milk. In Campania the milk of water buffalo creates outstanding butter, ricotta, and mozzarella. Small local dairies in the United States make fine quality milk products that can be found in specialty markets and farmers' markets.

Butter, *burro,* should always be unsalted with a sweet creamy flavor. Salt interferes with the flavor of butter and is often used to mask an inferior product. Look for fine quality sweet butter. Wrap butter well to avoid absorbing other flavors and odors and keep it up to one week in the refrigerator or up to three months in the freezer.

Heavy cream, *panna,* when full and rich in flavor, is sublime. Look for heavy cream produced by small local dairies. Avoid ultra-pasteurized cream; it whips poorly and has a dull flavor with a disagreeable aftertaste.

Eggs, *uova,* from farm-raised organically fed hens are far superior to those mass produced by steroid- and hormone-injected hens. Yolks of farm-fresh eggs should be plump and brightly colored; egg whites should be thick and gelatinous. Avoid eggs claiming to be fresh, farm-raised that are runny and flavorless. Purchase eggs from a vendor who has a rapid turnover. Always keep eggs refrigerated.

Mascarpone is often referred to as a cheese, though it technically does not fall into the cheese category. Mascarpone is made from cow's milk cream that has been drained of moisture. It should be luxuriously rich, with a texture like soft butter and a taste like fresh sweet cream. Both imported and domestic mascarpone come in small containers that can be found in refrigerated dairy cases or the cheese department of specialty markets and supermarkets.

Ricotta, which means "recooked" in Italian, is a cheese by-product made from the whey that remains after the production of cheese; it is not classified as a cheese. Ricotta produced in the United States is not always made from whey. Industrially produced ricotta that comes in freshness dated plastic containers is often made from either whole cow's milk or part skim cow's milk. It is usually bland, wet, and grainy. Ricotta should have a sweet, nutty flavor, with a texture that is dry and light-as-air. The best choice for ricotta is one made by a small dairy or by the cheese section of a specialty market. Sheep's milk and goat's milk ricotta also produced by small dairies are worth trying if available. It is best to use ricotta immediately, though it can be kept tightly covered in the refrigerator for one or two days.

CHEESE
formaggio

The extraordinary cheeses produced throughout Italy reflect rich gastronomic traditions that have endured for centuries. Many Italian cheeses are available in the United States and can be found at specialty markets and cheese shops. Cheese should be stored in the refrigerator, tightly wrapped in plastic. In order to experience its full flavor and proper texture serve cheese at room temperature.

Casera Valtellina is produced in the Alpine valley of Valtellina in the region of Lombardy, where traditional dairy techniques still prevail. Casera is used prominently in several of the classic dishes of the region—melted with buckwheat pasta and vegetables, known as *pizzoccheri* (see page 95) and batter dipped then fried to create an antipasto called *sciatt* (see page 94). This semi-hard cheese, produced from partly skimmed cow's milk, has a full nutty flavor. It comes in large flat wheels, which are cut into pie-shaped wedges.

Fontina d'Aosta is a grand Italian cheese produced in the Alpine region of Val d'Aosta in Piedmont and is made from cow's milk. Fontina is not only a fine eating cheese, it is considered one of the best cooking cheeses and is the principal ingredient in the Piedmontese specialty *fonduta* (see page 71), a creamy cheese sauce similar to a Swiss fondue. Fontina is produced in large round wheels. It has a thin toffee-colored rind and a semi-firm buff-colored interior that is mildly earthy and herbaceous in flavor. Fontina has many imitators but none can match its superb quality. The authentic Fontina d'Aosta can be identified by the imprint of a mountain in the center of the wheel with the name Fontina written across it.

Gorgonzola is the true sweetheart of Italian cheeses. This blue-veined cow's milk cheese is produced within designated areas of Lombardy and Piedmont. Gorgonzola comes in two versions—*gorgonzola dolce*, also known as sweet gorgonzola, and *gorgonzola naturale*, or aged gorgonzola. The dolce is a young cheese with a creamy color and texture, mildly sweet with a gentle tang. The more assertive aged gorgonzola is whiter in color and firmer in texture with a piquant flavor. While both are considered superb eating cheeses, they are often used in pasta sauces or served with steaming polenta.

Grana Padano is classified as a *grana*, a grainy-textured hard cheese suitable for grating. It could be considered a cousin to Parmigiano-Reggiano. This cow's milk cheese, which comes from the Po Valley of northern Italy, is aged a minimum of six months. Grana Padano is similar in appearance to Parmigiano. It has a golden straw color with a flaky texture, and is produced in large drum-shaped wheels stamped with its name. Grana Padano has a gentle, nutty flavor. Use it freshly grated with pasta, risotto, or soup. It can also be shaved over beef *carpaccio*.

Mozzarella. See page 148.

Parmigiano-Reggiano has been called the king of Italian cheeses. There is simply no finer cheese for eating or cooking. Parmigiano-Reggiano, often just called Parmigiano, is considered a grana, a grainy-textured hard cheese, suitable for grating. Production of Parmigiano is restricted to parts of Emilia-Romagna and a small section of Lombardy. It is made only from the first of May through mid-November, when the cows graze on green pastures, and must be aged a minimum of 14 months. Parmigiano has a straw-colored interior flecked with tiny crystals which create a texture that is smooth and crackly. The rind is a darker shade of straw. Its identifying feature is the name Parmigiano-Reggiano stamped repeatedly around the large wheel. It has a flavor that is mellow and nutty. Don't be fooled by imitators; other cheeses with similar names don't come close to the quality of Parmigiano-Reggiano. As an eating cheese, Parmigiano is a suitable accompaniment to fresh fruit, though it can stand on its own with a glass of sparkling white wine or an aged red. When cooking, it can be sprinkled into pasta, risotto, polenta, soups, and stuffings. Always grate Parmigiano-Reggiano just before serving.

Pecorino Toscano. See page 112.

Pecorino Romano is a hard, aged sheep's milk cheese produced near Rome and on the island of Sardinia. It has a creamy white interior and exterior, often covered with a protective black coating. Pecorino romano is a sharp, salty cheese with a bit of a bite. It is used primarily as a grating cheese, often sprinkled onto pasta, over soups, and blended into stuffings. Pecorino romano should always be grated just before serving.

Robiola Piemonte is produced in the region of Piedmont from sheep's, cow's, or goat's milk, or any combination of the three, enriched with cream. It is a soft, milky-white, rindless fresh cheese with a mousse-like texture. Robiola piemonte has a buttery flavor with a subtle tang. Several versions are found in the United States including those packaged under the brand names of Annabella la Morbida, Robiola Osella, and Robiola di Roccaverano. They are often shaped like small cubes, each wrapped in paper, and sealed in plastic trays. As an eating cheese robiola piemonte can be served at breakfast with crisp toasted bread or fresh fruit, or for lunch or dinner with a tossed salad. In Piedmont it is often used as a cooking cheese.

Stracchino, sometimes called Stracchino di Crescenza or simply Crescenza, is produced in the region of Lombardy. It is pure white inside and out with a soft edible rind. Stracchino comes in either small loaf shapes or paper-wrapped slabs. This soft cheese, made from cow's milk, has a milky flavor with a noted tang. Stracchino is a fine eating cheese, favorably enhanced when served with fresh fruit. It is sometimes used as a cooking cheese—popular in Liguria as a topping for focaccia (see page 118). This very young cheese should be consumed within one or two days.

Swiss Emmental, which comes from the valley of the Emme River in Switzerland, plays a small but significant role in the kitchen of Piedmont in spite of the abundance of fine cheeses produced within that region. Emmental is often referred to as Swiss cheese, but don't confuse this well-made Alpine cheese with the processed deli version. Emmental is produced from the milk of cows that graze in lush Alpine pastures. The butter-colored interior filled with holes gives Swiss emmental its distinctive appearance. Authentic Swiss emmental is produced in large wheels clearly stamped with the name Switzerland. It has a distinctive nutty-sweet flavor. Emmental can be added to salads and stuffings or melted in steaming soups.

Taleggio is primarily an eating cheese but it is used on occasion for cooking. This soft-textured high-fat cow's milk cheese produced in the northern part of Lombardy is easily identified by its eight-inch square shape and reddish rind. When allowed to ripen this cheese becomes soft and buttery in flavor with a subtle tartness. It is outstanding with fresh fruit and an aged red wine.

CURED MEATS
salumi

Fine quality domestic products as well as some imported from Switzerland provide excellent alternatives when cured meats produced in Italy are not available. They can be found in Italian markets and some specialty supermarkets.

Bresaola is a salt-cured, air-dried filet of beef produced in the Alpine valley of Valtellina in northern Lombardy. The delicately flavored meat is generally served thinly sliced as an antipasto. Bresaola imported from Switzerland is available in the United States.

Capocollo is a boned and rolled shoulder of pork, preserved with salt and seasoned with black pepper and spices. This savory cured meat from southern Italy is served thinly sliced as an antipasto and is often used as an ingredient in cooked dishes. A similar product called coppa, used in Italy's central regions, has a milder flavor. Domestically produced versions of capocollo and coppa are available in the United States.

Prosciutto is an aged, air-dried, salt-cured ham. It is more commonly known in Italy as *prosciutto crudo*, or raw ham, and is produced in many parts of the country. Prosciutto from Parma in Emilia-Romagna, from San Daniele in Friuli, and from Carpegna in the Marches are considered the finest. Though each one is slightly different, these are hams of silky texture with full sweet flavor. Their success is attributed to refined techniques, clear sweet air, and gentle breezes. All are available in the United States and are recommended over any other imported or domestic prosciutto. Using the finest quality prosciutto is imperative whether for eating it raw or for cooking. Prosciutto is best eaten soon after purchasing, but if well wrapped and refrigerated it can be kept for one or two days.

Pancetta is a cured pork product made from the same cut as bacon, but the similarity ends there. Pancetta is cured with salt, seasoned with crushed black peppercorns and spices, rolled and tied like salami, then air dried. American-style bacon is a smoked product and should not be substituted. Diced and sautéed, pancetta functions as the starting point for many cooked dishes—soups, stews, sauces, and stuffings. In Italy pancetta is often sliced and added to a mixed platter of salumi for an antipasto. A domestically produced version is available in the United States.

Speck is an Austrian-style smoke-cured, aged ham. It has always been an important product in the northern regions of Italy, particularly Alto-Adige, but it has gained popularity in the central regions of the country as well. Speck adds enormous flavor to pasta sauces and sauerkraut and when thinly sliced it can be served as antipasto. Speck has also become popular as a filling for *panini*, or small sandwiches, and as a topping for pizza.

PANTRY
la dispensa

Fine quality pantry products can be found in specialty markets and supermarkets. Mail order is a good alternative when products are difficult to find locally (see Mail Order Sources, page 189). Most pantry items ship well and the fine results are worth the small effort and shipping cost. Pantry items should all be stored in a cool, dry location shielded from direct sunlight.

Anchovies, *acciughe,* packed in sea salt, called *acciughe sotto sale,* are the finest available. They are meaty with a delightful briny flavor and are surprisingly less salty than those preserved in oil. The anchovies are packed whole with their heads removed and must be cleaned and filleted, a rather simple process. First rinse the anchovy under cold running water to wash away the surface salt. Split the anchovy open by inserting your fingertips into the stomach cavity. Separate the two halves; the backbone will remain attached to one side. Gently pry the backbone from the flesh and pull it away removing the tail. Rinse each fillet and pat dry with paper towels. Leave the remaining anchovies in the tin. Top them with a fresh layer of coarse sea salt and seal the tin with plastic wrap and store it in the refrigerator. Properly stored, the remaining anchovies should last for several months. Salt-packed anchovies come from Sicily in tins weighing slightly over a pound. Avoid purchasing them loose.

Anchovy fillets preserved in pure olive oil do not have the same delicate flavor and firm texture as the salt-packed ones, but those in jars from Sicily tend to be meatier and better than those in small tins.

Bread crumbs, *pangrattato,* are used as a stuffing for vegetables, meat, and poultry; as a crisp coating when deep-frying; and as a crunchy topping for casseroles or vegetables. To make bread crumbs save bits and pieces of leftover unseasoned firm-textured bread made from white flour. Allow the bread to dry completely in a brown paper bag or toast it lightly in the oven. Process small chunks in a food processor or blender until finely ground. If a very fine texture is desired, strain the crumbs through a sieve to eliminate larger pieces. Keep bread crumbs in the pantry tightly sealed in a jar or tin. Avoid commercially produced bread crumbs, particularly the seasoned variety, they are often stale and could contain undesirable ingredients.

Capers, *capperi,* add an unexpected burst of flavor and texture to salads, stuffings and sauces. They are tiny flower buds from a bush that grows freely in the Mediterranean. Those preserved in sea salt are best; they have a natural pungent taste and a crisp texture. Capers pickled in a vinegar brine are often soggy and the flavor of vinegar can be undesirably intrusive. Salt-packed capers come in either small glass jars or cellophane packets. Leave any unused capers in the salt, tightly sealed in the refrigerator up to 3 months. Use less salt when seasoning a dish with salt-packed capers.

Cornmeal, *polenta,* is a staple throughout most of northern Italy and often appears in the central regions as well. Polenta is the Italian name for both cornmeal and the thick, creamy porridge made from it. Polenta is available in fine, medium, or coarse grinds. The coarser textures make a stiffer polenta. Stone-ground cornmeal purchased directly from a mill produces extraordinary polenta. Cornmeal can be kept in a cool, dry location in a sealed container up to one month or in the freezer up to six months.

Dried beans and lentils, *fagioli e lenticche,* add excitement and variety to Italian menus year round. The freshness of dried beans is important. They should be less than two years old in order to cook evenly and hold their shape. Old, stale beans, even after long soaking, will never cook properly. Beans often sit in warehouses and on market shelves well beyond their prime. Look for a source that has a fast turnover. Purchasing direct from a grower is always a good option; check your local farmers' market. Store dried beans in a cool dry location tightly sealed in a jar for no longer than 1 year.

Dried herbs, *erbe secche,* can often fill in when fresh are not available. Dried oregano (often preferred over fresh in parts of southern Italy), marjoram, sage, thyme, bay leaves, and tarragon are all satisfactory when used discreetly. However, not all dried herbs are recommended. Parsley, basil, rosemary, and mint are best avoided. When substituting dried herbs for fresh, half to one third the amount is sufficient. Rub the dried herbs with the palms of your hands to release their fragrant oils.

Dried porcini mushrooms, *funghi porcini secchi,* impart remarkable flavor to sauces, soups, braised dishes, and risotto. The characteristic woodsy flavor of porcini mushrooms *(Boletus edulis)* is pleasantly intensified when dried. When fresh porcini are not available, or are too costly, consider dried porcini, though dried porcini cannot be substituted for fresh in all cases. Most dried porcini are sold in cellophane packets or bags; their quality can vary greatly so examine them well. Look for large pieces, preferably a larger percentage of caps than stems. Darker mushrooms are often more flavorful but not if extremely dark. Never buy porcini with lots of tiny holes, a sign of larvae infestation. Store the porcini tightly sealed in a glass jar or plastic container in a cool, dry cupboard (the refrigerator will do if necessary). Properly stored, porcini can be kept for years. As a matter of fact, their flavor is often heightened.

Dry pasta, *pasta secca,* is machine made on an industrial level from hard durum wheat flour, or semolina. When combined with water the semolina produces a firm pasta that retains a pleasant bite when cooked al dente. Dry pasta is in no way inferior to fresh pasta, called *pasta fresca.* The two products are distinctly different and should be handled accordingly. Dry pasta is always paired with sauces that measure up in character—hearty meat-based sauces or olive oil-based vegetable and seafood sauces sometimes seasoned with garlic and spicy chili pepper. Imported Italian dry pasta, sold in boxes under various brand names, produces excellent results when properly cooked and is the only dry pasta recommended.

Extra virgin olive oil, *olio extra vergine d'olive,* is produced throughout the central and southern regions of Italy and a few small pockets of the north. Tuscany is considered to produce the finest olive oil, but excellent oils come from other regions as well. The characteristics and quality of olive oil, like wine, are determined by soil, climate, and weather as well as the variety of olives, the ripeness at the time of harvest, and the method used in picking the fruit— handpicked, mechanically picked, or gathered after the olives have fallen to the ground. The method used to press olives is another essential factor in the quality of the oil.

The finest olive oils are produced on small estates using traditional methods. Olives are handpicked slightly underripe and are dried for two or three days to reduce their water content. The olives are brought to a local *frantoio*, or olive mill, where they are cold pressed between granite millstones into a thick paste. The paste is spread onto hemp mats that are sandwiched together between metal disks and pressed to extract the oil. The oil is transferred to a large centrifuge which spins out the natural water. This labor-intensive method produces the finest results and explains the very high price of estate-bottled extra virgin olive oils.

Commercially produced olive oil is pressed between steel plates or processed with chemical extractors. The steel presses become hot from friction, which heats the oil and destroys the flavor.

Extra virgin olive oil, the highest grade of olive oil, is made from the first pressing of the olives and has the least amount of oleic acid. The lower the acid the more full flavored and aromatic the oil. In order for an oil to be labeled extra virgin it must contain less than 1% acidity. Virgin olive oil, which is the next category, can have a maximum of 2% acidity. Pure olive oil is often produced from inferior oils that have been blended then chemically rectified and deodorized.

When selecting an olive oil, extra virgin olive oil stands out because it functions not only as an excellent cooking oil, but as a condiment complementing other ingredients while adding its own unique flavor and character. Personal preference is an important factor. When possible taste the olive oil before purchasing. Select one that appeals to your palate and is appropriate to your needs. Like wine, the character of certain olive oils will best complement certain foods.

Rustic, full-flavored olive oils are generally green in color and are usually produced in Tuscany, Umbria, the Marches, Lazio, and southern Italy. They are best when used as a condiment served at the table to drizzle over hearty full-flavored foods.

Fruity, herbal flavored olive oils are usually golden in color and are produced in Liguria and Lake Garda in northern Italy. They are excellent drizzled over more delicate dishes.

Light-flavored, less expensive extra virgin olive oils are appropriate when sautéeing and frying. Extra virgin olive oil is considered the best oil for frying not only for the flavor it imparts but because it has a high smoking point.

When purchasing fine quality olive oil beware of bargain prices. Purchase olive oil from a reliable source that has a good turnover. Be sure the vendor is properly storing his oils. At home olive oil should always be stored in glass decanters or bottles, never tins, which will impart an undesirable metallic flavor. Keep olive oil unrefrigerated in a cool dark place shielded from direct light. The full flavor of extra virgin olive oil diminishes as it ages, and it should be used within one year of production.

Honey, *miele,* is one of the oldest sweeteners known to man. There are more than three hundred varieties throughout the world including lavender, almond blossom, rhododendron, thyme, chestnut, Scottish heather, orange blossom, acacia, and raspberry blossom, just to name a few. The color, texture, and flavor of honey is determined by the nectar's source though it does not reflect its flavor—rosemary honey does not taste like rosemary, for example—and honeys derived from the same kind of flower but grown in different geographical locations can vary both in texture and flavor. Some honeys may be naturally thin and syrupy, while others may be thick, slightly crystallized, or even opaque. Each characteristic adds to the uniqueness of the variety. Keep in mind, the darker the honey, the more full flavored it will be. These varietal honeys have more character than commercially produced honey and are considerably more costly. The commercial variety that is simply labeled as honey is made from clover honey that has been processed to be consistent in flavor, color, and texture.

Rice, *riso,* in Italy, is generally of the short-grained variety, of which there are several types. It is used by Italians not only in the preparation of risotto but in salads, soups, stuffings, and a plenitude of pastries and desserts. Arborio is an excellent rice to use for any Italian preparation. It is by far the most widely used and abundantly available rice for risotto. It is classified as a superfino, the classification for a large plump grain. Risotto requires a rice that cooks up creamy while individual grains remain firm. Carnaroli, also classified as a superfino, is considered supreme for risotto. While preferable, it is not as easily available and tends to be more costly than Arborio.

Sea salt, *sale marino,* is a natural product derived from evaporated sea water and has a fuller flavor than ordinary table salt. It will enhance cooked dishes and add sparkle when used as a table salt. Sea salt, available in both fine and coarse grinds, should be used more discreetly than other salts.

Canned plum tomatoes, *pomodori pelati,* can be substituted in sauces, soups, and stews when fresh vine-ripened tomatoes are out of season. Italian San Marzano whole plum tomatoes, grown and canned near Naples, are the finest canned tomatoes available. The San Marzano tomato is prized as a plump, meaty tomato that ripens evenly and peels easily. When canned, the peeled tomatoes remain firm and have a sweet natural tomato flavor. Many brands are available but unfortunately quality varies. Try several before deciding on a favorite. Look for a tomato that softens and thickens quickly when cooked and is pleasantly sweet yet slightly acidic.

Tomato paste, *concentrato di pomodoro,* can add a touch of flavor and color to a sauce or soup. It should always be used discreetly. Imported Italian tomato paste has a fuller, fruitier flavor than the domestic kind and is conveniently available in tubes. Squeeze out the desired amount and store the tube in the refrigerator up to 3 months.

Wine vinegar, *aceto,* plays an important roll in the Italian kitchen—in sweet-and-sour sauces and marinades, for pickling, and for dressing salads. Today, there are many wine vinegars to choose from. A good wine vinegar must first begin with a good wine.

The wine is poured into a wooden barrel that already contains previously made vinegar. As the wine naturally converts to vinegar, some of the vinegar is drained off, more wine is added, and the process goes on and on. This natural procedure takes from one to six months for the vinegar to properly develop. Some producers will then continue aging their vinegar in wood for many years. Wood aging mellows and matures vinegar just as it does fine wine.

These natural vinegars differ greatly from the industrially produced vinegars that line supermarket shelves. Some vinegars can be processed in as little as one day using a high-heat method; the end result is a vinegar lacking flavor and character.

The label of a good quality wine vinegar should identify the wine it was made from and where the vinegar was produced. Naturally produced wine vinegar should be made from only one hundred percent wine; it should not contain preservatives or additives of any sort (keep in mind some wines do contain sulfites). Whether selecting a young vinegar or one that is more mature is a matter of personal preference. Nonetheless, a naturally processed wine vinegar, domestically produced or imported, is the best choice. Good quality wine vinegars can be found in a wide range of prices from very reasonably priced to more costly longer aged varieties.

FRESH PRODUCE
frutta e verdure

Fresh fruit and vegetables are essential to the Italian kitchen and are best when used in their proper season, purchased from local producers. For information on selecting seasonal produce see the entries under the headings In the Seasonal Market; for autumn see page 19, for winter see page 75, for spring see page 111, and for summer see page 145. These lists are by no means exhaustive but serve as a guide to the produce highlightled in the recipes of each chapter.

COMPOSING AN ITALIAN MEAL

Though the flavors and dishes may change from one region of Italy to the next, the sense of balance and harmony that is achieved in a well-composed Italian meal never falters. Each element of the meal serves as a separate course and each course acts as a prelude to the next. Not all meals are multi-course events, but each is carefully constructed so that every dish complements every other.

Antipasto is the first course to appear but it is not considered the first course of the meal. In Italian antipasto means "before the meal." Antipasti are one or more small plates of food intended to stimulate the appetite and prepare the palate for the courses that follow. It could be a simple plate of thinly sliced prosciutto or a more elaborate savory custard served with an appropriate sauce. In the regions of Piedmont and Apulia the antipasto course sometimes includes as many as eight or ten different plates. Antipasto is often skipped in a less formal meal. The first course, or *primo piatto,* then follows. This could be a bowl of soup, pasta, or risotto. The portion size is moderate since a second course, *secondo piatto,* follows. Meat, fish, poultry, or game are the common choices for secondo piatto but a seasonal vegetable, a wedge of grilled cheese, or a frittata could be a less filling alternative. The vegetable course, or *contorno* is served alongside the secondo piatto. Either a warm or cold vegetable might be offered. A salad would be the more likely choice when the secondo piatto is grilled or fried. Cheese or fresh fruit are to be expected as the next course. Special occasions might then warrant a dessert course, or *dolce*. A tiny cup of freshly brewed strong black coffee is served after the dolce, never with milk as it would be much too rich after such a complete and satisfying meal.

AUT

The flavors that speak of Italy are
the flavors of autumn—cardoons,
wild mushrooms, and white truffles;
apples, figs, and grapes; hazelnuts;
and full-bodied red wines.

Vegetables
verdure

Cardoons, *cardi,* a member of the thistle family like the artichoke, are cultivated for their stalks. Cardoons are silvery-gray in color with flat, wide, ribbed stalks like heads of celery. They are prized for their delicate flavor, reminiscent of artichokes. The small and medium stalks are the most tender and best to use when serving raw. The interior of the stalks, when cut, should be solid and fleshy, not hollow. Wrap and store cardoons in the refrigerator up to 4 days. Cardoons imported from southern Italy can be found in Italian markets from mid-autumn through early spring. Domestically grown cardoons can sometimes be found at farmers' markets between late spring and late fall.

Cauliflower, *cavolofiori,* a member of the Crucifera or mustard family along with broccoli, cabbage, and turnips, has a large white head of tightly closed, compact florets. The head of the cauliflower, known as the curd, should be white and free of discoloration; leaves should be bright green, moist, and crisp. Cauliflower is also available in small purple or pale green varieties. Cover and store cauliflower in the refrigerator up to 3 or 4 days. Cauliflower is available year round but is best in autumn.

Leeks, *porri,* are the sweet member of the onion and garlic family, and resemble giant scallions. Their long white cylindrical stalks which extend into long, dark green leaves should always have their root ends attached. Select leeks that are firm; avoid wilted leaves, split, oversized bulbs or signs of yellowing. Leeks must be washed thoroughly as they tend to trap grit between the layers of leaves. Loosely wrap and store them in the refrigerator up to 1 week. Leeks are widely available year round although they are at their best from late spring through late fall.

Mushrooms, *funghi,* are available in a wide range of sizes, shapes, and textures. Cultivated mushrooms have a mild earthy flavor. The white button mushroom is best known, but also available are cremini, portobello (overgrown cremini), shiitake, oyster mushrooms, and pom poms. Wild mushrooms have an earthy woodsy flavor. A favorite of most mushroom lovers is the porcini *(Boletus edulis)* also known as *cèpes.* Porcini are prized for their distinct heady aroma and wild flavor. They abound in parts of Italy and France and are also found in North America particularly in the Northwest. They have large rounded caps with thick meaty stems and range in color from white to dark brown. They appear in the markets from late summer through late fall and occasionally in late spring. Other wild mushrooms available

sporadically are morels, chanterelles, hedgehog, and the brightly colored lobster mushrooms. When selecting wild mushrooms, small is usually considered better. Wild mushrooms found in specialty produce markets, farmers' markets, as well as some specialty supermarkets, are considered to be perfectly safe. Gathering mushrooms in the wilds can be very risky. It is not recommended unless accompanied by a trained expert. Many varieties are highly toxic and some even deadly. Mushrooms, whether wild or cultivated, should be plump, firm, and moist. Avoid those that are dehydrated, shriveled or soggy. Reject mushrooms with small holes, a sign of worms. Store mushrooms in the refrigerator in brown paper bags, not plastic. When extremely fresh they can be kept for up to 2 days. Wild mushrooms and the more exotic varieties of cultivated mushrooms are available in farmers' markets and specialty produce markets and can be ordered by mail (see Mail Order Sources, page 189). Each variety of wild mushroom has its own season.

Potatoes, *patate,* are available in a multitude of colors, sizes and shapes. There are three basic categories: low-moisture/high-starch; medium-moisture/medium-starch; and high-moisture/high-starch. Low-moisture/high-starch potatoes have dry mealy flesh and are good for baking, roasting, mashing, frying, or making gnocchi; so-called baking potatoes or russets fall into this category. Medium-moisture/medium-starch potatoes are good for roasting and can also be used for gnocchi; all yellow-fleshed potatoes are medium-moisture, including Yukon Gold and Carola. High-moisture/low-starch potatoes have a moist waxy flesh and are often referred to as boiling potatoes for their ability to hold their shape when boiled; some varieties are the eastern potato and the Long Island potato. Potatoes should be firm, never soft or wrinkled. Avoid potatoes that are damp or those with dark spots, gashes, or cracks. Reject potatoes that are sprouting or those with green-tinged skins. Potatoes should be handpicked and should always be stored unwashed in a brown paper or burlap bag in a cool, dark, dry place. A dry cellar or cupboard is best, where they will keep for several weeks. If refrigerated, potatoes should be used within 2 weeks. Potatoes are harvested from early summer through early winter; they are then kept in cold storage (conditions similar to those underground) where they remain in good condition for several months. Just-harvested potatoes, locally grown by small producers, are optimum and can be found at farmers' markets and farm stands.

Savoy cabbage, *cavolo verza,* is the most flavorful of all cabbages. It has crinkled, ruffled leaves with a matte finish. The head is looser and less compact than other heading cabbages. Savoy cabbage ranges in color from dark to light green. Select one that is solid and heavy with dark green, firm outer leaves with no sign of browning or yellowing. The stem should be closely trimmed, white, and moist. Avoid cabbage with black spots on the stem. Cover and store in the refrigerator for up to 1 week. Savoy cabbage enjoys the autumn chill and continues to thrive into early winter. It then goes into cold storage until early spring. The best Savoy cabbage can be found at farmers' markets and farm stands.

Spinach, *spinaci,* is available in two varieties, one with dark green crinkly leaves and the other with flat, smooth, pale green leaves. Spinach grows in small bunches with short to medium-length stems. Avoid spinach with thick, tough stems, overgrown leaves, or leaves that are yellowed or wilted. Spinach should have a sweet earthy fragrance. Refrigerate unwashed spinach tightly covered up to 2 days. Spinach must be washed thoroughly because it tends to be gritty. Spinach is available year round but grows best in spring and autumn when it can be purchased at farmers' markets and farm stands.

Turnips, *rape,* are another member of the Crucifera or mustard family. The variety most often used in Italy has a round root with white skin, tinged with purple at the top. Small young turnip roots are sweeter and more tender; older, overgrown ones become bitter and woody. If the turnip roots are still attached to their tops, the turnip greens should be bright in color, never yellowed. Remove and store the tops in the refrigerator tightly covered and separate from the roots up to 2 days. Cover and store turnip roots in the refrigerator up to 2 weeks. Turnip roots are available year round but are sweetest and most tender during spring and autumn. Look for locally grown turnips at farmers' markets and farm stands.

Fruit
frutta

Apples, *mele,* are best when just harvested and purchased close to their source. In September and October, local farmers' markets and farm stands abound with a vast selection of apples to fulfill all needs— eating out-of-hand, baking, cooking, and puréeing into applesauce. At their peak, apples are crisp, succulently moist and fragrant. Select apples that are firm with smooth skins. They should be free of bruises and gouges. Cover and refrigerate unwashed apples immediately after purchasing. (Apples left unrefrigerated quickly become overripe and mealy.) After harvest, many apple varieties are preserved in a controlled atmosphere storage which preserves the flavor and texture of some varieties better than others.

Figs, *fichi,* are bulbous in shape with soft pliable skin and come in shades of green, gold, and purple (called black). When ripe, the interior of a fig, consisting of many tender edible seeds, is sweet and pulpy. Figs should be plump and tender. Avoid figs that are shriveled or bruised. Figs are generally harvested ripe and are ready to eat when purchased. Loosely cover and store unwashed figs in the refrigerator for up to 3 days. Serve figs at room temperature. Figs are available in specialty produce markets from early summer through mid-fall.

Grapes, *uva,* grown in the United States for wine production as well as for the table, for the most part come from California. The American slip-skin variety of table grapes, which include Concords, are grown in the eastern states. Select plump grapes with a dusty bloom that are firmly attached to woody stems. Loosely cover and store unwashed grapes in the refrigerator for up to 5 days. Grapes taste best served at room temperature. California table grapes are widely available most of the year, while the slip-skin varieties are harvested in September and October and can be found at farmers' markets and farm stands.

Pears, *pere,* unlike most other fruit, ripen after they have been harvested. Select firm pears that are free of blemishes and soft spots. Those that are tender at the market are likely to bruise before they reach your home. Allow pears to soften slightly at room temperature. Some varieties will yellow when ripe, others will develop russeting, or speckling of the skin. Loosely cover and store ripe pears in the refrigerator up to 4 days. Pears should always be served at room temperature. Though pears are widely available most of the year, they are best in late summer through mid-fall. The tastiest pears are those purchased from local producers.

Plums, *prugne,* fall under two categories: Japanese style, considered clingstones, or European style, considered freestones. Japanese plums are round with skins in shades of red, black-red, yellow, and green. The juicy flesh of Japanese plums is either red or yellow. Japanese-style plums are excellent for eating out-of-hand. European-style plums are oval with blue or purple skins and are best for cooking, preserving, and drying as prunes. They have golden flesh that is meaty and not so juicy. Select plums that are plump and yield to gentle pressure. Avoid plums that are shriveled or those with soft spots or bruises. Plums can be left to soften slightly at room temperature, then refrigerated up to 3 days. Plums taste best served at room temperature. Japanese-style plums are harvested from June through September. European-style plums are a fall fruit, available in September and October. The finest quality plums are those locally grown.

CLOCKWISE STARTING LEFT, *luscious golden persimmons. Pecorino Sardo, or sheep's milk cheese from Sardinia, sold from a truck at the market. Cavolo verza, or Savoy cabbage. Potatoes shipped in loose soil to preserve freshness. Unloading flats of persimmons at the Asti market in Piedmont. The vendemmia, or grape harvest, at the Viberti vineyards in Vergne.*

TRUFFLE HUNT

Though white truffles are found in other parts of Italy, Alba is considered the capital of white truffles, and the tartufo d'Alba *commands the highest price. The white truffle is not pure white in color. It ranges from creamy white to a tawny gray-brown and looks like a gnarled potato with many small dimples. Sizes can vary greatly. The largest are most impressive but the small to medium size ones are favored as being the most aromatic and flavorful. The fragrance of a white truffle can be described as musky; it is often associated with the aroma of fresh herbs and garlic. Unlike the black truffle, white truffles are eaten raw. Their pungent aroma is unleashed as they are shaved into delicate slivers. Though traditionalists contend the only real way to savor a truffle is shaved over an egg gently sautéed in butter, the Piedmontese favor truffles with a thin fresh pasta called* tajarin *or over a warm cheese sauce called* fonduta. *They also use truffles to enhance polenta, omelets, and* brasato, *a braised roast of beef that has been marinated in red wine.*

Light fog drifts through the wooded field like gentle waves as Giovine Tersillo arrives with his English setter at his side. There is a chill in the autumn air. Twilight is fast approaching and the pair face a long night ahead. Giovine is a *trifolau*, an experienced truffle hunter, and has been one for more than 50 years. Tonight he has brought Mirca, one of his two trained dogs, to assist him in his search for the white diamonds of Alba. The gems they seek are not precious stones but fragrant truffles that grow hidden beneath the soil of the Langhe and Roero zones of Piedmont. *Tartufi d'Alba*, the white truffles of Alba, unpredictably attach themselves to the roots of oak, willow, poplar, linden, and hazelnut trees. The fungi (once believed to appear beneath a tree that was struck by lightning) are sniffed out by trained dogs, then unearthed by the trifolau. The trifolau and their canine companions often hunt through the night in secret locations.

The development of a truffle begins when climatic conditions are just right, usually late in August. It then takes several weeks for the truffle to mature. The hunting season peaks during the cold, damp autumn months, from September through December. Thousands of trifolau rummage the hillsides near streams and along riverbanks, returning to the same site that rewarded them the year before. Providing the root was not damaged, it will produce one truffle a year. The scarcity of truffles determines the cost, which fluctuates from one year to the next, often reaching levels of pure extravagance.

Mirca scours the field, sniffing enthusiastically, as Giovine commands her to his side. The dog responds obediently, eyeing Giovine attentively as he removes a small sack from his jacket pocket. Grasping the sack tightly, Giovine allows Mirca a quick sniff of a concealed truffle, a reminder of the dog biscuit she will receive as payment for a find. Mirca dashes off in eager pursuit. Suddenly the dog's demeanor changes. As Mirca begins to dig, Giovine extends his long bent-wood cane, the kind always carried by a trifolau, catching Mirca's leather collar with its crook. Mirca retreats. As she contentedly accepts a biscuit, Giovine claims the truffle. He wraps it in a large cotton handkerchief and tucks it into his pocket as he directs Mirca to another section of the field.

The flavor of a white truffle
diminishes quickly. If you must keep a truffle
for a day or two, store it in the lowest part
of the refrigerator wrapped in a paper towel.
Use a damp, soft mushroom brush or toothbrush
to clean the truffle just before serving.

During truffle season Ester Carnero of
La Luna e i Falò (see page 37) shaves white
truffles over her cardi con fonduta, LEFT,
sautéed cardoons topped with a warm cheese
sauce (see page 71). Cardoons from the town
of Nizza Monferrato are called cardi gobbi.
They are grown with their stalks partially
covered with soil. They develop a unique curved
shape and tender white flesh.

AL BUON PADRE

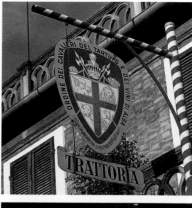

In 1920 when Antonio Giuseppe Viberti purchased a small inn and farmhouse in the hamlet of Vergne, it served as a rest stop for hungry and weary travelers. The inn was conveniently situated at *la porta delle Langhe*, the gateway to the Langhe hills, in the municipality of Barolo, the majestic wine-growing zone of Piedmont. Toni d'Giuspin, as Antonio was known, greeted his guests, who often journeyed from the cities of Turin and Cuneo, with a good, solid Piedmontese meal, freshly baked bread, and wine made in his small cantina. He offered them a warm and comfortable place to sleep and provided stables to shelter their horses and mules. It was not long before Antonio's inn was affectionately referred to as Al Buon Padre, a testimony to the way Antonio doted on his guests, just like a good father.

That same warm hospitality is now provided at Al Buon Padre by Giovanni Viberti, one of Antonio's three sons, and Giovanni's wife, Maria. Giovanni presides over the twenty-five-acre estate, which produces more than forty thousand bottles of well-respected wines. Maria upholds the traditions and standards of a classic Piedmontese kitchen, established by her mother-in-law, Giovanna. The stables for the animals are gone and the wine cellar and inn have moved to a new structure not far from the original. The old cellar, below the *trattoria*, now serves as an aging room and *enoteca*, a place to taste and purchase the wines of the estate. Giovanni's brother, Luigi, and his wife, Pasqualina, maintain the *panetteria* adjacent to the trattoria. Here, they still produce the handmade baked goods (breads, *torte*, *crostate*, and *biscottini*) that were once made by Antonio and Giovanna. The tiny well-organized kitchen, where Maria prepares for as many as sixty, remains as before. The only addition has been a gas-burning stove, which she uses for boiling large pots of water to cook her handmade pasta. She fires up her old wood-burning stove each morning to manage the bulk of the work.

Guests at Al Buon Padre are no longer passing by en route to other points. Piedmont has become an important destination for wine enthusiasts and for those with a passion for fine food. Each fall, particularly during the months of September and October, during *vendemmia,* the wine harvest, visitors make the pilgrimage to the

Giovanni Viberti, OPPOSITE, blankets his wife Maria's handmade tajarin, *thin ribbons of pasta, with shavings of white truffle. ABOVE, the Viberti family, left to right, Maria, Gianluca, Patrizia, and Giovanni.*

Vergne

Luigi Viberti, TOP, *working in the* panneteria, *where he bakes handmade breads and* grissini, ABOVE, *that measure more than a yard long.* OPPOSITE, *Maria Viberti's* bagna caûda, *a warm anchovy sauce, is served with roasted peppers,* Peperoni alla Bagna Caûda.

wine-producing zones. The picturesque, sloping hills of the Langhe are where some of Italy's finest wines are produced.

Weekends at the trattoria are particularly busy during vendemmia and Maria begins her preparation several days ahead by making *tajarin,* delicate golden strands of pasta, considered by some to be the most important dish of the Langhe. Maria has perfected her technique for rolling out silky thin sheets of dough and cutting them as fine as hay. She makes the tajarin three or four times each week and uses as many as sixty eggs at a time.

The countryside surrounding Alba, the capital city of the Langhe, is the sacred ground of the white truffle, and thousands of its admirers will be there to celebrate its advent. *La Fiera del Tartufo,* a truffle fair held in the old city of Alba, a short distance from Vergne, extends through the month of October, the height of truffle season. After the festivities many of the visitors will spill out of the city into the nearby wine-growing villages to sample the local dishes and to drink the wines that have made Piedmont world renowned.

Maria will dress her tajarin with sweet butter infused with sprigs of fresh rosemary and sage. As the tajarin is served, Giovanni will arrive at the table with a small basket of truffles and his *tagli-atartufi,* a small flat implement with a razor-sharp blade used to shave the truffles into paper-thin shards. He will ask the question the hungry crowd waits to hear, "*Tartufi?*" And there will surely be numerous takers, regardless of the extra charge.

While Maria works in the kitchen, she can watch the activity in the vineyards progressing, as Gianluca, her eldest son, decides on the precise moment to begin the harvest in each of their six vineyards. Gianluca, who studied wine growing and production as well as oenology at the Istituto Tecnico Agrario ed Enologico in Alba, organizes the harvest and takes responsibility for the production and aging of the Viberti wines—Barolo, Dolcetto d'Alba, Barbera d'Alba and Chardonnay. Three of the Viberti vineyards, each facing a different direction, grow nebbiolo grapes for the

production of their Barolo wines (nebbiolo takes its name from *nebbia,* the fog that blankets the lowlands during the vendemmia*).* Gianluca attributes the combination of weather and soil rich in limestone for the success achieved in this small area south of the Tanaro River, the official growing zone for Barolo wine.

Maria is joined in the kitchen on weekends by her daughter Patrizia, who spends most of the week in Alba, where she teaches. The tables in the two small dining rooms of the trattoria are dressed in neatly pressed white linen and set with porcelain dinnerware. Each place setting includes the appropriate crystal glasses for serving Viberti wines. In the center of each table is a neat stack of *grissini,* the slender, crisp breadsticks that originated in Turin. Each one, hand rolled by Luigi in the panetteria, measures more than a yard in length. Giovanni arranges the crystal decanters on the credenza in the front dining room for decanting the older vintages. Decanting the wine will oxygenate it to bring forth its full flavor and bouquet. After long hours in the vineyards and *cantina,* Gianluca freshens up to join the family and help with the service.

The meal commences when a small wooden cutting board is brought to the table with *salame crudo,* a hard dry salami made by Luigi, followed by two or three additional antipasti. Next comes the tajarin. As Maria passes the steaming plates through a small window that opens into the front dining room, she sneaks an occasional glance at her guests. For *secondo piatto,* or second course, Maria often prepares a braised roast or stew that has been bathed in red or white wine. A meal at Al Buon Padre would not be complete without Gianluca's favorite dessert, *bûnet,* a delicate steamed chocolate flan scented with rum and Marsala wine and dripping with caramel sauce.

As the evening comes to an end, the Vibertis finally relax. The family gathers around a table for dinner. Claudio, the younger son, joins them to discuss the events of the day. Maria carries each course from the kitchen and Giovanni pours the wine. This, after all, is their family tradition.

Peperoni alla Bagna Caûda
Roasted Peppers in Warm Anchovy Sauce

Anchovies, garlic, and olive oil, ingredients used in the traditional warm dipping sauce bagna caûda, were originally brought to Piedmont from the coastal region of Liguria. Bagna caûda, which means hot bath in Piedmontese dialect, is usually served as a dip with crisp raw vegetables. Maria Viberti serves her version with bell peppers that have been slow-roasted in the oven; she cooks the sauce in a double boiler until all of the ingredients are melted together. The tender sweet peppers are split in half and the warm sauce is spooned into their hollows.

Maria prefers to make bagna caûda with a pure olive oil instead of extra virgin. She feels the bold flavor of extra virgin would be too pronounced.

    4   RED, YELLOW, OR ORANGE BELL PEPPERS
    6   LARGE CLOVES OF GARLIC
    6   SALT-PACKED ANCHOVIES, FILLETED (SEE PAGE 12) AND FINELY
        CHOPPED
    ⅓   CUP (3 FL OZ/80 ML) PURE OLIVE OIL
    PINCH OF SEA SALT

1. Preheat the oven to 300°F (150°C).

2. Place the whole peppers on a baking sheet and roast for 1 hour. Rotate them after the first 30 minutes, then again after 15 minutes. The peppers should remain firm and hold their shape. If they begin to soften, remove them from the oven immediately. Let the peppers cool slightly.

3. Cook the garlic cloves in a small pot of boiling water for 20 to 30 minutes, or until they are very soft. Let the garlic cool, then peel and mash the pulp with a fork. Combine the anchovies with the garlic and mash them together to make a smooth purée.

4. When the peppers are cool enough to handle, peel, core, and seed them. Cut the peppers in half lengthwise and drain them, hollow side down, on paper towels.

5. Combine the garlic purée with the olive oil and salt in the top of a double boiler. Cook the mixture over simmering water, stirring often, for 30 minutes.

6. Arrange the pepper halves, hollow side up, on a serving platter. Spoon the warm sauce into the hollows and serve immediately.

MAKES 4 TO 6 SERVINGS

Note: The pepper halves can be reheated in a 300°F (150°C) oven for 5 minutes before filling with sauce, if you prefer to serve them warm.

Tajarin al Coltello
Thin Pasta Ribbons

Tajarin are the finest, most delicate of all handmade pasta, each strand barely measuring 1/16 inch in width. Maria Viberti dries her tajarin in mounds that resemble small stacks of hay.

    3¼ CUPS (14 OZ/400 G) UNBLEACHED ALL-PURPOSE FLOUR
    4   LARGE EGGS
    2   TEASPOONS EXTRA VIRGIN OLIVE OIL
    PINCH OF SEA SALT

1. To make the pasta dough for the tajarin, use the flour, eggs, olive oil, and salt as directed on page 188, the section entitled Making the Dough. The dough will be kneaded and stretched in a manual pasta machine. Line 2 trays or baking sheets with cotton kitchen towels and dust lightly with flour.

2. Divide the dough into 4 equal portions and knead in the pasta machine as directed in the section entitled Kneading the Dough in a Pasta Machine. Stretch the dough as directed in the section entitled Stretching the Dough in a Pasta Machine. Stretch the dough 1 piece at a time as thin as possible, taking it to the last setting on the dial. Using a fluted pastry wheel, cut each sheet of pasta into 10-inch (25-cm) lengths and arrange them side by side, on the towel-lined trays. Dry the pasta slightly, turning the sheets occasionally to dry them evenly. The surface should be dry to the touch, but the pasta should remain flexible.

3. When the pasta has dried sufficiently, lightly flour both sides of each sheet of dough and stack five of them together. Fold the stack lengthwise in half and using a large chef's knife, slice the pasta crosswise into very fine strands, no wider than 1/16 inch (2 mm). Gently toss the strands to separate them and transfer them to the towel-lined trays. Dust with flour and toss again. Continue to stack and cut the pasta.

MAKES 6 SERVINGS

ABOVE, Maria Viberti's Tajarin al Coltello, thin handmade ribbons of pasta, dry in trays covered with a cotton kitchen towel. FAR LEFT AND LEFT, Maria stretches pasta into thin sheets and drapes them over the kitchen counters to dry. RIGHT, she cuts the tajarin by hand on a wooden cutting board.

Tajarin con Tartufi

*Thin Pasta Ribbons with Herb Butter
and White Truffles*

*The aroma of white truffles is intoxicating as Giovanni Viberti shaves
thin slivers over steaming mounds of* tajarin, *the delicate egg pasta his wife
Maria makes by hand. The tajarin is first tossed in butter infused with
the fragrance of fresh rosemary and sage.*

For the Herb Butter

- 8 TABLESPOONS (4 OZ/125 G) UNSALTED BUTTER
- 1 SPRIG OF ROSEMARY
- 1 SPRIG OF SAGE
- SEA SALT

TAJARIN AL COLTELLO (THIN PASTA RIBBONS, PAGE 28)
SEA SALT

- 1 MEDIUM FRESH WHITE TRUFFLE, BRUSHED CLEAN WITH
  A SOFT BRUSH

1. Fill a very large pot (at least 8 quarts/8 liters) with water and
bring it to a rapid boil.

2. To make the herb butter, melt the butter with the rosemary
and sage in a sauté pan large enough to hold the tajarin when cooked.
The butter should not brown. When melted, remove the herb sprigs
and season with sea salt to taste.

3. When the water in the pot has come to a boil, add salt to taste.
Lift the towels containing the tajarin, one at a time, and slide the pasta
into the boiling water. (Do not use your hands to handle the tajarin,
or it will shatter.) Cover the pot just until the water returns to a boil.
Uncover and boil the tajarin for 12 seconds, or just until it is tender.
Drain in a large colander, reserving some of the cooking water.

4. Transfer the tajarin to the sauté pan with the herb-infused
butter and toss over very low heat until well coated. If the pasta seems
dry, add some of the reserved cooking water. Serve the tajarin immediately in wide shallow pasta bowls and use a truffle slicer or vegetable
peeler to shave the truffle into paper-thin slivers over each serving.
MAKES 6 SERVINGS

Tajarin con Tartufi, *OPPOSITE.*

Tajarin con Sugo di Carne

Thin Pasta Ribbons with Meat Sauce

Maria Viberti's sugo di carne, which she makes with ground veal, is
more delicate than most meat sauces. A richer sauce would clearly overwhelm
her tajarin.

For the Meat Sauce

- 2 LARGE ONIONS, COARSELY CHOPPED
- 1½ TEASPOONS COARSELY CHOPPED FRESH ROSEMARY LEAVES
- ¼ CUP (2 FL OZ/60 ML) EXTRA VIRGIN OLIVE OIL
- 1½ POUNDS (675 G) GROUND VEAL
- 3 CUPS (24 FL OZ/725 ML) CANNED TOMATOES, DRAINED AND
  CHOPPED
- ½ TO 1 CUP (8 TO 16 FL OZ/125 TO 250 ML) MEAT BROTH
  (FOR HOMEMADE, SEE PAGE 187)
- SEA SALT

TAJARIN AL COLTELLO (THIN PASTA RIBBONS, PAGE 28)
SEA SALT

- 1 CUP (4 OZ/125 G) GRATED PARMIGIANO-REGGIANO, FOR SERVING

1. To make the meat sauce, combine the onions and rosemary on
a cutting board and chop them together until very fine. Heat the
olive oil in a medium-size, heavy, flame-proof casserole over medium-
low heat. Add the onion mixture and cook until the onion is very
tender and golden, 20 to 25 minutes. If the onion begins to brown
before it has softened, add 1 or 2 tablespoons of water and continue to
cook. (Be sure all of the water has evaporated before adding the veal.)

2. Add the ground veal and raise the heat to medium. Sauté the
veal, crumbling it with a fork, until cooked through. Stir in the tomatoes, ½ cup (4 fl oz/125 ml) of the broth, and salt to taste. Simmer the
sauce, uncovered, for 1½ hours, stirring occasionally. Add more broth
if the sauce becomes very thick and sticks to the bottom of the pan.

3. Fill a very large pot (at least 8 quarts/8 liters) with water and
bring it to a rapid boil. Add salt to taste. Lift the towels containing the
tajarin, one at a time, and slide the pasta into the boiling water. (Do
not use your hands to handle the tajarin, or it will shatter.) Cover the
pot just until the water returns to a boil. Uncover and boil the tajarin
for 12 seconds, or just until it is tender. Drain the tajarin in a large
colander and transfer it to a large shallow serving bowl. Pour over the
meat sauce and toss the tajarin until it is well coated with sauce. Serve
immediately with a bowl of Parmigiano for sprinkling.
MAKES 6 SERVINGS

Vitello Arrosto allo Chardonnay

Veal Braised in Chardonnay with Vegetable Sauce

Maria Viberti braises a large veal roast with Viberti Chardonnay and a batutto, finely chopped aromatic vegetables and herbs that serves as the base for many soups, sauces, and stews. At the end, she purées the vegetables with the pan juices.

3 TABLESPOONS (1½ FL OZ/45 ML) EXTRA VIRGIN OLIVE OIL
2 POUNDS (900 G) BONELESS VEAL ROAST, TIED (TOP ROUND OR RUMP)
1 LARGE ONION, CUT INTO ½-INCH (1.5-CM) DICE
1 MEDIUM CARROT, CUT INTO ½-INCH (1.5-CM) DICE
1 CELERY STALK, CUT INTO ½-INCH (1.5-CM) DICE
1 SPRIG OF ROSEMARY
2 BAY LEAVES
1 GARLIC CLOVE
5 WHOLE CLOVES
½ CUP (4 FL OZ/125 ML) CHARDONNAY OR OTHER DRY WHITE WINE
SEA SALT AND FRESHLY GROUND BLACK PEPPER
MEAT BROTH (FOR HOMEMADE, SEE PAGE 187)

1. Heat the olive oil in a large, heavy casserole over medium-high heat. Add the veal roast and brown it on all sides. Transfer the roast to a platter.

2. Add the onion, carrot, celery, rosemary, bay leaves, garlic, and cloves. Sauté, stirring often, until the vegetables are golden. Return the roast to the casserole, pour over the chardonnay, and bring it to a boil. Season the roast with salt and pepper. Cover the casserole and simmer, turning and basting the roast occasionally for 1½ to 2 hours, or until tender when pierced with a fork.

3. Transfer the roast to a cutting board and discard the rosemary stem, bay leaves, and whole cloves. Cover the roast with aluminum foil. To make the sauce, pass the vegetables and pan juices through a food mill fitted with the fine disk or purée the mixture in a food processor. Thin with meat broth, if desired. Season the sauce with salt and pepper to taste. Reheat if necessary. Thinly slice the veal roast and serve each portion with 1 or 2 spoonfuls of sauce.

MAKES 4 TO 6 SERVINGS

OPPOSITE, Giovanni Viberti slices Vitello Arrosto allo Chardonnay *in the dining room of Al Buon Padre. He then ladles the puréed vegetable sauce over the braised veal. In autumn, the veal is paired with* Cavolfiore Fritto, *breaded and fried cauliflower.*

Cavolfiore Fritto

Breaded and Fried Cauliflower

Maria Viberti likes to serve fried cauliflower with her vitello arrosto. The florets are encased in a crisp crumb crust and are always meltingly tender. To achieve a fine-textured crust, use homemade bread crumbs (see page 13) and sift the crumbs to eliminate the larger pieces.

1 HEAD CAULIFLOWER, CORED AND CUT INTO FLORETS
2 LARGE EGGS, LIGHTLY BEATEN
1 CUP (2 OZ/60 G) FINE DRY BREAD CRUMBS
PURE OLIVE OIL, FOR FRYING
SEA SALT

1. Fill a large pot (at least 6 quarts/6 liters) with water and bring it to a rapid boil. Plunge the cauliflower into the water and boil it for 2 minutes. Drain the cauliflower, refresh it under cold water, and drain it again. Dry the cauliflower on paper towels.

2. Dip the cauliflower into the beaten eggs, then coat with bread crumbs. Place the breaded cauliflower on a tray and refrigerate it for at least 1 hour.

3. Heat 1 inch (2.5 cm) of olive oil in a large, heavy skillet with high sides, over medium heat. When the oil is hot, add the cauliflower, several pieces at a time. Fry the cauliflower until golden brown on one side, then turn and brown the other side. Using a slotted spoon, remove the cauliflower from the skillet, drain on paper towels, then sprinkle with salt. Fry the remaining cauliflower in the same way. Serve immediately.

MAKES 6 SERVINGS

The Viberti vineyards *produce and export four classic Piedmontese wines, Barolo, Dolcetto d'Alba, Barbera d'Alba, and Chardonnay. Giovanni Viberti, samples a late vintage Barolo in the aging room below the trattoria.*

Zabajone Al Buon Padre

Warm Zabaglione with Espresso Coffee

Maria Viberti spikes her warm zabaglione with a well-aged Marsala wine and brewed espresso. She occasionally serves it with a slice of torta di nocciole, a traditional Piedmontese hazelnut cake (page 46). Her husband, Giovanni, prefers his with a glass of 15- to 20-year-old Barolo—Viberti, of course. This recipe, which serves two, can be multiplied to serve as many as desired.

> 4 LARGE EGG YOLKS
>
> 2 TABLESPOONS SUGAR
>
> LARGE PINCH OF UNBLEACHED ALL-PURPOSE FLOUR
>
> 2 TABLESPOONS FRESHLY BREWED ESPRESSO COFFEE
>
> 1 TEASPOON WHOLE MILK
>
> ¼ CUP (2 FL OZ/60 ML) DRY MARSALA WINE

1. Fill the bottom of a double boiler with 1 inch (2.5 cm) of water. Heat the water until it simmers.

2. Combine the egg yolks, sugar, and flour in the top of the double boiler. Blend the mixture with a wire whisk and place it over the simmering water. Beat the egg yolk mixture constantly. As the sugar dissolves, the mixture will become runny; it will thicken to the consistency of heavy cream. This should take no longer than 5 minutes. At that point, pour in the espresso, milk, and Marsala wine. Continue to beat until the zabaglione becomes thick and fluffy with the consistency of lightly whipped cream. This will take another 5 minutes. Rest the zabaglione for 10 minutes or just until tepid, stirring occasionally. Pour the zabaglione into 2 small dessert bowls and serve immediately.

MAKES 2 SERVINGS

Bûnet al Cioccolato, *a chocolate flan,* RIGHT. Zabajone Al Buon Padre, OPPOSITE, *warm zabaglione.*

Bûnet al Cioccolato

Steamed Chocolate Flan with Caramel Syrup

This classic steamed flan served in Piedmont is named for its bonnetlike shape. The bûnet is made with crushed amaretti cookies and steamed in a mold coated with caramel. Maria Viberti's chocolate version—adored by her son Gianluca—includes rum, Marsala wine, and cocoa.

Maria always serves the bûnet with pesche in burnia, *peaches preserved in a light syrup, made in summer with fruit picked from the trees that grow in the vineyards. You can serve the bûnet alone or with any preserved summer fruit.*

> ½ CUP (3½ OZ/100 G) SUGAR
>
> 4 LARGE EGGS
>
> 2½ TABLESPOONS UNSWEETENED COCOA POWDER
>
> 1 CUP (8 FL OZ/250 ML) WHOLE MILK
>
> 1 TABLESPOON WHITE RUM
>
> 1 TABLESPOON DRY MARSALA WINE
>
> ⅓ CUP (1½ OZ/45 G) AMARETTI COOKIES, CRUSHED

1. Preheat the oven to 250°F (120°C). Warm a 4-cup (1-liter) kugelhopf or ring mold in the oven while making the syrup.

2. Heat ¼ cup (1¾ oz/50 g) of the sugar in a small, heavy saucepan over medium-low heat. Do not stir until the sugar begins to melt around the edges of the pan. Stir with a wooden spoon until the sugar dissolves into a smooth syrup that is nutty brown in color. Quickly pour the syrup into the warm mold and rotate the mold to evenly coat the surface. The caramel syrup will be very hot, so be sure to wear protective oven mitts when handling the saucepan and while coating the mold. Set the mold on a wire rack to cool completely. The caramel will harden and crack.

3. Bring a kettle of water to a boil, to use for a bain-marie.

4. Beat the eggs in a large bowl with a wire whisk until foamy. Add the remaining ¼ cup (1¾ oz/50 g) sugar and continue to beat until the sugar is dissolved. Blend in the cocoa, then add the milk, rum, and Marsala wine. Stir in the amaretti cookies and pour the mixture into the caramelized mold. Cover the mold with aluminum foil and place it in a large pot. Fill the pot with enough of the boiling water to come halfway up the sides of the mold. Steam the bûnet in the gently simmering water for 15 minutes, or until a paring knife inserted into the center comes out clean. Remove the mold from the water, cool thoroughly on a cooling rack, then refrigerate.

5. Twenty minutes before serving, unmold the bûnet onto a shallow serving platter. Spoon any syrup that remains in the mold over the flan.

MAKES 6 SERVINGS

LA LUNA E I FALÒ

I n *La Luna e i Falò* (The Moon and the Bonfires), a novel by Cesare Pavese, the author depicts a ritual still performed each year in the month of August in the Monferrato Astigiano zone of Piedmont. In hopes of a good harvest, the farmers of Canelli and San Stefano Belbo gather old grapevines and set them aflame under the radiance of the full moon. The glow of the fires, scattered throughout the hills, is an awesome sight. For Franco Carnero, La Luna e i Falò represents a dream come true on one of those hillsides in the village of Canelli.

Ester Carnero, ABOVE, re-creates antique recipes of the Monferrato Astigiano zone of Piedmont in her restaurant kitchen. Gnocchetti Verdi con Funghi Porcini, OPPOSITE, are tiny green potato dumplings tossed with a sauce that celebrates the fresh porcini mushrooms of fall.

Franco and his wife, Ester, run La Luna e i Falò, a small inn and farm in a quiet community where life has changed little in the last thirty years. Canelli remains unaffected by the overwhelming tourism that has forever altered the pattern of life in nearby villages. Franco first visited the village of Canelli, which borders the Langhe and Monferrato Astigiano wine-growing zones of Piedmont, in 1969, while on a hunting trip with friends. Overcome by the beauty of the hillsides and the imposing landscape, he and Ester found and purchased a run-down house with an extraordinary view on a small plot of land. They drove to Canelli each Sunday from the industrial city of Turin, where they ran a successful restaurant. They planted a garden and vineyard and made the necessary repairs on the house. Franco dreamed of escaping from a hectic lifestyle to produce wine and maintain his small farm. Eventually, they left Turin and dedicated themselves to the restoration of the house and the development of the land.

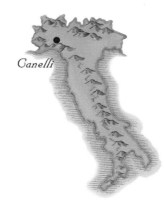

Canelli

The restoration process was monumental. It seems that the area had once been so impoverished that local builders, unable to afford traditional bricks, built many of the old homes with handmade bricks formed from the only materials available to them: their white limestone-rich soil and their Moscato wine. When the mixture dried, it was as hard as stone. The brick structures were coated with stucco to protect them from the dampness, which could cause the bricks to melt like bars of white chocolate in the blazing sun. To the astonishment of the Carneros, their home was built entirely of these provisional bricks, and if they intended to stay, the bricks had to be replaced.

Wine production commenced slowly and the cost of the restoration set them back

*The vineyards of La Luna
e i Falò, OPPOSITE TOP,
where Franco Carnero cultivates
the grapes for his Moscato
d'Asti. OPPOSITE LEFT, the
elegantly furnished sitting
area where guests can gather for
an* aperitivo *before dinner.
OPPOSITE CENTER, the geese
at La Luna e i Falò make
wonderful watchdogs—they
create quite a ruckus when
strangers approach. OPPOSITE
RIGHT, Franco prepares a table
for arriving guests. BELOW, a
small chapel on the drive that
leads to La Luna e i Falò.*

financially. With few choices left to them, the Carneros decided to once again open a restaurant.

This time it would be different, a small, more manageable restaurant in their country home. Word quickly spread among their old clients in Turin who were pleased to know they could again satisfy their hunger for Ester's fine cooking. La Luna e i Falò became an immediate success.

Franco's garden flourished. He soon provided Ester with fruits, vegetables, herbs, and nuts to use in her spacious kitchen, where she researches and revives old regional recipes to which she adds her personal touch. Franco's vineyard produces more than five thousand bottles of wine each year, to serve and sell at their restaurant.

La Luna e i Falò is now a handsome red brick and stucco structure with a sweeping view of thirty towns and villages. The entrance of the house is behind a series of arches that form a sheltered portico. The dining room and connecting living room where guests meet for dinner are furnished with bold renaissance pieces, oriental rugs, and a fine collection of artwork. Large crockery bowls filled with seasonal fruits and vegetables gathered from the garden rest on tables and sideboards throughout the house.

Ester works with great skill; her kitchen experience began at a tender age under the tutelage of her parents; her father was from Emilia-Romagna, her mother from the Veneto. Ester describes her cuisine as Astigiano, in the style of the province of Asti, but she lends to it other small influences. One such influence, in particular, is the use of duck, common in both Emilia and the Veneto. Franco and Ester raise a silent duck called *anatra muta*, which is prized for its large, meaty breast.

In true Piedmontese style, Ester begins her meals with several antipasti. Many of the recipes were uncovered through her research. She often serves *tartrà*, individual flans delicately seasoned with fresh herbs and Parmigiano-Reggiano. Another find is her *antica salsa*, a puréed sauce made from fresh figs and sweet peppers, which she spoons over thin slices of roasted veal. Franco

accompanies the antipasti with his Cortese, a white wine with a light fruity aroma and taste. He serves his Dolcetto, a young, dry red wine, with both the pasta and the meat course.

Franco takes pride in being the pasta maker of the family. He rolls out tender sheets of golden egg pasta which Ester stuffs and shapes either like small pillows or like candy wrappers with twisted ends. He also cuts the sheets into thin strands for *taglierini* and makes *gnocchetti verdi*, tiny green cushions of potato dough. Ester prepares all of the sauces and fillings, which reflect the season.

Twice each week, Ester shops at the large outdoor market in Canelli to purchase seasonal fruits and vegetables not grown in their garden as well as meats, local cheeses, and other dairy products. During the fall she can find porcini mushrooms. They are usually gathered in the woods of Sassello, a village in the maritime Alps.

During the fall, hazelnuts, which can be found throughout the area, are ready for harvesting. Ester is provided with an abundance of hazelnuts that grow on the grounds of La Luna e i Falò. She uses them in savory as well as sweet dishes, including her *torta di nocciole*, a dense, buttery hazelnut cake, made with amaretti cookies.

Desserts have always been a favorite of Ester's; she has been preparing them since she was a child. She usually serves a sampling of two or three on a plate, assuming her guests love them as much as she does. Franco pours each guest a chilled glass of his Moscato d'Asti to sip with dessert. Moscato d'Asti is a sparkling sweet white wine, similar to Asti Spumante, though slightly less fizzy. Canelli is noted for the production of both Asti Spumante and Moscato d'Asti, both made from the Moscato Bianco grape.

Franco offers guests coffee and grappa as the meal comes to a close. Both he and Ester often join them for conversation that usually centers around the food, the wine, and the beauty of the Langhe and Monferrato Astigiano zones that won Franco's heart nearly thirty years ago.

For Franco Carnero, La Luna e i Falò

represents a dream come true

on a hillside in the village of Canelli.

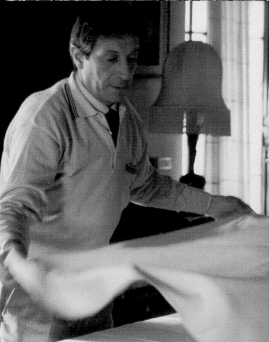

Tartrà con Intingolo

Savory Herb Flan with Tomato Herb Sauce

Ester Carnero is known for her refined use of the fresh herbs that are always close at hand in her garden. She blends them in combinations that intermingle with other ingredients but never intrude. She uses herbs for their digestive properties as well as for the intricate quality they add to a dish.

Ester serves her tartrà, *a savory herb and cheese flan that bakes in individual ramekins, with a chunky red wine-laced* intingolo, *or sauce. The intingolo is made with small bits of prosciutto, onion, celery, and tomatoes. It simmers with fresh rosemary and sage. When the sauce is ready Ester stirs in another blend of herbs. The combination is ambrosial. Tartrà is served in Piedmont as an antipasto though at one time it served as a* piatto unico, *or one-dish meal, during cold winter months.*

For the Herb Flan

1½ TABLESPOONS (1½ OZ/40 G) UNSALTED BUTTER
 1 BAY LEAF
½ MEDIUM ONION, FINELY GRATED
 3 LARGE EGGS
 1 LARGE EGG YOLK
 1 CUP (8 FL OZ/250 ML) WHOLE MILK
½ CUP (4 FL OZ/125 ML) HEAVY CREAM
¾ TEASPOON FINELY CHOPPED ROSEMARY LEAVES
¾ TEASPOON FINELY CHOPPED SAGE LEAVES
 2 TEASPOONS GRATED PARMIGIANO-REGGIANO
¼ TEASPOON FRESHLY GRATED NUTMEG
SEA SALT AND FRESHLY GROUND BLACK PEPPER

For the Tomato Herb Sauce

½ OUNCE (15 G) IMPORTED ITALIAN PROSCIUTTO OR PANCETTA, COARSELY CHOPPED
½ MEDIUM ONION, COARSELY CHOPPED
½ CELERY STALK, COARSELY CHOPPED
 3 TABLESPOONS (1½ FL OZ/45 ML) EXTRA VIRGIN OLIVE OIL
¾ TEASPOON FINELY CHOPPED ROSEMARY LEAVES
¾ TEASPOON FINELY CHOPPED SAGE LEAVES
 1 BAY LEAF
¼ CUP (2 FL OZ/60 ML) DRY RED WINE
 2 CUPS (16 FL OZ/500 ML) CANNED ITALIAN TOMATOES, DRAINED AND FINELY CHOPPED
SEA SALT AND FRESHLY GROUND BLACK PEPPER
 2 TEASPOONS FINELY CHOPPED MIXED HERB LEAVES SUCH AS BASIL, MARJORAM, MINT, OR THYME

1. Preheat the oven to 400°F (200°C). Oil and flour six 6-ounce ramekins or custard cups. Bring a large kettle of water to a boil, to use for a bain-marie.

2. To prepare the herb flan, melt the butter in a small skillet. Add the bay leaf and grated onion. Cook over low heat until the onion is lightly golden, about 10 minutes. Remove the bay leaf and let the onion cool.

3. Whisk the whole eggs and the egg yolk in a large bowl. Stir in the milk, heavy cream, rosemary, sage, Parmigiano, nutmeg, and the onion. Blend well and season with salt and black pepper.

4. Arrange the ramekins in a small roasting pan that is at least 2 inches (5 cm) deep. Pour the custard mixture into the ramekins and add enough boiling water to the roasting pan to reach halfway up the sides of the ramekins. Carefully place the pan in the oven and bake the flans for 40 minutes, or until they are puffed and golden brown on top.

5. To prepare the tomato herb sauce, combine the prosciutto, onion, and celery on a cutting board and chop them together until very fine. Heat the olive oil in a large saucepan. Add the prosciutto mixture, the rosemary, sage, and bay leaf. Cook until the celery and onion are tender, about 15 minutes. Pour in the red wine and simmer briskly until half of the wine has evaporated. Add the tomatoes and salt and pepper to taste and simmer briskly for 15 minutes. Discard the bay leaf, stir in the mixed herbs, and remove the sauce from the heat.

6. Slide the flans out of the ramekins and serve them with the tomato herb sauce.

MAKES 6 SERVINGS

Vitello in Antica Salsa di Peperoni e Fichi

Roast Veal with Sweet Pepper and Fig Sauce

Ester Carnero discovered an old Piedmontese recipe that combines the autumnal flavors of fresh figs and bell peppers. The fruit and vegetables simmer in a sauce that is later puréed and spooned over sliced roasted veal, which Ester serves as an antipasto. She occasionally serves the same sauce with bollito misto, *a mixture of boiled meats that could include beef, veal, pork, tongue, chicken, or cotechino sausage, a type of pork sausage seasoned with nutmeg and cloves.*

The roasted veal can also be served with the pan juices as a meat course accompanied by roasted potatoes (see page 97) or a mixed green salad. As a meat course the veal will make 4 to 6 servings.

For the Roast Veal

  2 TABLESPOONS (1 FL OZ/30 ML) EXTRA VIRGIN OLIVE OIL
  2 POUNDS (900 G) BONELESS VEAL ROAST, TIED
     (BOTTOM ROUND, LOIN, OR SHOULDER)
  1 MEDIUM ONION, CUT IN HALF
  1 SPRIG OF ROSEMARY
  1 SPRIG OF SAGE
  1 BAY LEAF
     SEA SALT AND FRESHLY GROUND BLACK PEPPER
  1 CUP (8 FL OZ/250 ML) DRY WHITE WINE

For the Sweet Pepper and Fig Sauce

  1 POUND (450 G) FRESH FIGS
  3 TABLESPOONS (1½ FL OZ/45 ML) EXTRA VIRGIN OLIVE OIL
  2 MEDIUM RED BELL PEPPERS, CORED AND CUT INTO
     1-INCH (2.5-CM) PIECES
  1 MEDIUM YELLOW BELL PEPPER, CORED AND CUT INTO
     1-INCH (2.5-CM) PIECES
  ½ CELERY STALK, CUT INTO 1-INCH (2.5-CM) PIECES
     SEA SALT AND FRESHLY GROUND BLACK PEPPER

1. To prepare the roast veal, heat the olive oil in a large, heavy flame-proof casserole over medium-high heat. Add the veal, and surround it with the onion, rosemary, sage, and bay leaf. Brown the veal evenly on all sides. If the onion becomes dark, remove it from the pan and return it when the roast has finished browning. Season the roast with salt and pepper. Pour over the white wine, cover the pan, and simmer slowly for 1 hour, turning the roast every 15 minutes, until a meat thermometer registers 140°F (60°C) (medium).

2. To prepare the sauce, slip the skin off the figs. Cut the figs into quarters and combine them in a medium saucepan with the olive oil, red and yellow peppers, celery, and salt and black pepper to taste. Cover and simmer the mixture for 40 minutes, stirring occasionally, until the vegetables are very tender. Purée the mixture through a food mill fitted with the fine disk or in a food processor.

3. When the roast is ready, transfer it from the pan to a carving board. Cover it with aluminum foil and let it rest for 10 minutes. The pan juices can be reserved for use at another time. Thinly slice the veal. Arrange 3 or 4 slices on each plate and lightly coat each slice with a spoonful of the sauce. This dish can be served either warm or at room temperature.

MAKES 8 SERVINGS

Note: The pan juices can be strained and thickened slightly with flour, then used as a sauce with fresh pasta.

The view from the upper level of the house affords a panorama of the surrounding towns and villages, RIGHT.

Vitello in Antica Salsa di Peperoni e Fichi, *LEFT, a roast veal with a sweet pepper and fig sauce is served as antipasto.* Tartà con Intingolo, *BELOW, is a savory flan served with a sauce of fresh herbs and tomatoes.*

Gnocchetti Verdi con Funghi Porcini

Tiny Green Gnocchi with Fresh Porcini Mushroom Sauce

Franco Carnero prepares gnocchetti verdi, *tiny green potato dumplings scarcely the size of a hazelnut. To add color as well as flavor he uses a combination of leafy greens and fresh herbs that his wife, Ester, cooks ahead. She varies the mixture of greens according to availability and whim. She then pairs the herbaceous freshness of the gnocchetti with the earthiness of porcini mushrooms, creating a delightful autumn* primo piatto, *or first course.*

To achieve a light-as-air texture it is important not to add too much flour to the gnocchetti dough. The more flour worked in, the tougher the gnocchetti will be. To avoid overflouring, squeeze the greens well after they have been cooked, then blot away excess moisture with a paper towel. It is also important to use a potato that is low in moisture but high in starch like a russet, also known as Idaho. Never use a new potato, or a boiling potato; they contain too much moisture, and would require additional flour.

For the Gnocchetti

1½ POUNDS RUSSET POTATOES, SCRUBBED

4 LARGE EGG YOLKS

½ CUP (4 OZ/125 G) COOKED LEAFY GREENS, SUCH AS SPINACH (SEE PAGE 141), SWISS CHARD LEAVES, NETTLES, OR BORAGE, SQUEEZED VERY DRY AND FINELY CHOPPED (SEE NOTE)

1½ CUPS (6 OZ/180 G) UNBLEACHED ALL-PURPOSE FLOUR

For the Porcini Mushroom Sauce

1 POUND (450 G) FRESH PORCINI MUSHROOMS (SEE NOTE)

5 TABLESPOONS (3 OZ/85 G) UNSALTED BUTTER

4 TABLESPOONS (2 FL OZ/60 ML) EXTRA VIRGIN OLIVE OIL

1 MEDIUM ONION, CHOPPED

1 SMALL CLOVE OF GARLIC, FINELY CHOPPED

2 TABLESPOONS CHOPPED ITALIAN FLAT-LEAF PARSLEY LEAVES

SEA SALT AND FRESHLY GROUND BLACK PEPPER

½ CUP (2 OZ/60 G) GRATED PARMIGIANO-REGGIANO, PLUS ADDITIONAL FOR SERVING

1. To prepare the *gnocchetti*, place the whole potatoes in a large pot filled with cold water to cover the potatoes by 2 inches (5 cm). Bring the water to a boil and cook for 20 to 25 minutes or until the potatoes are tender when pierced with a small paring knife. Drain the potatoes and let them rest just until they are cool enough to handle. If the potatoes cool completely they will become gummy. Peel the potatoes and cut them into chunks. Purée them through a food mill fitted with the fine disk. (If a food mill is not available, use a potato ricer or a sieve, not a food processor.)

2. Line a large tray or baking sheet with a cotton kitchen towel. Lightly dust the towel with flour.

3. Combine the potatoes with the egg yolks and spinach in a large bowl. Blend in 1 cup (4 oz/120 g) of the flour, then turn the dough out onto a wooden pastry board or work surface. Knead the dough with the remaining ½ cup (2 oz/60g) of flour. Incorporate only as much of the flour as needed to make the dough smooth but still slightly sticky. The rest of the flour will be used while cutting the gnocchetti.

4. Divide the dough into 8 equal portions. Work with 1 piece of dough at a time, keeping the other portions of dough covered with wax paper. Roll the dough on the unfloured pastry board into a rope ½ inch (1.25 cm) thick. Cut the rope into small nuggets ½ inch (1.25 cm) long. Transfer the gnocchetti to the towel-lined tray and lightly dust them with flour. Roll and cut the remaining dough in the same way. Cover the gnocchetti with another towel. They can be refrigerated up to 1 or 2 hours until they are ready to be cooked.

5. To prepare the sauce, use a dry pastry brush or paper towel to clean the fresh porcini mushrooms. Brush away any surface soil or grit but do not soak the mushrooms in water. Trim off the dry end of the stems and finely chop the mushrooms.

6. Heat the butter and olive oil in a sauté pan large enough to hold the gnocchetti until the butter is melted. Add the onion and sauté over low heat until the onion is very tender and golden, about 15 minutes. Add the garlic and cook for 1 minute. Add the mushrooms, raise the heat to medium-high, and cook for 2 to 3 minutes. Stir in the parsley, and salt and pepper to taste and cook for 1 minute more. Remove the pan from the heat.

7. Fill a very large pot (at least 8 quarts/8 liters) with water and bring it to a rapid boil over high heat. Add salt to taste. Add the gnocchetti and cover the pot just until it returns to a boil. After the gnocchetti rise to the top of the pot, cook them for 2 minutes more.

8. Heat the porcini mushroom sauce over medium heat. Add ⅓ cup (3 fl oz/80 ml) of the water from the boiling gnocchetti. Simmer the sauce while the gnocchetti continue to cook.

9. When they are ready, use a large skimmer to transfer the gnocchetti to the pan of sauce. Lower the heat, sprinkle over ½ cup (2 oz/60 g) Parmigiano, and gently toss the gnocchetti until they are evenly coated with the sauce and the cheese has melted. Transfer the gnocchetti to a large serving platter and serve immediately with a bowl of Parmigiano for sprinkling.

MAKES 4 SERVINGS

Notes: 1. Ester combines 2 or 3 leafy greens in equal amounts which she boils separately until wilted. She squeezes out all of the moisture, then chops them together very fine.

2. When fresh porcini mushrooms are not available the mushroom sauce can be made with 1 pound of any cultivated or wild mushrooms that can be purchased in specialty markets (see page 19) and 1 ounce of dried porcini mushrooms. Clean the fresh mushrooms as directed in Step 5 and finely chop them. Soak the dried porcini mushrooms in ½ cup (4 fl oz/125 ml) of warm water for 15 minutes. Lift them out of the soaking liquid, reserving the liquid. Scrape off any grit left on the porcini and finely chop them. Strain the liquid through a double layer of cheesecloth. Use the fresh cultivated or wild mushrooms and the dried porcini mushrooms for the fresh porcini mushrooms in Step 6. Substitute ⅓ cup (3 fl oz/80 ml) of the porcini liquid for the water added to the sauce from the gnocchetti pot in Step 8.

Anitra all'Uva

Braised Duck with Wine Grapes

Ester Carnero sometimes blends the pulp of fresh fruit into the pan juices of her braised duck. Her choice of fruit is, of course, determined by the season. During vendemmia, *the wine harvest, Ester uses a combination of green and red wine grapes from the vineyards at La Luna e i Falò—Moscato Bianco, Barbera, or Dolcetto. The grapes are simmered briefly then puréed with the pan juices and aromatic vegetables that were braised with the duck. Whole grapes are added again at the end and cooked briefly.*

If wine grapes are not available, any table grape can be used. Muscat table grapes are an excellent choice. They become available in mid-fall, imported from Sicily or shipped from California.

1   WHOLE DUCK (4 TO 5 POUNDS/1.8 TO 2.2K)

4   TABLESPOONS (2 OZ/60 G) EXTRA VIRGIN OLIVE OIL

SEA SALT AND FRESHLY GROUND BLACK PEPPER

1   MEDIUM ONION, CUT INTO SMALL CHUNKS

1   CELERY STALK, CUT INTO SMALL CHUNKS

7   TEASPOONS FINELY CHOPPED MIXED HERB LEAVES, SUCH AS
    OREGANO, ROSEMARY, SAGE, AND THYME

2   SMALL BAY LEAVES

⅔   CUP (5½ FL OZ/160 ML) DRY WHITE WINE

10   GREEN AND 10 RED WINE OR TABLE GRAPES, PLUS 1½ CUPS
     (10 OZ/300 G) MIXED GREEN AND RED GRAPES

1. Remove the liver and gizzards from the cavity of the duck and reserve them for another use. Rinse the duck inside and out and dry it

well. Heat 2 tablespoons (1 oz/30 g) of the olive oil in a large flame-proof casserole over medium-high heat. Add the duck and brown evenly on all sides. Transfer the duck to a platter and drain off the fat in the casserole.

2. When the duck has cooled, season the cavity with salt and pepper and fill it with half of the onion and celery and 2 teaspoons of the chopped herbs. Rub the surface of the duck with an additional 2 teaspoons of the herbs and season with salt and pepper.

3. Heat the remaining 2 tablespoons (1 fl oz/30 ml) olive oil in the casserole over medium heat. Add the duck and scatter around it the remaining celery, onions, and the bay leaves. Cook, stirring the vegetables often, until they are lightly golden, about 10 minutes. Pour over the white wine and bring it to a boil. Simmer until half of the wine has evaporated. Pour in 2 cups (16 fl oz/250 ml) of hot water and bring the liquid back to a boil. Partially cover the pan and simmer for 1 hour, turning the duck every 20 minutes. Stir 10 green and 10 red grapes into the casserole and simmer another 30 minutes or until the duck is fully cooked. (To test the duck for doneness, pierce the meaty portion of the thigh with a small paring knife. If the juices run clear, the duck is fully cooked. If the juices are pink, cook the duck 15 minutes more and test it again.)

4. Transfer the duck from the casserole to a shallow platter and cover it with aluminum foil. Discard the bay leaves and purée the contents of the casserole through a food mill fitted with the fine disk. Discard the solids left in the mill. (If a food mill is not available, pass the mixture through a sieve.) Degrease the sauce and pour it back into the casserole. Simmer the sauce briskly until it has thickened slightly. Stir in the remaining 1½ cups (10 oz/300 g) of grapes and the remaining 3 teaspoons of herbs. Simmer the sauce for 2 to 3 minutes and season it with salt and pepper to taste. Cut the duck into small serving pieces, removing the skin, if desired. Arrange it on a shallow serving platter. Spoon the sauce and the grapes over the duck and serve immediately.

MAKES 4 SERVINGS

Note: If you are not serving the duck immediately, purée the sauce and thicken it, but do not add the grapes and herbs as indicated in Step 4. When ready, reheat the cut-up duck in the sauce, remove it, and degrease the sauce again. Stir the grapes, herbs, and salt and pepper to taste into the sauce and simmer for 2 to 3 minutes.

Ester Carnero describes her cuisine as

Astigiano, in the style of the province of Asti.

Panna Cotta dell' Antico Piemonte

Cream Pudding with Caramel Syrup

Panna cotta, which means cooked cream, is a dessert that has gained wide popularity throughout Italy though its roots are in Piedmont. It combines scalded milk and heavy cream with rum, Marsala, and vanilla. A small proportion of gelatin is added to give the mixture a pudding-like texture after it has been chilled. The panna cotta is poured into a form that has been coated with caramel. When the dessert is unmolded, it sits in a syrupy caramel sauce. Ester Carnero prepares her panna cotta most often in a loaf pan but it can also be made in a ring mold or individual ramekins.

⅔ CUP (4½ OZ/140 G) SUGAR
1¾ CUPS (14 FL OZ/435 ML) WHOLE MILK
2¼ TEASPOONS UNFLAVORED GELATIN (SEE NOTE)
2 CUPS (16 FL OZ/500 ML) HEAVY CREAM
1 CUP (3½ OZ/110 G) CONFECTIONERS' SUGAR
2 TABLESPOONS (1 FL OZ/30 ML) WHITE RUM
1 TABLESPOON DRY MARSALA WINE
1½ TEAPOONS VANILLA EXTRACT

1. Preheat the oven to 250°F (120°C). Warm a 9 x 5-inch (23 x 12.5-cm) loaf pan in the oven while making the syrup.

2. Heat the sugar in a small heavy saucepan over medium-low heat. Do not stir until the sugar begins to melt around the edges of the pan. Stir with a wooden spoon until the sugar dissolves into a smooth syrup that is nutty brown in color. Quickly pour the caramel syrup into the warm loaf pan and rotate the pan to evenly coat the surface. The caramel syrup will be very hot, so be sure to wear protective oven mitts when handling the saucepan and while coating the loaf pan. Set the pan on a wire rack to cool completely. The caramel will harden and crack.

3. Pour ¼ cup (2 fl oz/60 ml) of the milk into a small bowl. Sprinkle over the gelatin and set aside. The gelatin will become spongy in texture. Scald the remaining 1½ cups (12 fl oz/375 ml) of milk in a small saucepan over medium heat. Remove the pan from the heat and add the gelatin mixture. Stir until it is completely dissolved.

4. In another saucepan, combine the heavy cream with the confectioners' sugar and warm over medium heat. Stir constantly with a wooden spoon until the cream is very warm and the sugar is completely dissolved. (Do not boil.) Pour the cream mixture into a large bowl, combine it with the milk mixture and let it cool completely.

5. When cool, stir in the rum, Marsala, and vanilla. Pour the mixture through a strainer into the caramelized loaf pan. Refrigerate the pan overnight or until the panna cotta becomes firm. Unmold the panna cotta onto a shallow, rectangular serving platter and refrigerate it until you are ready to serve. Slice the panna cotta and spoon some of the caramel syrup over each slice.

MAKES 8 SERVINGS

Note: Ester uses just enough gelatin for the panna cotta to hold its shape while remaining light and creamy in texture. If you prefer it slightly firmer, use an additional ¼ teaspoon gelatin. In order for the panna cotta to unmold and slice easily, it must be kept very cold.

Torta di Nocciole delle Langhe

Classic Hazelnut Cake of the Langhe

A favorite dessert in Piedmont, this dense, buttery cake is made from ground hazelnuts. Ester's version is one that is eaten throughout the Langhe zone. Her husband, Franco, suggests serving it with a chilled glass of Moscato d'Asti.

1¾ CUPS (7 OZ/210 G) UNBLEACHED ALL-PURPOSE FLOUR
2 TEASPOONS BAKING POWDER
2 CUPS (10 OZ/300 G) BLANCHED HAZELNUTS (SEE NOTE)
3 LARGE EGGS
¾ CUP (5 OZ/150 G) SUGAR
7 TABLESPOONS (3½ OZ/110 G) UNSALTED BUTTER, MELTED AND
    COOLED TO ROOM TEMPERATURE
¼ CUP (2 FL OZ/60 ML) BREWED ITALIAN ESPRESSO COFFEE
¼ CUP (2 FL OZ/60 ML) WHOLE MILK
2 TABLESPOONS (1 FL OZ/30 ML) LIGHT RUM
1 TABLESPOON PURE OLIVE OIL
1 TEASPOON VANILLA EXTRACT
8 AMARETTI COOKIES, CRUSHED

1. Preheat the oven to 375°F (190°C). Butter a 9-inch (23-cm) cake pan and lightly dust with flour.

2. Sift the flour and baking powder together. Spread the hazelnuts on a baking sheet and toast them in the oven for 10 minutes, or until they are golden brown. Cool completely. When cool, finely grind the nuts in a food processor.

3. Beat the eggs and sugar in a large bowl for 1 minute using an electric mixer on high speed. Switch the speed to low and blend in the melted butter, coffee, milk, rum, olive oil, and vanilla. When well blend-

ed, stir in the ground nuts and amaretti cookies. Add the flour mixture and beat on low, just until the flour has dissolved. Pour the mixture into the cake pan. Bake on the center shelf of the oven for 40 to 45 minutes, or until a toothpick inserted into the center of the *torta* comes out clean. Cool for 10 minutes on a cooling rack, then turn the torta out of the pan. Reverse the torta and cool it completely before serving.

MAKES 8 SERVINGS

Note: If blanched hazelnuts are not available, toast hazelnuts with their skins, as directed in Step 2. When cool, rub off the skins with a cotton kitchen towel. (It may not be possible to remove the entire skin.)

PAGE 44, Anitra all'Uva, *Braised Duck with Wine Grapes.*
PAGE 45, Panna Cotta dell'Antico Piemonte, *Cream Pudding with Caramel Syrup.* ABOVE, Torta di Nocciole delle Langhe, *Classic Hazelnut Cake of the Langhe.*

LA VIRANDA

*Lorella and Claudio Solito,
ABOVE, have run the
country farmhouse restaurant,
La Viranda, for more than
ten years. OPPOSITE, savoy
cabbage is stuffed with a
combination of fall vegetables
and cheese to make
Caponet. These savory little
bundles are served as an
antipasto.*

*San
Marzano
Oliveto*

Sunday, the traditional day of rest for Italians, is a
day to gather with family and friends and journey
out to the countryside to explore its treasures.
It is a day to visit historic villages, to view works of
art in small churches, or simply to mill about a
crowded piazza. The crisp autumn weather and the
excitement inspired by the harvest stimulate the appetite of
many Italians to escape into farm country to celebrate the season
with a hearty Sunday lunch.

The countryside once abounded with rustic family-run restaurants specializing in
well-prepared, humble foods of the locality. Today the possibilities are not as numerous,
but the best places are easily identifiable when driving back roads through small villages.
They are often unassuming structures, devoid of any signposts. The only distinguishing
feature is a crowded parking area, overflowing with vehicles on a Sunday afternoon.
Sounds of laughter, mingled with the rattling of pots and pans and the clinking of glasses
and dishes, are often heard through open windows, shattering the rural silence.

One such jewel of a place is a large, white modest farmhouse set among the
expanse of vineyards and fruit orchards in the sleepy village of San Marzano Oliveto in
the Monferrato zone of Piedmont. La Viranda is not the kind of restaurant you often
read about in tourist guidebooks. It is a country restaurant steeped in tradition, a place
that anyone who appreciates simple, authentic food yearns to discover.

San Marzano Oliveto is permeated with the essence of autumn. The air is sweet.
It is filled with the fragrance of ripening fall fruit—apples, pears, plums, figs, quince,
persimmons, and wine grapes. Entering La Viranda, you are tantalized by the heady scent
of slow-cooked meats braising in hearty local wines. There are glorious undertones
of cooked fruit and caramelized sugar. These are the comforting aromas of Piedmont.

Sunday lunch in Italy is the important meal of the day, served between one and
three in the afternoon. Guests begin arriving at La Viranda shortly before opening and
by two it is filled to capacity. The atmosphere is lively and jovial; there is a warm
holidaylike spirit. Groups of family and friends gather at long trestle tables to feast on

dishes that rekindle cherished memories—visions of grandmothers, mothers, and aunts in flour-dusted aprons busy working in cluttered, steamy kitchens. As bottles bearing the La Viranda label are uncorked, glasses are hastily filled. Guests raise their glasses to toast family and friendship as worn wooden cutting boards topped with hand-made salami wrapped in cotton towels are delivered to tables with baskets of crusty bread. After a brief pause the excitement once again heightens as energetic young women emerge from the kitchen carrying platters of handmade pasta. They exchange conversation with guests as though they, too, were part of the family and celebration.

Hearty meat dishes are the common offerings for secondo, the course that follows the pasta. They are prepared in the traditional Monferrato style: bathed in wine, perfumed with branches of herbs, cooked over a low fire, and accompanied by simple side dishes, or *contorni*.

Readying the dessert course behind the scenes is a brother-and-sister team committed to respecting family traditions and "old ways." They serve a sampling of regional desserts best accompanied by a chilled glass of their esteemed sparkling dessert wine, Moscato d'Asti.

Lorella and Claudio Solito have run their country farmhouse restaurant for more than ten years. Lorella, who is reserved and soft-spoken, brings with her the knowledge and the spirit of her grandmother's kitchen, where her culinary experience began. Under the loving guidance of her *nonna*, Lorella started by assisting with the *dolci*, the traditional desserts of the Piedmont. The creamy puddings, nut cakes, and fruit tarts Lorella serves to her guests are those she and her family have always eaten at home.

Claudio puts other responsibilities aside and joins Lorella in the kitchen on weekends to assist in the preparation of the pasta, sauces, and some of the antipasti. Claudio also cures most of the pork products. He makes more than seventeen hundred pounds of salami each year, in addition to pancetta and *coppa*, a rolled shoulder of pork cured with white wine and

seasoned with ground cloves. Processing begins in late fall, after the wine harvest, and continues through early spring.

Most of La Viranda's sixty acres, which were once a cattle farm, are now vineyards. The land is maintained by a cooperative of family farmers who joined forces in the interest of preserving the abandoned vineyards of the Monferrato. Lorella and Claudio are members of the cooperative, which furnishes them with high-quality products used in the restaurant—meat, poultry, eggs, cheese, milk, butter, and all of their fresh vegetables. Claudio produces the wines he serves and sells at La Viranda. San Marzano Oliveto lies within the wine growing province of Asti, and Claudio produces some of its best wines—Barbera d'Asti, Dolcetto d'Asti, and Freisa d'Asti, as well as a Cabernet Sauvignon, Cortese del Piemonte, and the sweet, sparkling Moscato d'Asti.

Most of the fruit trees in the orchard were planted by the previous owner. They produce sweet and sour cherries, peaches, nectarines, plums, figs, quince, and several varieties of apples and pears. Lorella preserves the fruit, starting in early summer and continuing through fall when the last quince is pulled from the tree. She makes several kinds of jams and jellies and floats stone fruit in syrup or douses it in spirits. She captures the essence of apples in her apple nectar and blends fragrant honey with toasted hazelnuts from La Viranda's trees. Her *mostarda*, an old-fashioned fruit and nut conserve sweetened with grape must, is made with a blend of apples, pears, quince, figs, and crushed nuts. The mostarda is served as a condiment with boiled meats or local cheeses. Lorella also jars marinated vegetables in olive oil, whole tomatoes with basil leaves, and a tomato conserve. Many of her products are proudly displayed on a shelf in the restaurant.

As the sound of the espresso machine echoes through the dining room, contented guests prepare to leave, often taking home a taste of the Monferrato countryside—Claudio's wines, Lorella's preserves, or simply a basket of apples.

OPPOSITE, a bowl of Agnolotti La Viranda, *ravioli served with butter and sage. BELOW, the coffee bar at La Viranda. On weekends, Claudio, BOTTOM, trades farm chores for kitchen duty.*

For every cook in Piedmont, there must surely be a recipe for agnolotti.

Insalata Borghese
Chicken and Roasted Pepper Salad

Lorella serves this salad as a cold antipasto in fall when the sweet, fleshy red and yellow peppers for which Piedmont is renowned are in season.

3 RED BELL PEPPERS

3 YELLOW BELL PEPPERS

2 WHOLE FREE-RANGE CHICKEN BREASTS, POACHED

8 OUNCES (240 G) SWISS EMMENTAL CHEESE

3 TABLESPOONS (1½ OZ/45 G) SALT-PACKED CAPERS

3 SALT-PACKED ANCHOVIES, FILLETED (SEE PAGE 12)

1 TABLESPOON DIJON MUSTARD

6 TABLESPOONS (3 FL OZ/90 ML) EXTRA VIRGIN OLIVE OIL

SEA SALT

10 LARGE BASIL LEAVES

1. Preheat the broiler. Arrange the whole peppers on a broiler pan or baking sheet. Roast them under the broiler, until they are evenly blistered, but not charred. Let the peppers rest until cool enough to handle.

2. Remove the skin and debone the chicken breasts. Cut the meat into ⅜ by 1¾-inch (1 by 4.5-cm) julienne strips. Cut the cheese in the same way and combine them in a large bowl.

3. Peel and core the roasted peppers. Cut them into julienne strips, the same size as the chicken and cheese. Add to the bowl.

4. Soak the capers in 3 changes of cold water to remove the salt. Drain and dry them with paper towels. Finely chop the anchovies.

5. To make the dressing, whisk the mustard with 1 tablespoon (½ fl oz/15 ml) of the olive oil in a small bowl. Add the remaining olive oil, 1 tablespoon (½ fl oz/15 ml) at a time. Season with salt to taste.

6. Pour the dressing over the ingredients in the large bowl. Add the anchovies and capers and gently toss. Tear the basil into small pieces, add to the bowl, and toss again. Serve immediately.

MAKES 8 SERVINGS

Caponèt
Cabbage Leaves Stuffed with Mixed Vegetables

These savory little cabbage bundles are a traditional Piedmontese antipasto. Lorella uses savoy cabbage, called cavolo verza, *which has a delicate texture and richly intense cabbage flavor. The* caponèt *are stuffed with a combination of cheese and fall vegetables that include cardoons, the stalk of an edible thistle. If unavailable, use the bottoms of two medium artichokes that have been trimmed (see note,*

page 136) and cooked just until tender. The artichoke, a cousin of the cardoon, has a very similar taste and is harvested a second time in early fall; the first harvest is in spring. The vegetable stuffing yields enough to make 48 very small cabbage rolls.

2 LARGE SAVOY CABBAGES, CORED

1 LARGE STALK CARDOON

JUICE OF ½ LEMON

3 CUPS (18 OZ/500 G) CAULIFLOWER FLORETS

2 MEDIUM CARROTS, CUT INTO ½-INCH (1.25-CM) DICE

2 SMALL WHITE TURNIPS, CUT INTO ½-INCH (1.25-CM) DICE

1 SMALL ONION, FINELY CHOPPED

2 TABLESPOONS CHOPPED ITALIAN FLAT-LEAF PARSLEY LEAVES

½ CUP (2 OZ/60 G) SHREDDED FONTINA D'AOSTA CHEESE

½ CUP (2 OZ/60 G) SHREDDED SWISS EMMENTAL CHEESE

⅓ CUP (1½ OZ/45 G) GRATED PARMIGIANO-REGGIANO

SEA SALT AND FRESHLY GROUND BLACK PEPPER

4 LARGE EGGS, LIGHTLY BEATEN

2 TABLESPOONS (1 OZ/30 G) UNSALTED BUTTER

½ CUP (4 FL OZ/125 ML) MEAT BROTH OR VEGETABLE BROTH (FOR HOMEMADE, SEE PAGE 187)

1. Fill a large pot (at least 6 quarts/6 liters) with water and bring it to a boil. Add salt to taste. Line 2 large trays or baking sheets with paper towels for draining the vegetables.

2. Separate enough large cabbage leaves to make 48 rolls. Very large leaves make 4 rolls, medium leaves make 2. Cook the whole leaves, 3 at a time, in the boiling water for 2 minutes, or just until they are flexible. Using a large skimmer or strainer, remove them from the pot and transfer them to a tray. Continue to boil the water.

3. Cut enough of the remaining cabbage into 1-inch (2.5-cm) pieces to measure 1 cup. Cook the cabbage for 10 minutes, or until tender, and transfer it to the other tray. When the cut-up cabbage is cool, squeeze out all of the moisture, then pat it dry with paper towels. (Any cabbage that remains can be reserved for another use.)

4. To prepare the cardoon for cooking, fill a bowl with cold water and stir in lemon juice. Trim away the leafy edges of the cardoon. Pull off the tough fibrous strings, as for a celery stalk. Cut the cardoon into 2-inch (5-cm) pieces and soak in the lemon water.

5. Replenish the water in the pot as necessary and bring it back to a boil. Cook the cauliflower in the boiling water for 5 minutes, or until tender, and transfer it to the tray with the diced cabbage. Cook the carrots, then the turnips, in the same way, for 7 to 8 minutes each or until tender, and transfer them to the tray. Cook the cardoon in the boiling water until tender, 30 to 45 minutes, and add it to the tray of vegetables.

6. Preheat the oven to 400°F (200°C).

7. Combine the diced cabbage, cauliflower, carrots, turnips, and cardoon on a cutting board and chop them together until very fine. Transfer the vegetables to a large bowl. Add the onion, parsley, fontina, emmental, and Parmigiano. Season with salt and pepper to taste, then blend in the eggs.

8. Remove the spine of the whole cabbage leaves and cut each one into pieces that are at least 4 x 5 inches (10 x 12 cm). Place 1 tablespoon of the vegetable mixture on the center of each piece. Fold in the sides of the leaf to cover the filling, then roll up the leaves. Arrange the rolls, side by side, in a buttered baking pan. Cut the butter into small pieces and scatter them over the cabbage rolls. Pour the broth into the pan and bake the cabbage rolls, uncovered, for 30 minutes, or until they are piping hot and lightly browned on top. Serve immediately.

MAKES 12 SERVINGS

Rollata di Coniglio
Boned Rabbit Stuffed with Vegetables and Herbs

This boneless rabbit, stuffed with prosciutto and fresh herbs, is rolled around a whole carrot and celery stalk that creates a striking affect when sliced. The rollata can also be made with a chicken of equal size that has been skinned, butterflied, and boned. Boning a rabbit or chicken, if you are not experienced, is a job best left to your butcher. Order ahead to give him ample time.

2 MEDIUM CARROTS, PEELED

2 MEDIUM CELERY STALKS

SEA SALT AND FRESHLY GROUND BLACK PEPPER

1 WHOLE RABBIT (3 POUNDS/1.4 K), BONED

1 TEASPOON FINELY CHOPPED THYME LEAVES, PLUS 1 SPRIG
   OF THYME

1 TEASPOON FINELY CHOPPED ROSEMARY LEAVES, PLUS 1 SPRIG
   OF ROSEMARY

1 TEASPOON FINELY CHOPPED SAGE LEAVES, PLUS 1 SPRIG OF SAGE

2 OUNCES (60 G) IMPORTED ITALIAN PROSCIUTTO, THINLY SLICED

1 BAY LEAF

2 TABLESPOONS (1 FL OZ/30 ML) EXTRA VIRGIN OLIVE OIL

2 TABLESPOONS (1 OZ/30 G) UNSALTED BUTTER

1 MEDIUM ONION, CUT INTO 1-INCH (2.5-CM) PIECES

1 LARGE CLOVE OF GARLIC, CRUSHED

1 CUP (8 FL OZ/250 ML) DRY WHITE WINE

1 CUP (8 FL OZ/250 ML) MEAT BROTH
   (FOR HOMEMADE, SEE PAGE 187)

1. Cut 1 carrot and 1 celery stalk into 1-inch (2.5-cm) pieces, leave others whole. Fill a large pot (at least 6 quarts/6 liters) with water and bring it to a boil. Salt the water to taste and blanch the whole carrot and celery stalk for 2 minutes. Drain and refresh the vegetables under cold water and dry them with paper towels.

2. Extend the rabbit on a flat work surface. Remove any visible fat. Season with salt and pepper and sprinkle with the chopped thyme, rosemary, and sage leaves. Layer the prosciutto slices over the herbs, slightly overlapping. Arrange the blanched carrot and celery across the neck end of the rabbit. Roll the rabbit around the vegetables, tuck in the ends, and tie it like a roast with twine.

3. Make an herb bouquet with the bay leaf and sprigs of thyme, rosemary, and sage. Tie it together with twine.

4. Heat the olive oil and butter in a large, heavy flame-proof casserole over medium-high heat. Add the roast and brown it well on all sides. Remove it from the pan to a large platter and season with salt and pepper to taste. Add the cut-up carrot, celery, and onion to the casserole. Cook the vegetables over medium heat until golden brown. Add the garlic and cook for 1 minute more. Return the rabbit to the casserole and pour over the white wine. Raise the heat to medium-high, bring the wine to a boil, and reduce it by one third. Pour in the broth and add the herb bouquet. Cover the pan and simmer the rabbit slowly for 1½ hours, rotating it every 20 minutes.

5. Remove the rabbit from the casserole and cover with aluminum foil. Strain the pan juices and return them to the casserole. Simmer briskly to thicken slightly. Season with salt and pepper if needed. Slice the roast and moisten the slices with the pan juices.

MAKES 6 SERVINGS

LEFT, Lorella prepares a cheese board using a selection of cheeses typical of the Monferrato zone of Piedmont and produced by their farm cooperative.

Agnolotti La Viranda
Spinach- and Meat-Filled Ravioli

For every cook in Piedmont, there must surely be a recipe for agnolotti. *These pillows of overstuffed pasta, also called ravioli, are filled with a multitude of ingredients. They often include one or more meats and vegetables in combination with rice, cheese, and aromatic herbs and spices.*

The savory filling Lorella uses for her agnolotti combines Rollatine di Vitello *(recipe follows), with a classic* Arrosto di Vitello e Maiale *(page 56). The meats are ground together with cooked spinach and rice, then blended with eggs, cheese, and nutmeg. A rather lengthy procedure when you consider the time it takes to first prepare the meats. To get the most out of the time you invest, make the rollatine for dinner the night before and set aside half of the meat rolls and ⅓ cup (3 fl oz/80 ml) of the pan juices. You will be left with three portions. The arrosto can also be made the day before. The agnolotti can be served with melted butter and sage or the pan juices from the arrosto. They can also be cooked and served in a homemade meat broth (see page 187).*

For the Filling
- 1   POUND (450 G) SPINACH, STEMMED AND WELL WASHED
  (SEE PAGE 141)
- SEA SALT
- 2   TABLESPOONS (1 OZ/30 G) UNSALTED BUTTER
- 2   TABLESPOONS PLUS ¾ CUP (3 OZ/90 G) GRATED
  PARMIGIANO-REGGIANO
- ¾   CUP (4 OZ/120 G) ARBORIO RICE
- ½   RECIPE ROLLATINE DI VITELLO (RECIPE FOLLOWS), COOLED,
  WITH ⅓ CUP (3 FL OZ/80 ML) PAN JUICES
- ARROSTO DI VITELLO E MAIALE (PAGE 56), COOLED AND DRAINED
- 6   LARGE EGGS
- ½   TEASPOON FRESHLY GRATED NUTMEG

For the Pasta
- 7   CUPS (30 OZ/840 G) UNBLEACHED ALL-PURPOSE FLOUR
- 10   LARGE EGGS
- 5   TEASPOONS EXTRA VIRGIN OLIVE OIL
- ¼   TEASPOON SEA SALT

- 12   TABLESPOONS (6 OZ/185 G) UNSALTED BUTTER
- 20   SMALL FRESH SAGE LEAVES
- 1   CUP (4 OZ/120 G) GRATED PARMIGIANO-REGGIANO, PLUS
  ADDITIONAL FOR SERVING

1. To make the filling, place the spinach with only the water that clings to its leaves in a large heavy skillet. Sprinkle with a pinch of salt, cover the skillet, and cook over medium heat, stirring, until it is wilted, 7 to 8 minutes. Drain the spinach, refresh it under cold water, and drain again. Squeeze out all of the water. Pat the spinach dry with paper towels and finely chop it. Heat the butter in a small skillet over medium heat. Add the spinach and cook until it is dry. Stir in the 2 tablespoons of Parmigiano-Reggiano and season with salt to taste. Cool the spinach completely.

2. Fill a large saucepan with water and bring it to a boil. Add salt to taste, and stir in the rice. Simmer until tender, 18 to 20 minutes. Drain the rice, then transfer it to a bowl and stir in ⅓ cup (3 fl oz/ 80 ml) of the pan juices from the rollatine. Cool the rice completely.

3. When all of the filling ingredients are cool, grind the spinach, rice, rollatine, and the *arrosto* through a meat grinder into a large bowl. Add the eggs, ¾ cup (3 oz/90 g) of the Parmigiano, nutmeg and salt to taste. Blend the mixture thoroughly.

4. To make the pasta dough for the *agnolotti*, use the flour, eggs, oil, and salt as directed on page 188, the section entitled Making the Dough. The dough will be kneaded and stretched in a manual pasta machine. Line 3 trays or baking sheets with cotton kitchen towels and dust lightly with flour.

5. Divide the dough into 10 equal portions and knead in the pasta machine as directed in the section entitled Kneading the Dough in a Pasta Machine.

6. Stretch the dough as directed in the section entitled Stretching the Dough in a Pasta Machine. Stretch the dough, one piece at a time, as thin as possible, taking it to the last setting on the dial. The agnolotti must be stuffed as soon as each piece of dough has been stretched.

7. Arrange the long sheet of dough on a lightly floured pastry board or work surface and cut it in half. Use 1 half at a time and keep the other half covered with a towel. Arrange the filling in a row of small mounds ½ inch (2.5 cm) from a long edge of the sheet, using a scant teaspoon of the filling mixture for each mound and spacing them ½ inch (2.5 cm) apart. Dip a small brush into water and lightly moisten the dough around the filling. Fold the sheet of dough length-wise in half to cover the mounds. Gently press the dough around the fillings and ease out any air bubbles while sealing the dough. Cut the agnolotti into small squares, leaving a ¼-inch (0.6-cm) border around the filling. (Reserve the scraps to serve in broth.) Transfer the agnolotti to one of the towel-lined trays. Continue to make agnolotti using the remaining pieces of pasta dough. Cover the agnolotti with cotton towels until they are ready to be cooked.

8. To cook the agnolotti fill a very large pot (at least 8 quarts/ 8 liters) with water and bring it to a rapid boil. Add salt to taste. Stir

in the agnolotti and cover the pot, just until the water returns to a boil. Uncover and boil the agnolotti, stirring occasionally, for 4 to 5 minutes, or until tender.

9. Meanwhile, melt the butter with the sage leaves in a sauté pan large enough to hold the agnolotti. Do not allow the butter to brown. When the agnolotti are ready, remove them from the pot with a large skimmer or strainer being sure to drain them well. Add the agnolotti to the pan. Sprinkle with Parmigiano and carefully toss over low heat until the agnolotti are evenly coated with butter and the cheese has melted. Transfer the agnolotti to a large serving platter and serve immediately, with a bowl of Parmigiano for sprinkling.

MAKES 10 SERVINGS

Note: The pan juices from the arrosto can be thickened with a pinch or two of flour and used as a sauce for homemade pasta.

Guests of La Viranda can take home a little taste of the Monferrato which Lorella preserves in jars, LEFT.

Rollatine di Vitello

Braised Veal Rolls

Lorella serves these rollatine, *or little veal rolls, as a meat course, or* secondo piatto, *sometimes adding potatoes to the pan. She always makes enough to put some aside for the stuffing in her* agnolotti *(see page 54), a Piedmontese ravioli. If you are preparing the rollatine for agnolotti set aside half of the meat rolls and ⅓ cup (3 oz/80 ml) of the pan juices before they have been reduced.*

2 OUNCES (60 G) IMPORTED ITALIAN PROSCIUTTO,
  COARSELY CHOPPED

1 SMALL ONION, COARSELY CHOPPED

2 SMALL CLOVES OF GARLIC, COARSELY CHOPPED

2 TABLESPOONS COARSELY CHOPPED ITALIAN FLAT-LEAF
  PARSLEY LEAVES

½ TEASPOON CHOPPED ROSEMARY LEAVES, PLUS 1 SPRIG
  OF ROSEMARY

1½ POUNDS (12 OZ/675 G) (12 PIECES) VEAL SCALOPPINE, PREFERABLY
  CUT FROM THE TOP ROUND, LIGHTLY POUNDED

3 TABLESPOONS (1½ FL OZ/45 ML) EXTRA VIRGIN OLIVE OIL

4 LARGE CANNED TOMATOES, DRAINED AND FINELY CHOPPED

½ CUP (4 FL OZ/125 ML) DRY WHITE WINE

⅔ CUP (5½ FL OZ/160 ML) MEAT BROTH (FOR HOMEMADE,
  SEE PAGE 187)

8 SMALL SAGE LEAVES

SEA SALT AND FRESHLY GROUND BLACK PEPPER

1. Combine the prosciutto, onion, garlic, parsley, and chopped rosemary on a cutting board. Chop them together until very fine. Arrange the scaloppine on a work surface and spoon equal amounts of the filling mixture onto the center of each. Roll up the scaloppine, tucking in the sides to enclose the filling. Tie rolls with butcher's twine.

2. Heat the olive oil in a medium-size heavy sauté pan over medium-high heat. Add 6 meat rolls and brown them evenly on all sides. Transfer them to a small platter. Brown the remaining rolls and add them to the platter. Add the tomatoes to the pan, and simmer briskly for 2 minutes. Pour in the white wine and simmer 2 minutes more. Return the meat rolls to the pan and pour the meat broth over them. Add the sprig of rosemary and the sage leaves. Season with salt and black pepper to taste.

3. Gently simmer the meat rolls, partially covered, turning occasionally, for 35 minutes, or until tender. Transfer the meat rolls to a shallow serving platter and snip off the twine. Continue to simmer the sauce to thicken it slightly. Discard the rosemary stem and spoon the sauce over the rollatine.

MAKES 6 SERVINGS

Variation: Lorella sometimes cooks the rollatine with potatoes. Peel 1 pound (16 oz/450 g) of small potatoes, preferably Yukon Gold, and cut them into 1½-inch (3.8-cm) chunks. Place the potatoes in a large saucepan and fill the pan with cold water to cover the potatoes by 2 inches (5 cm). Add salt to taste. Boil the potatoes 10 to 12 minutes or just until they are tender. Add the potatoes to the pan with the rollatine during the last 10 minutes of cooking. Remove the potatoes and rollatine from the pan while reducing the sauce.

Arrosto di Vitello e Maiale

Braised Veal and Pork Chunks

These tender chunks of veal and pork can be served with mashed potatoes as a side dish, or contorno.

2 TABLESPOONS (1 FL OZ/30 ML) EXTRA VIRGIN OLIVE OIL

¾ POUND (12 OZ/350 G) BONELESS VEAL SHOULDER, CUT INTO 2-INCH (5-CM) CHUNKS

¾ POUND (12 OZ/350 G) BONELESS PORK SHOULDER, CUT INTO 2-INCH (5-CM) CHUNKS

⅔ CUP (5½ FL OZ/160 ML) DRY WHITE WINE

1 SPRIG OF ROSEMARY

5 SMALL SAGE LEAVES

SEA SALT AND FRESHLY GROUND BLACK PEPPER

1. Heat the olive oil in a small heavy flame-proof casserole over medium-high heat. Add half of the meat and brown well on all sides. Transfer the meat to a small platter. Add the remaining meat and cook it in the same way. Return all of the meat to the pan and pour over the white wine. Add the rosemary, sage, and salt and pepper to taste. Partially cover the pan and simmer gently. Turn the pieces occasionally and cook for 50 minutes, or just until the meat is tender.

2. To thicken the pan juices, if desired, transfer the meat with a slotted spoon to a small serving bowl. Simmer the juices briskly until they have thickened as desired. Taste for additional seasoning and pour the pan juices over the meat. Serve the arrosto immediately.

MAKES 4 SERVINGS

Torta di Mele con Prugne

Double-crusted Apple-Plum Tart

Lorella uses a tart green apple just picked from the fruit orchards of La Viranda for her apple and plum tart. Her pastry crust is crisp and buttery yet sturdy enough to contain the pale pink juices that seep from the fruit.

For the Pastry Dough

2⅓ CUPS (10 OZ/280 G) UNBLEACHED ALL-PURPOSE FLOUR

¼ CUP (2½ OZ/50 G) SUGAR PLUS ADDITIONAL FOR SPRINKLING

1 LARGE EGG, LIGHTLY BEATEN

PINCH OF SEA SALT

7 TABLESPOONS (3½ FL OZ/110 ML) WHOLE MILK, TEPID

5 TABLESPOONS (2½ OZ/75 G) UNSALTED BUTTER, SOFTENED

For the Filling

4 TABLESPOONS (2 FL OZ/60 ML) UNSALTED BUTTER

2 POUNDS (32 OZ/900 G) GRANNY SMITH APPLES, PEELED, CORED, AND CUT INTO ¾-INCH (2-CM) SLICES

1 POUND (16 OZ/450 G) ITALIAN PRUNE PLUMS OR EMPRESS PLUMS

2 TABLESPOONS (1 FL OZ/30 ML) APPLE JUICE

⅔ CUP (4½ OZ/140 G) SUGAR

1 TABLESPOON LIGHT RUM

1. To make the pastry dough, mound the flour on a pastry board or work surface, or pour it into a bowl. Make a well in the center and add ¼ cup (2½ oz/50 g) sugar, the egg, a pinch of salt, milk, and softened butter. Blend the ingredients in the well with a fork. Gradually incorporate the flour to make a soft ball of dough. Knead the dough gently for 1 minute, or until it is smooth and very tender. Wrap the dough in wax paper and let it rest at room temperature for at least 30 minutes.

2. Preheat the oven to 375°F (190°C).

3. To make the filling, melt the butter in a large skillet. Add the apple slices and sauté over medium-high heat, stirring often, until the apples are al dente. Do not allow the apples to become soft. Stir in the plums, apple juice, and sugar. Cook, tossing constantly, until the sugar is dissolved. Add the rum and continue to cook until the juices have thickened. Let the apple mixture cool completely.

4. When the apples are cool, lightly dust the pastry board or work surface with flour and roll out two thirds of the dough to a 15-inch (38-cm) round. Carefully roll the dough onto the rolling pin then lower it into an 11-inch (28-cm) tart tin. Gently press the dough into the corners and against the sides of the tin. Allow the excess dough to hang over the sides. Spoon the cooled apple mixture into the shell. Roll out the remaining piece of dough into a 10-inch (25-cm) round. Cover the apple mixture with the round of dough and fold the overhanging excess dough over the top pastry round, letting the dough drape casually. Sprinkle with sugar and bake in the center of the oven for 45 to 50 minutes, or until golden brown. Cool the *torta* completely on a cooling rack.

MAKES 8 SERVINGS

The fruit trees at La Viranda produce the apples and plums that Lorella uses in this rustic tart, Torta di Mele con Prugne, *OPPOSITE.*

BORGO SPANTE

The road leading to Borgo Spante winds from the Umbrian hill town of Orvieto that was once the ancient Etruscan settlement of Volsinii. It meanders through thousands of shimmering olive trees, miles of sheep-grazing pastures, and countless fields of tobacco. A small hand-painted wooden sign that reads simply *Spante* sits on the side of the road. A quick turn to the left, as the sign indicates, takes you down a narrow lane. The small fifteenth-century farming compound can be glimpsed at the end of the lane. Borgo Spante is the home of the Faina family. The imposing stone villa became the family's country residence in 1752. The villa is surrounded by small buildings, once the homes of *contadini* and their families, who farmed Spante's land and maintained it as a self-sufficient community. The compound includes a bell tower, a chapel, a small schoolhouse, a barn, and stables.

Borgo Spante rests in a corner of paradise. The region of Umbria, known as the "green heart of Italy," lies between the regions of Tuscany to the north and Latium (which includes the city of Rome) to the south. Umbria is a gentler, quieter, and less visited region, which has preserved its beauty throughout the centuries. Its steep green hills, lush deep valleys, and cultivated fertile plains generously provide the local people with abundance and variety for their tables.

Borgo Spante has always been a magical place for Claudia Spatola. As a young girl, Claudia spent summers visiting with her maternal grandmother, Maria Maio Faina, who lived in the villa. Claudia became fascinated with nature and enjoyed exploring Spante's broad expanse. She developed a passion for foraging while wandering through the woods and fields collecting edible herbs, greens, wild mushrooms, and nuts.

Claudia returned to Spante after a long absence. Much of the land that once stretched for nearly a thousand acres had been sold, and the compound was abandoned. The villa and its grounds suffered greatly from neglect and was an entangled web of overgrown vines and shrubs. The vegetation that had already strangled the cultivated land threatened to destroy the structures, including the villa. In spite of her family's

Caterina Carradini, ABOVE, *hand rolls bread dough speckled with bits of prosciutto and pancetta into small rolls that resemble snails.* Lumachelle *are a specialty of the area near Orvieto in the region of Umbria.* OPPOSITE, *Crostata di Caterina, a dessert tart made with two fillings and topped with nuts from the trees at Borgo Spante.*

Orvieto

The kitchen at Borgo Spante,
is filled with rustic details.
TOP, an old sweep-broom for
the hearth made in a style
still found in the markets at
Orvieto hangs next to a
well-worn cutting board and
an enamel strainer used
for scooping pasta from boiling
water. The gate leading to
the garden, ABOVE, is framed
by an arbor entangled with
overgrown vines.

fears, at just eighteen years of age Claudia moved into the villa; she was determined to preserve what remained of Spante and to undertake its restoration, an ongoing process.

Caterina Carradini, the wife of a contadino, still lived with her husband and daughter in near isolation in a small cottage on the grounds. She and Claudia developed a warm friendship and shared the desire to see Spante's rebirth. After several difficult and lean years (at times Claudia could only pay Caterina for her efforts in friendship), they managed to refurbish the villa and, with the help of Caterina's husband, to clear and replenish the land—replanting olive and fruit trees and establishing a small kitchen garden.

Claudia decided to restore and convert three of the small dwellings into vacation apartments to help finance the cost. Caterina prepared home-cooked meals for the guests. To Claudia's surprise, word of Spante's beauty and fine hospitality spread rapidly, and the increased demand for accommodations encouraged her to restore additional space. Borgo Spante became a comforting retreat for those desiring a tranquil setting.

Caterina now cooks in the rustic kitchen of the villa for Claudia and her family, who delight in visiting Spante. She cooks in a modest Umbrian country style. Her dishes are slow-simmered and always robust in flavor.

Activity in the kitchen centers around the *caminetto*, a large open hearth. Besides heating the kitchen, the caminetto renders many functions. A *paiolo*, or large iron cauldron, hangs from a heavy chain over the burning logs and is used for cooking polenta or boiling pasta. Beneath the floor of the hearth, behind a closed door, is a small bin called a *scaldavivande* which functions as a warm chamber for rising yeast dough or as a place to heat dinner plates. Caterina uses the floor of the hearth for baking traditional Umbrian flatbreads and to simmer pots filled with soups, sauces, or stews.

A tall terra-cotta urn filled with the dense green olive oil pressed in early winter from the fruit of Spante's olive trees stands near the

caminetto. The warmth of the fire keeps the oil from congealing during cold winter months. Umbrian olive trees produce an oil of prime quality and provide a generous yield.

The old wooden table in the center of the kitchen serves as a worktable as well as a place to eat less formal meals. It is here that Caterina kneads the dough for breads and pizzas, cuts thick coarse-textured strands of pasta, called *umbrichelli*, and rolls out the pastry for tarts.

On early mornings in fall Caterina often finds the kitchen filled with baskets of field greens and herbs still glistening with dew, as well as wild mushrooms, nuts, or fresh fruit—figs, apples, pears or big red pomegranates—gathered by Claudia during her walks. Field greens might be tossed as a salad or cooked as a side dish. Herbs find their way into soups, salads, and stews. Chestnuts are roasted in the caminetto while almonds, walnuts, hazelnuts, and pinenuts, if not used at once in one of Caterina's crusty confections, are tucked away for other occasions. Caterina always arranges a bowl of fresh fruit and nuts to serve with local sheep's milk cheese at the close of a meal or as a light snack.

Claudia can rely on the frequent autumn rains to provide the conditions necessary for edible wild mushrooms to grow, and Caterina has many uses for them. She dips whole mushrooms into batter and fries them, turns them into sauces for pasta and polenta, adds them to frittatas, and always reserves a generous supply of mushrooms to store for the winter. She strings sliced mushrooms like pearl necklaces and hangs them near the caminetto to dry and preserves marinated mushrooms in olive oil.

Borgo Spante can once again sustain itself—the fruit trees produce a diversity of fruit; the vines yield grapes for wine; the kitchen garden supplies the vegetables; and Mother Nature provides the rest. As Spante once again prospers, Claudia is rewarded for her years of sacrifice, and she is delighted to share its magic with others.

Sun-dappled fall fruit in the kitchen at Borgo Spante, ABOVE. Claudia flavors her purée of fava beans with a hint of wild fennel, Crostini dei Morti, ABOVE RIGHT. These ancient ledgers, RIGHT, have recorded the Faina family recipes since the Renaissance. BELOW, Claudia's mushrooms dry by the caminetto.

Lumachelle

Snail-shaped Rolls with Prosciutto and Pancetta

These traditional Umbrian rolls are one of Caterina's specialties. She dices thin slices of prosciutto and pancetta and then blends them into the dough.

4 TEASPOONS ACTIVE DRY YEAST

1½ CUPS (12 FL OZ/375 ML) WARM WATER (105-115°F/40-46°C)

4 TO 4½ CUPS (17 TO 19 OZ/480 TO 540 G) UNBLEACHED
ALL-PURPOSE FLOUR

1 CUP (4 OZ/120 G) GRATED PARMIGIANO-REGGIANO

¼ CUP (1 OZ/30 G) FINELY DICED IMPORTED ITALIAN PROSCIUTTO

¼ CUP (1 OZ/30 G) FINELY DICED PANCETTA

2 TABLESPOONS (1 FL OZ/30 ML) EXTRA VIRGIN OLIVE OIL

SEA SALT AND FRESHLY GROUND BLACK PEPPER

1. Sprinkle the yeast over ½ cup (4 fl oz/125 ml) of the water in a small bowl. Stir until the yeast is dissolved. Mound 4 cups (17 oz/480 g) of the flour on a pastry board or work surface. Make a well in the center and add the yeast mixture, the remaining 1 cup (8 fl oz/250 ml) water, the Parmigiano, prosciutto, pancetta, olive oil, ½ teaspoon salt, and ¼ teaspoon black pepper. Blend the ingredients in the well with a fork then begin to incorporate the flour, blending until the mixture forms a soft ball of dough. Knead for 10 minutes, incorporating some of the remaining flour, until it is no longer sticky. The dough should be smooth and very tender.

2. Transfer the dough to a large well-oiled bowl. Rub the dough against the bowl to coat it with oil. Cover the bowl with a cotton kitchen towel and let the dough rest in a warm, draftfree place for 1 hour, or until doubled in size.

3. Oil and flour 2 large baking sheets. When the dough is ready, turn it out onto the lightly floured pastry board, and knead the dough for 2 minutes to force out any air bubbles. Cover the dough with the towel and let it rest for 5 minutes.

4. Divide the dough into 20 equal pieces. Roll each piece into a 12-inch-long (30-cm-long) rope. Wind the rope into a coil and tuck the loose end under. Arrange the rolls on the baking sheets 1 inch (2.5 cm) apart. Cover with towels and let the rolls rest in a warm draftfree place for 45 minutes, or until they have risen 50 percent in size.

5. About midway in the rising, preheat the oven to 400°F (200°C).

6. Place the baking sheets on 2 racks in the oven. Stagger them so they are not one on top of the other. Bake the rolls for 25 to 30 minutes, or until golden. Reverse the position of the baking sheets after 18 minutes, so they bake evenly. Slide the *lumachelle* onto a large cooling rack to cool.

MAKES 20 ROLLS

Lumachelle, *snail-shaped rolls,* OPPOSITE, *serve as a satisfying* merenda, *or afternoon snack, with fresh fruit and cheese. As a variation, Caterina sometimes twists the rolls into a shape she calls* sorelluce, *which means little sisters. She rolls each portion of dough into a 12-inch-long (30-cm-long) rope, folds it in half and twists 2 times.*

Frittata di Cipolle

Onion Frittata

Caterina makes a frittata with red onions she has gently braised for 1½ hours. The onions become caramelized and practically melt. The frittata can be served as an antipasto or as a light meal accompanied by a tossed green salad.

  1   POUND (450 G) RED ONIONS, SLICED ¼ INCH (0.6 CM) THICK
 4½ TABLESPOONS (2½ FL OZ/65 ML) EXTRA VIRGIN OLIVE OIL
SEA SALT AND FRESHLY GROUND BLACK PEPPER
  8   LARGE EGGS
  ⅓ CUP (1½ OZ/45 G) GRATED PARMIGIANO-REGGIANO

1. Combine the onions with 3 tablespoons (1½ fl oz/45 ml) of the olive oil and a pinch of salt in a medium-size heavy sauté pan. Cover the pan and cook the onions over very low heat, stirring occasionally, for 30 minutes. Reduce the heat if the onions start to brown. After 30 minutes, add 2 tablespoons of water and continue to cook the onions, covered, for 30 minutes more. Raise the heat slightly and cook the onions for another 30 minutes. The onions will brown lightly and a rich brown glaze will form at the bottom of the pan. Stir frequently, scraping the glaze and blending it into the onions. After 1½ hours of cooking, the onions should be golden brown and very creamy in texture. Season with salt and black pepper to taste and let them cool in the pan.

2. Beat the eggs in a large bowl with a wire whisk and stir in the onions. Add the Parmigiano and season with salt and pepper.

3. Heat the remaining 1½ tablespoons olive oil in a 9-inch (23-cm) seasoned omelet pan or nonstick skillet over medium-low heat. When the oil is hot, pour in the egg mixture. As the eggs set, use a fork to push the edges toward the center of the pan. Tilt the pan slightly to allow the raw egg to fill the bare section. Do this until the frittata is almost completely set and the bottom is golden brown. (The top of the frittata will still be runny.) If the frittata browns too fast, lower the heat.

4. Invert the frittata onto a large plate. Carefully slide it back into the pan, top side down, to cook the uncooked side. When the frittata is golden brown underneath, slide it onto a serving plate and let it cool for at least 10 minutes before serving. The frittata can be served warm or at room temperature.

MAKES 6 SERVINGS

Crostini dei Morti

Puréed Fava Beans with Toasted Bread

Crostini dei Morti is a traditional antipasto that is served in Umbria on November 2 to comemmorate Il Giorno dei Morti, literally the Day of the Dead, or All Souls' Day. A thick purée made from dried fava beans is ladled over grilled or toasted bread that has been rubbed with garlic. Use split, dried, shelled fava beans. Whole beans have thick rubbery skins that are tedious and messy to remove.

  8   OUNCES (240 G) SPLIT DRIED FAVA BEANS, SOAKED OVERNIGHT
      IN COLD WATER TO COVER BY 1 INCH (2.5 CM)
SEA SALT
  ⅛ TEASPOON FENNEL SEEDS
  2   TABLESPOONS (1 FL OZ/30 ML) EXTRA VIRGIN OLIVE OIL, PLUS
      ADDITIONAL TO SERVE AT THE TABLE
  6   SLIGHTLY DRY SLICES FIRM-TEXTURED COUNTRY-STYLE BREAD
      (FOR PANE TOSCANO, SEE PAGE 78), SLICED ½ INCH (1.25 CM)
      THICK
  1   CLOVE OF GARLIC

1. Drain the beans in a colander and transfer them to a heavy pot. Fill the pot with 5 cups (1.2 liters) cold water and ¼ teaspoon of salt. Bring to a boil, reduce the heat, and simmer, uncovered, for 1½ hours, or until tender and falling apart. Stir the beans occasionally and adjust the heat as necessary to keep them at a simmer. If the beans stick to the bottom of the pot, add some water. When ready, the mixture should be very thick.

2. Purée the beans in a food mill fitted with the coarse disk or process in a food processor. If using a food processor, let the mixture cool slightly before puréeing. Take care not to overprocess, the mixture should have a coarse texture.

3. Return the purée to the pot. Add the fennel seeds and 2 table-spoons (1 fl oz/30 ml) olive oil. Simmer the purée for 30 minutes, stirring frequently. When ready, the mixture should be thick but pourable. Season with additional salt to taste.

4. Preheat the oven to 400°F (200°C).

5. Cut the bread slices into 2 or 3 pieces each. Place them in a single layer on a baking sheet and toast the bread in the oven for 10 minutes. Turn the slices and toast them for 6 to 8 minutes more, or until lightly browned on both sides. The bread can also be toasted on a grill. While it is hot, rub 1 side of the bread with the garlic. Place the bread in wide shallow soup bowls, 2 or 3 pieces per serving.

Spoon the warm purée on top and serve immediately. Pass a cruet of extra virgin olive oil at the table for drizzling.

MAKES 6 SERVINGS

Note: When the fava bean purée cools it becomes very thick. To reheat it, add 2 or 3 tablespoons of water and stir over medium-low heat until the purée softens.

Umbrichelli

Umbrian Handmade Pasta

Umbrichelli, *a rustic Umbrian handmade pasta similar to thick spaghetti, are sometimes hand rolled one strand at a time. Caterina prefers to stretch a portion of the dough into a thick sheet. She presses a ridged wooden rolling pin over the dough, to perforate long thick strands. The strands can then be pulled apart or cut with a pizza wheel.*

   6 CUPS (26 OZ/720 G) UNBLEACHED ALL-PURPOSE FLOUR
⅛ TEASPOON SEA SALT

1. To make the pasta dough, use the flour, salt, and 1½ cups (12 fl oz/375 ml) water as directed on page 188, the section entitled Making the Dough. Knead the dough entirely by hand until smooth and tender, about 10 minutes. It is not necessary to use all of the flour. Excess flour will make the dough tough and dry. The remaining flour will be used when stretching and cutting the pasta. Flour the dough lightly, wrap it in plastic wrap, and let it rest for 5 minutes.

2. Line 3 trays or baking sheets with cotton kitchen towels and dust lightly with flour.

3. Divide the dough into 6 equal portions. Work with 1 piece of dough at a time, keeping the unused portions wrapped in plastic wrap. Lightly dust a pastry board or work surface with flour and roll out the dough to a long narrow strip ⅛ inch (0.4 cm) thick. Flour both sides and firmly roll a ridged wooden pasta rolling pin lengthwise once across the dough. Do not roll back and forth. The ridges of the rolling pin will impress deep grooves into the dough. Separate the strands of dough by gently pulling them apart. If they do not separate easily, use a pizza cutting wheel to cut through the grooves. If a ridged rolling pin is not available, use a long-bladed slicing knife and cut the dough into ⅛-inch-wide (0.4-cm-wide) strands. Transfer the strands to one of the towel-lined trays. Arrange the strands side by side without touching. Dust lightly with flour and cover the tray with a cotton towel. Roll out and cut the remaining pieces of dough in the same way.

MAKES 6 SERVINGS

Umbrichelli all'Arrabbiata

Umbrian Handmade Pasta with Spicy Tomato Sauce

The spicy tomato sauce Caterina makes for her hand-rolled umbrichelli *also goes well with any imported Italian dried spaghetti.*

For the Sauce
  ¼ CUP (2 FL OZ/60 ML) EXTRA VIRGIN OLIVE OIL
  2 SMALL CLOVES OF GARLIC, FINELY CHOPPED
  2 SMALL HOT RED CHILI PEPPERS, CHOPPED
3¼ CUPS (28 FL OZ/800 ML) CANNED TOMATOES,
     DRAINED AND CHOPPED
  3 TABLESPOONS CHOPPED ITALIAN FLAT-LEAF PARSLEY LEAVES
SEA SALT

  1 RECIPE UMBRICHELLI (PRECEDING RECIPE)
SEA SALT

1. Heat the olive oil in a large heavy saucepan over medium heat. Add the garlic and chili peppers and cook until the garlic is golden. Pour in the tomatoes and bring to a boil. Add 1 tablespoon of the parsley and season with salt to taste. Simmer, uncovered, for 35 minutes. Season with additional salt to taste.

2. While the sauce is simmering, fill a very large pot (at least 8 quarts/8 liters) with water and bring it to a rapid boil. Add salt to taste. Stir in the pasta and cover the pot until it returns to a boil. Uncover and boil the pasta for 3 to 5 minutes, or until al dente. Drain the pasta and transfer to a large serving bowl. Pour the sauce on top, sprinkle with the remaining 2 tablespoons parsley, and toss. Serve immediately.

MAKES 6 SERVINGS

Polenta di Spante

Polenta with Two Sauces

Caterina prepares two sauces for her polenta, one a tomato-based meat sauce and the other an olive oil-based mushroom sauce. She serves the polenta on a wooden board in the old-fashioned farmhouse style.

For the Meat Sauce

    3   TABLESPOONS (1½ FL OZ/45 ML) EXTRA VIRGIN OLIVE OIL
    2   LARGE PORK CHOPS (1 POUND/450 G), BONED AND CUT INTO
        2-INCH (5-CM) CHUNKS, BONES RESERVED
    4   OUNCE (120 G) SLICE OF PANCETTA, CUT INTO 1-INCH
        (2.5-CM) CHUNKS
    1   POUND (450 G) SWEET ITALIAN SAUSAGE, WITHOUT FENNEL SEEDS,
        CUT INTO 2-INCH (5-CM) PIECES
    1   MEDIUM CARROT, FINELY CHOPPED
    1   MEDIUM CELERY STALK, FINELY CHOPPED
    1   SMALL ONION, FINELY CHOPPED
    1   SMALL CLOVE OF GARLIC, FINELY CHOPPED
    5   SMALL BASIL LEAVES, TORN INTO SMALL PIECES
    ⅔   CUP (5½ FL OZ/160 ML) RED WINE
    4   CUPS (32 FL OZ/1 LITER) CANNED TOMATOES, WITH THE JUICE,
        COARSELY CHOPPED
    1   SMALL HOT RED CHILI PEPPER, CHOPPED
    SEA SALT AND FRESHLY GROUND BLACK PEPPER

For the Mushroom Sauce

    1½ POUNDS (675 G) FRESH PORCINI MUSHROOMS (SEE NOTE)
    ⅓   CUP (3 FL OZ/85 ML) OLIVE OIL
    1   SMALL HOT RED CHILI PEPPER, CHOPPED
    ¾   CUP (6 FL OZ/185 ML) MEAT BROTH (FOR HOMEMADE,
        SEE PAGE 187)
    SEA SALT
    1   TABLESPOON CHOPPED ITALIAN FLAT-LEAF PARSLEY LEAVES

For the Polenta

    1¼ CUPS (6 OZ/185 G) FINELY GROUND YELLOW CORNMEAL
    SEA SALT
    ¾   CUP (3 OZ/90 G) GRATED PARMIGIANO-REGGIANO, PLUS
        ADDITIONAL FOR SERVING

1. To prepare the meat sauce, heat the olive oil in a large sauté pan over medium-high heat. Add the pork, pork bones, pancetta, and sausage. Cook the meat until it is well browned on all sides and a rich brown glaze has formed at the bottom of the pan. Add the carrot, celery, onion, garlic, and basil. Reduce the heat to medium and cook until the vegetables are tender, 15 to 20 minutes. Pour in the red wine and increase the heat to medium-high. Cook until half of the wine has evaporated. Add the tomatoes and chili pepper. Season with salt and black pepper to taste. Simmer for 1½ hours. Remove the bones before serving.

2. To prepare the mushroom sauce, clean the mushrooms. Trim away the dry end of the stems, brush away any soil or grit, and wipe the mushrooms clean with a damp cloth. Coarsely chop the mushrooms and combine them with the olive oil, chili pepper, and broth in a large saucepan. Season with salt to taste. Cover the pan and simmer the sauce briskly for 15 to 20 minutes, or until it has thickened slightly.

3. To prepare the polenta, bring 7 cups (1.7 liters) of water to a rolling boil in a medium-size heavy pot. Hold a fistful of cornmeal over the pot. Stir constantly while letting the cornmeal slip through your fingers in a slow steady stream into the pot. When all of the cornmeal has been added, lower the heat. Simmer for 45 minutes, stirring often, or until the polenta is thick but still pourable. Season with salt to taste.

4. While the polenta is simmering, oil a large wooden pastry or cutting board. Reheat the sauces. When the polenta is ready, pour it out onto the wooden board and quickly spread it with a wet metal spatula. Spoon some of the meat sauce over half of the polenta. Stir the parsley into the mushroom sauce and pour several large spoonfuls over the other half. Sprinkle ¾ cup (3 oz/90 g) Parmigiano over the sauces and serve additional cheese at the table. Pour the rest of the sauces into bowls and serve them at the table as well.

MAKES 6 SERVINGS

Note: When fresh porcini mushrooms are not available, the mushroom sauce can be made with 1½ pounds (675 g) of any fresh cultivated or wild mushrooms that have been purchased in specialty markets (see page 19) and ½ ounce (15 g) of dried porcini mushrooms. Clean the fresh mushrooms as directed in Step 2 and coarsely chop them. Soak the dried porcini mushrooms in ⅓ cup (3 fl oz/85 ml) of warm water for 15 minutes. Lift them out of the soaking liquid, reserving the liquid. Scrape off any grit left on the porcini and coarsely chop them. Strain the liquid through a double layer of cheesecloth. Add meat broth to the liquid to measure ¾ cup (6 fl oz/185 ml). Use the mixture in place of the meat broth alone. Use the fresh cultivated or wild mushrooms and the dried porcini mushrooms in place of the fresh porcini mushrooms. If the sauce is too watery, simmer, uncovered, until it has thickened slightly.

OPPOSITE, Polenta di Spante.

It is considered a show of true friendship for Italians to eat their polenta together from the same board.

Patate della Contadina
Creamy Potato Casserole

This potato casserole is layered with thin slices of prosciutto and a creamy white cheese sauce. During times of hardship, a farmer's wife would have served this type of a casserole as a piatto unico, or a one-dish family meal, which could be assembled with ingredients that were produced on the farm. It provided nourishment and comfort after a long day of hard outdoor work.

3½ POUNDS (1.6 K) YUKON GOLD OR RUSSET POTATOES, PEELED
SEA SALT AND FRESHLY GROUND BLACK PEPPER
  6 TABLESPOONS (3 OZ/90 G) UNSALTED BUTTER
  ¼ CUP (1 OZ/30 G) UNBLEACHED ALL-PURPOSE FLOUR
3¾ CUPS (30 FL OZ/900 ML) WHOLE MILK
  1 CUP (4 OZ/120 G) GRATED PARMIGIANO-REGGIANO OR
    PECORINO ROMANO
  ⅛ TEASPOON FRESHLY GRATED NUTMEG
  3 OUNCES (90 G) IMPORTED ITALIAN PROSCIUTTO, THINLY SLICED

1. Place the whole potatoes in a large pot with cold water to cover by 2 inches (5 cm). Add salt to taste. Bring to a boil and cook the potatoes until tender when pierced with a paring knife. Drain and transfer them to a large bowl. Smash the potatoes with a potato masher or a fork. They should remain chunky. Season with salt and pepper to taste.

2. Preheat the oven to 425°F (215°C). Butter a 13 x 9 x 2-inch (32 x 23 x 5-cm) oval or rectangular baking pan that is at least 2 inches (5 cm) deep.

3. Melt 5 tablespoons (2½ oz/75 g) of the butter in a heavy saucepan over medium heat. Stir in the flour and cook until the mixture becomes foamy. Pour in the milk and stir until it reaches a boil. Reduce the heat and simmer for 1 minute. Add ¾ cup (30 oz/90 g) of the Parmigiano and stir until it is melted and the sauce is smooth. Remove from the heat and season it with nutmeg, salt, and black pepper to taste.

4. Arrange half of the potatoes in an even layer at the bottom of the baking pan. Place half of the prosciutto on top. Spoon half of the cheese sauce over the prosciutto, spreading it evenly. Layer the remaining potatoes, prosciutto, and cheese sauce in the same way, ending with the sauce. Sprinkle the top of the casserole with the remaining ¼ cup (1 oz/30 g) Parmigiano and dot it with the remaining 1 tablespoon (½ oz/15 g) butter. (The casserole can be made ahead up to this point. Cover the baking pan and refrigerate. Remove the pan from the refrigerator 20 minutes before baking.)

5. Bake the casserole 30 to 35 minutes, or until golden and bubbly.
MAKES 8 SERVINGS

Spezzatino di Pollo con Torta al Testo
Savory Chicken Stew with Umbrian Flatbread

Fresh or dried chili peppers add zest to this chicken stew. Caterina serves it with a stack of torta al testo, *crisp flatbreads baked on the floor of the hearth. The breads can also be baked on terra-cotta tiles in a conventional oven (see page 78). Select a free-range chicken that is meaty and lean. Ask the butcher to cut the chicken into small pieces using a meat saw to avoid splintered bones.*

For the Umbrian Flatbread
2½ TEASPOONS ACTIVE DRY YEAST
1¼ CUPS (10 FL OZ/300 ML) WARM WATER (105 TO 115°F/40 TO 46°C)
  4 TO 4½ CUPS (16 TO 18 OZ/450 TO 525 G) UNBLEACHED
    ALL-PURPOSE FLOUR
SEA SALT
  1 TABLESPOON EXTRA VIRGIN OLIVE OIL

For the Chicken Stew
  1 SMALL CLOVE OF GARLIC, FINELY CHOPPED
  ½ MEDIUM ONION, COARSELY CHOPPED
  1 SMALL CARROT, COARSELY CHOPPED
  ½ CELERY STALK, COARSELY CHOPPED
  ½ TEASPOON COARSELY CHOPPED FRESH ROSEMARY LEAVES
  1 FREE-RANGE CHICKEN (3½ TO 4 POUND/1.5 TO 1.75 K),
    CUT INTO 18 PIECES
  ⅓ CUP (3 FL OZ/80 ML) EXTRA VIRGIN OLIVE OIL
  2 SMALL HOT RED CHILI PEPPERS, CHOPPED
SEA SALT
  ¾ CUP (6 FL OZ/185 ML) DRY WHITE WINE
  1 CUP (8 FL OZ/250 ML) CANNED TOMATOES,
    DRAINED AND CHOPPED

1. To make the flatbread, sprinkle the yeast over ½ cup (4 fl oz/125 ml) warm water in a small bowl. Stir until the yeast is dissolved. Mound 4 cups (16 oz/450 g) of the flour on a pastry board or work surface. Make a well in the center and add the yeast mixture, ½ teaspoon salt, olive oil, and the remaining ¾ cup (6 fl oz/185 ml) water. Blend the ingredients in the well with a fork then begin to incorporate the flour, add just enough of the flour to make a soft ball of dough. Knead the dough with some of the remaining flour for 1 minute.

2. Transfer the dough to a large well-oiled bowl. Rub the dough

against the bowl to coat it with oil. Cover the bowl with a cotton kitchen towel and let the dough rest in a warm draftfree place for 1 hour, or until doubled in size.

3. While the dough is rising, arrange terra-cotta tiles or a pizza stone on the center shelf of the oven as directed on page 78. Preheat the oven to 475°F (245°C). Allow 30 minutes for the oven and the tiles to preheat.

4. When the dough is ready, turn it out onto the lightly floured pastry board, and knead for 2 minutes to force out any air bubbles. Cover the dough and let it rest for 5 minutes.

5. Divide the dough into 4 equal pieces. Work with 1 piece of dough at a time. Flour the remaining pieces and cover them with the towel. Flatten the dough slightly. Lightly flour a ridged wooden rolling pin and roll out the dough ¼ inch (0.6 cm) thick. Prick with a fork and transfer the dough to a floured pizza peel or rimless baking sheet. Slide the dough directly onto the hot tiles. Bake for 7 to 9 minutes, or until golden around the edges and puffy. Cool on a cooling rack. Roll out and bake the remaining pieces of dough in the same way.

6. To make the chicken stew, combine the garlic, onion, carrot, celery, and rosemary in a food processor and process to a coarse purée. Heat a large heavy sauté pan over medium-high heat and add the chicken pieces. Cover the pan and cook, turning the pieces from time to time, until the chicken has rendered all of its fat and water and has become golden in color, about 15 minutes. Remove the chicken and drain off the fat and liquid.

7. Return the chicken to the pan and pour the olive oil over it. Add the chili peppers and season the chicken with salt to taste. Spoon the puréed vegetables over the chicken and partially cover the pan. Briskly simmer the mixture for 20 minutes, turning the chicken and stirring the sauce occasionally. Pour in the white wine and simmer for 15 minutes. Stir in the tomatoes, reduce the heat and simmer slowly for 15 minutes more. If the mixture appears dry at any time, reduce the heat and cover the pan tightly. Taste for additional seasoning. Serve the stew hot with the flatbreads.

MAKES 4 SERVINGS

Misticanza
Sautéed Mixed Greens

Misticanza is a mix of mild and peppery field greens that Caterina first blanches, then sautées in olive oil with garlic and chili peppers If it is served hot, additional extra virgin olive oil can be served in a cruet on the table for drizzling over. If the misticanza is at room temperature, surround it with wedges of fresh lemon.

1½ POUNDS (675 G) MIXED GREENS SUCH AS SPINACH, SWISS CHARD LEAVES, DANDELION GREENS, ESCAROLE, CHICORY, OR BROCCOLI RABE, TRIMMED AND THOROUGHLY WASHED

SEA SALT

3 TABLESPOONS (1½ FL OZ/45 ML) EXTRA VIRGIN OLIVE OIL

2 CLOVES OF GARLIC, CRUSHED

1 TO 2 SMALL HOT RED CHILI PEPPERS

1. Fill a large pot (at least 6 quarts/6 liters) with water and bring it to a boil. Add salt to taste. Stir in the greens and boil for 3 to 5 minutes, or just until tender. Drain, refresh under cold water, and drain again. Squeeze to eliminate all of the water then coarsely chop.

2. Heat the olive oil in a large sauté pan over medium heat. Add the garlic and chili peppers and cook just until the garlic is lightly golden. Add the greens and sauté until heated through. Remove the garlic and season with salt to taste.

MAKES 6 SERVINGS

Torta al Testo, a crisp flatbread that bakes on the floor of the hearth, accompanies this spicy chicken stew, Spezzatino di Pollo, RIGHT. Caterina sweeps hot embers aside and spreads the thinly stretched yeast dough onto the smoldering hearth, ABOVE. The embers are shoveled over the dough, and the bread is baked until crisp and golden. The ash-coated breads are then dusted clean, RIGHT.

Crostata di Caterina

Dessert Tart with Two Fillings

Almonds and walnuts that grow on the grounds of Borgo Spante are used to garnish Caterina's large dessert tart made with two fillings. Half of the tart is filled with a lemon-scented pastry cream and the other half is filled with a blend of ricotta and chocolate. Caterina tops the pastry cream with walnuts and the ricotta with almonds then bakes the tart until golden. She serves guests a thin slice from each half.

Caterina prepares the ricotta filling with a sheep's milk ricotta. If it is not available, use fresh homemade ricotta usually found at specialty food shops and markets that specialize in Italian products.

For the Pastry Dough

2½ CUPS (10 OZ/300 G) UNBLEACHED ALL-PURPOSE FLOUR
2 LARGE EGGS
1 LARGE EGG YOLK
½ CUP (3½ OZ/100 G) SUGAR
1 TABLESPOON WHOLE MILK OR BRANDY
½ TEASPOON GRATED LEMON ZEST
PINCH OF SEA SALT
¼ TEASPOON BAKING POWDER
8 TABLESPOONS (4 OZ/125 G) UNSALTED BUTTER, SOFTENED

For the Pastry Cream

1 CUP (8 FL OZ/250 ML) WHOLE MILK
1 2-INCH (5-CM) PIECE OF LEMON ZEST
2 LARGE EGG YOLKS
¼ CUP (1¾ OZ/50 G) SUGAR
2 TABLESPOONS UNBLEACHED ALL-PURPOSE FLOUR
½ TEASPOON VANILLA EXTRACT

For the Ricotta Filling

1¼ CUPS (10 OZ/300 G) RICOTTA
3 TABLESPOONS (1½ OZ/45 G) SUGAR
1½ TABLESPOONS CHOPPED SEMISWEET CHOCOLATE

18 WHOLE BLANCHED ALMONDS, FOR GARNISH
18 WALNUT HALVES, FOR GARNISH
CONFECTIONERS' SUGAR, FOR DUSTING (OPTIONAL)

1. To prepare the pastry dough, mound the flour on a pastry board or work surface, or pour it into a bowl. Make a well in the center and add the eggs, egg yolk, sugar, milk, lemon zest, a pinch of salt, and the baking powder. Beat the ingredients in the well with a fork. Add the butter, mash it with the fork, and blend it with the ingredients in the well. (The butter will remain lumpy.) Gradually incorporate the flour, blending the mixture to form a ball of dough. If using a bowl, turn the dough out onto a pastry board or work surface. Knead the dough gently until it is smooth. Wrap the dough in wax paper and let it rest in a cool place for at least 1 hour. (The dough can be refrigerated briefly, but do not let it become too firm.)

2. To prepare the pastry cream, combine the milk and lemon zest in a medium-size heavy saucepan. Heat the milk over medium-low heat until it is scalded. Meanwhile, blend the egg yolks and sugar in a medium bowl with a wire whisk. Add the flour and stir until it is completely dissolved. Slowly whisk one third of the scalded milk into the egg yolk mixture. Add the remaining milk all at once and blend thoroughly. Pour the mixture back into the saucepan and return it to the heat. Stir constantly until the custard has thickened. Remove from the heat and stir in the vanilla. Continue to stir for 1 minute. Remove the lemon zest and pour the custard into a bowl. Smooth the top with a rubber spatula and place a buttered round of wax paper on the surface to prevent a skin from forming. Let cool to room temperature.

3. To prepare the ricotta filling, combine the ricotta, sugar, and chocolate in a small bowl and blend thoroughly.

4. Preheat the oven to 400°F (200°C).

5. Place two thirds of the pastry dough on a lightly floured wooden pastry board or work surface. Flour a wooden rolling pin and roll out the dough to a 14-inch (35-cm) round ¼ inch (0.6 cm) thick. Carefully roll the dough onto the rolling pin, then lower it into an 11-inch (28-cm) pan. Gently press the dough into the corners and against the sides of the tart pan. Trim off the excess dough. Roll a portion of the trimmings, into a rope that is ⅜ inch (1 cm) thick and 11 inches (28 cm) long. Place the rope across the center of the tart shell to divide the shell in half. Spread the pastry cream over half of the tart shell, then spread the ricotta filling over the other half. Use the remaining dough and trimmings to make additional ⅜-inch-thick (1-cm-thick) ropes. Arrange them over the filling in a lattice pattern. Place an almond in each square of the lattice, over the ricotta filling. Place the walnut halves over the pastry cream.

6. Bake the tart on the center shelf of the oven for 40 to 45 minutes, or until the crust is golden. Cool the tart completely on a cooling rack. Dust with confectioners' sugar before serving, if desired.

MAKES 8 SERVINGS

Cardi con Fonduta e Tartufi
Cardoons with Cheese Sauce and White Truffles

Ester Carnero of La Luna e i Falò (see page 37) pours fonduta over sautéed cardoons and tops the dish with shaved white truffles. Fonduta, a warm cheese sauce, is one of Piedmont's best known specialties.

8   OUNCES (240 G) FONTINA
    D'AOSTA CHEESE
¾   CUP (6 FL OZ/185 ML) WHOLE
    MILK
1   HEAD OF CARDOONS (2½ LBS/1 K)
JUICE OF 1 LEMON
SEA SALT
2   TABLESPOONS (1 OZ/30 G)
    UNSALTED BUTTER, SOFTENED
2   LARGE EGG YOLKS
2   TABLESPOONS (1 FL OZ/30 ML)
    PURE OLIVE OIL
1   MEDIUM WHITE TRUFFLE,
    BRUSHED CLEAN WITH A SOFT
    BRUSH

1. Begin the fonduta at least 2 hours before serving. Cube the fontina cheese and place in the top of a double boiler. Pour the milk over the cheese and refrigerate for at least 2 hours.

2. To prepare the cardoons, fill a large bowl with cold water and add the juice of ½ lemon. Separate the cardoons into individual stalks. Trim off the dry ends and the leafy edges. Pull off the strings, as with celery and cut into 1½-inch (3.8-cm) pieces. Soak them in the lemon water.

3. Fill a large pot (at least 6 quarts/6 liters) with water and bring it to a rapid boil. Add salt to taste and the juice of ½ lemon. Add the cardoons and simmer until tender, 30 to 45 minutes. Drain and pat dry with paper towels.

4. To cook the fonduta, place the top of the double boiler containing the cheese and milk over simmering water. Add the butter and egg yolks and stir constantly with a wire whisk until the butter and cheese have melted and become thick and creamy, about 15 minutes. Remove from the heat and stir for 1 minute more. Let the sauce rest over the hot water while sautéing the cardoons.

5. Heat the olive oil in a large skillet. Add the cardoons and sauté just until heated through. Season with salt to taste. Transfer the cardoons to a serving platter and pour the fonduta over. Shave the truffle into thin slivers over the fonduta using a truffle slicer or vegetable peeler. Serve immediately.

MAKES 6 SERVINGS

Osso Buco con Funghi Porcini
Veal Shanks with Porcini Mushrooms

In this version of braised veal shanks from Umbria, the shanks are thinly sliced and simmered with fresh porcini mushrooms.

3   POUNDS VEAL SHANKS, SLICED
    ¾ INCH (2 CM) THICK
½   CUP (4 FL OZ/125 ML) EXTRA
    VIRGIN OLIVE OIL
UNBLEACHED ALL-PURPOSE FLOUR
    (FOR DREDGING)
SEA SALT AND FRESHLY GROUND
    BLACK PEPPER
1   LARGE ONION, CHOPPED
1   CUP (8 FL OZ/250 ML) DRY
    WHITE WINE
1   CUP (8 FL OZ/250 ML) MEAT
    BROTH (FOR HOMEMADE,
    SEE PAGE 187)
8   OUNCES (225 G) FRESH PORCINI
    MUSHROOMS

1. Tie each piece of shank around the middle with butcher's twine to hold it together. Heat ¼ cup (2 fl oz/60 ml) of the olive oil in a 12-inch (30-cm) sauté pan over medium-high heat. When the oil is hot, lightly dredge half of the veal in flour and cook until it is golden brown on both sides. Transfer to a large platter, season with salt and pepper, and cook the remaining pieces in the same way.

2. When all of the veal has been browned and removed from the pan, add the remaining ¼ cup (2 fl oz/60 ml) olive oil and the onion and cook over low heat until golden, about 15 minutes. Pour in the wine. Simmer, uncovered, for 5 minutes while scraping up the brown bits at the bottom of the pan with a wooden spoon.

3. Return the veal to the pan. Add the broth, cover, and simmer, turning the pieces occasionally, for 1 hour and 15 minutes, or until the veal is fork tender.

4. To clean the fresh mushrooms, trim away the dry end of the stems, brush off any soil or grit, and wipe them clean with a damp cloth. Coarsely chop and stir the porcini into the sauce. Cover the pan and simmer for 15 minutes more, or until the mushrooms are cooked.

MAKES 6 SERVINGS

Pears with Gorgonzola
Pere con Gorgonzola

Serve these fresh pears with sweet gorgonzola and walnuts as a cheese course after *secondo piatto*.

6   TABLESPOONS (1½ OZ/45 G)
    CHOPPED WALNUTS
4   PEARS, PEELED, CORED, AND
    CUT INTO THIN WEDGES
4   OUNCES (120 G) GORGONZOLA
    DOLCE
HONEY, FOR DRIZZLING

1. Preheat the oven to 400°F (200°C).

2. Place the walnuts on a baking sheet and toast for 6 to 7 minutes or until golden.

3. Arrange the pear wedges on 4 individual dessert plates. Crumble the gorgonzola over the pears and top with toasted walnuts. Drizzle honey over each serving and serve immediately.

MAKES 4 SERVINGS

T E R

In winter Italian cooking leans toward root vegetables, legumes, and dark leafy greens, cooked in an open hearth that warms the stomach as well as the kitchen.

Vegetables
verdure

Celery root, *sedano rapa,* also referred to as celeriac, is a variety of celery bred for its root as opposed to its stalk. The tan bulbous root has long thin leafy stems that should be trimmed immediately after purchasing. Celery root has a flavor similar to that of celery and parsley. Once the rough skin has been peeled the exposed white flesh must be soaked in cold water acidulated with lemon juice to prevent discoloration. Select small roots that feel firm and heavy for their size. Avoid roots with soft spots or splits. Refrigerate loosely covered up to 10 days. Celery root is available at specialty produce markets and farmers' markets from early autumn through winter.

Fennel, *finocchio,* a Mediterranean native related to carrots and parsley, is a cultivated aromatic vegetable with a delicate, slightly sweet flavor reminiscent of licorice. It is eaten both raw and cooked (wild fennel is used exclusively as an herb). It has broad white leaves that form a fleshy bulb. The leaves are topped with celery-like stalks and feathery greens. When selecting fennel look for bulbs that are firm, solid, and moist with bright, fresh-looking greens. Rounded bulbs are more tender and less fibrous that flatter ones. Avoid brown spots or splitting. Remove the stalks and store the bulb loosely covered in the refrigerator up to 3 days. Fennel is widely available from early fall through spring.

Escarole, *scarola,* is a member of the chicory family. It has broad, wavy edged, crisp leaves that grow in large heads. Outer leaves are dark green with white ribs; the inner leaves and heart are paler and slightly yellow. Escarole is milder in flavor than other chicories and can be served raw or cooked. It must be washed thoroughly as it tends to be very sandy. When choosing escarole look for leaves that are crisp in texture. Store escarole loosely wrapped in the refrigerator for up to 3 days. Escarole is available from early fall to late spring in Italian markets that carry fresh produce.

Radicchio, *radicchio,* is a chicory known for its brilliant red color and slightly bitter, peppery flavor. Until recently most of the radicchio in the United States was imported from Italy; California has now become a major supplier. Close to a dozen varieties of radicchio grow in Italy. The most common types found in the United States are radicchio di Verona, which grows in small rounded heads with deep burgundy-red leaves with white ribs and veins and radicchio di Treviso, which looks similar to endive with its pointed tapered heads of loosely overlapping leaves that range in color from pink to very dark maroon. Both types can be used raw or cooked. Store radicchio in the refrigerator wrapped in paper towels and sealed in a plastic bag for no longer than 4 days.

Tuscan black cabbage, *cavolo nero,* also called Tuscan black kale or lacinato kale is a member of the cabbage family. It has narrow, very dark green curly leaves with a texture similar to American kale. Select Tuscan black cabbage with firm brightly colored leaves. Avoid those that are yellowing. Cover and store in the refrigerator up to 3 days; long storage could cause the leaves to become bitter. Tuscan black cabbage is available from late fall through winter and is usually found in Italian produce markets and some specialty food stores.

Winter squash, *zucca,* is harvested in fall but abundantly available in winter due to its excellent storage capabilities. The numerous varieties of winter squash have tough skins, dry dense flesh, and hollow inner cavities containing tough seeds. Good substitutes for the large pumpkin-like varieties used in Italy are butternut squash, buttercup squash, and hubbard squash. Winter squash should be heavy for its size, have firm deeply colored shells with a dull finish, and be free from cuts or soft spots. Store winter squash in a cool, dark, dry, well-ventilated place. It will keep for several weeks or months. Winter squash is widely available from September through March.

Fruit
frutta

Oranges, *arance,* are used for both eating and juice. There are three basic types of oranges: sweet oranges, which include navels, Valencias and blood oranges; loose-skinned oranges, which include Mandarins, clementines, and tangerines; and bitter oranges, which include the Seville orange. Loose-skinned oranges have "zipper" skins and easily divide into segments. Bitter oranges are usually too sour or astringent to eat raw and are best for cooking, marmalade, and liqueurs. Choose fruit that is heavy for its size, evenly shaped, and without soft spots. Oranges are always picked when ripe and color can vary from bright orange to dull orange tinged with green. Store oranges at room temperature for 1 week or unwrapped in the refrigerator for up to 2 weeks. Fresh oranges are widely available year round, depending on their variety, but they are at their peak from late fall through winter.

PANE TOSCANO

Pane toscano, ABOVE, *a staple*
of the Tuscan kitchen, might
find its way into soup, crostini,
fettunta, *or* panzanella.
OPPOSITE TOP AND BOTTOM
LEFT, *Janet Hansen prepares*
Pane all'Anice e Alloro, *an*
impressive anise and laurel-scented
bread that is shaped to resemble
a laurel leaf crown. OPPOSITE
BOTTOM RIGHT, *two versions*
of Janet's Tuscan flatbread. The
top one, Schiaccia con Fricioli,
is made with pancetta cracklings.
The lower one, Schiaccia
con Ricotta, *uses sheep's milk*
ricotta and is scented with
fennel. An egg wash gives them
both a rich mahogany glaze.

Nothing ranks quite as high in importance in the diet of an average Tuscan as bread. The dense, saltless loaves of *pane toscano,* or Tuscan bread, make their appearance at nearly every meal, from toasted slices served with fresh butter and jam at breakfast to thick chunks that soak up the juices of a hearty soup in the evening. Pane toscano has a thick hard crust that keeps the bread moist and fresh for several days. As the bread begins to age it takes on new life. The absence of salt allows the bread to dry rather than turn stale, and the dry bread soaks up liquid while maintaining a firm texture, never becoming pasty. A bread lacking salt might sound bland and dull, but pane toscano is yeasty and fragrant. The absence of salt also balances the full flavor of Tuscan foods. It is said that Tuscans, thought by many to be frugal, eliminated salt in their bread long ago as a means of protesting a tax on salt.

Pane toscano has a multitude of functions. As *crostini* it acts as a foil for a vast array of tasty spreads with which to begin the meal. Crostini are thin toasted slices that can be served either hot or cold and can be topped with creamy mixtures made from mushrooms, olives, artichokes, beans, or chicken liver. Toppings can also include cured meats, cheese, or softened butter blended with anchovies, capers, fresh herbs, or truffles.

As *fettunta,* which means oily slice, pane toscano is thickly sliced, toasted on an open grill, rubbed with garlic, then doused with extra virgin olive oil and sprinkled with sea salt. Fettunta, called *bruschetta* in other parts of Italy, often serves as a midday snack. It can also be dressed with a mixture of tomatoes, basil, and olive oil.

Slices of pane toscano turn a simple bowl of soup into truly hearty fare. In a Tuscan salad called *panzanella,* the bread is crumbled and tossed with fresh basil and sun-ripened tomatoes at their peak. Forcemeat made with pane toscano, enriched with cheese and seasonings, is used as a stuffing for meat, poultry, and vegetables. Pane toscano is cubed and fried to serve as croutons sprinkled over a soup, grated for bread crumbs. Lastly, but no less importantly, pane toscano serves as a kind of edible utensil for nudging morsels of food onto the fork and mopping the plate.

The Tuscan appetite for bread *extends beyond* pane toscano *to include a collection of rustic-style loaves, flatbreads, and buns enriched and flavored with olive oil, honey, herbs, spices, olives, dried fruit, or nuts. Other Tuscan breads derive character from stone-ground whole wheat flour, chestnut flour, chickpea flour, or cornmeal.*

Several of the breads made in the Maremma, a territory in the province of Grosseto at Tuscany's southernmost end, are demonstrated by Janet Hansen at her farmhouse cooking school.

The flatbread of Tuscany, similar to focaccia or pizza, is called schiaccia *or* schiacciata, *from the verb* schiacciare, *which means to flatten. The Maremma version Janet prepares, called* Schiaccia con Ricotta, *is oval in shape with a long slit cut through the center. The dough, made with sheep's milk ricotta and a pinch of ground fennel seeds, is brushed with an egg wash before baking. Any good quality fresh ricotta can be used. Her* Schiaccia con Fricioli, *a winter flatbread, uses cracklings made from pancetta blended into the dough in place of ricotta.* Pane dei Morti, *literally bread of the dead, is associated with* il giorno dei morti, *the day of the dead, or All Souls' Day, November 2. This flatbread is made with walnuts, raisins, and dried figs. In addition to flatbreads, Janet also prepares an anise and laurel-scented bread shaped to resemble a laurel leaf crown called* Pane all'Anice e Alloro.

Janet's classes focus on the foods of Maremma, Italian regional cooking, and the foods of the Middle Ages and Renaissance, the subjects of her book, I fuochi del Medioevo/I fornelli del Rinascimento, *published in Italy.*

Pane Toscano
Tuscan Bread

FOR THE STARTER

5½ TEASPOONS ACTIVE DRY YEAST

1 CUP (8 FL OZ/250 ML) WARM WATER (105° TO 115°F/40° TO 46°C)

1½ CUPS (6 OZ/180 G) PLUS 2 TABLESPOONS UNBLEACHED ALL-PURPOSE FLOUR

FOR THE DOUGH

1 CUP (8 FL OZ/250 ML) WARM WATER

SEA SALT

4⅓ CUPS (18 OZ/510 G) UNBLEACHED ALL-PURPOSE FLOUR

1. To make the starter, pour the warm water into a large bowl. Sprinkle the yeast over the water and stir until dissolved. Add 1½ cups (6 oz/180 g) flour and blend until the mixture is smooth. Scrape down the sides of the bowl with a rubber spatula and sprinkle with the remaining 2 tablespoons of flour. Cover the bowl with a large cotton kitchen towel and let the dough rest in a warm draftfree place for at least 1 hour or overnight.

2. To make the dough, stir the warm water and a large pinch of salt into the starter. Add 3 cups of the flour, 1 cup (4 oz/120g) at a time, blending thoroughly before adding the next. Sprinkle 1 cup (4 oz/120g) of flour onto a pastry board or work surface. Turn out the dough onto the pastry board and knead in all of the flour, about 10 minutes. The dough will be very sticky and difficult to handle at the beginning. After all of the flour has been incorporated, the dough will be easier to handle but still tender.

3. Transfer the dough to a very large well-oiled bowl. Rub the dough against the the bowl to coat it with oil. Cover the bowl with the towel. Let it rest again in a warm draftfree place for 30 to 45 minutes or until doubled in size.

4. Punch down the dough and turn it out onto a lightly floured pastry board. Spread out the towel and dust it with the remaining ⅓ cup (1 oz/30 g) of flour. Knead the dough for 2 minutes. Shape the dough into a flat, wide loaf, about 14 inches (35 cm) long. Loosely wrap the dough in the towel, leaving enough room in the towel for the dough to rise. Let the dough rest again in a warm draftfree place until doubled in size, for 30 to 45 minutes.

5. Arrange terra-cotta tiles or a pizza stone on the center shelf of the oven (see instruction box, to right). Preheat the oven to 400°F (200°C). Allow 30 minutes for the oven and the tiles to preheat.

6. When the dough is ready, roll it out of the towel directly onto the hot tiles or stone. Make one or more lengthwise slashes on the top of the bread, using a sharp knife or razor. Bake for 55 to 60 minutes, or until lightly browned with a thick, hard crust. Turn the bread on its side and knock on its bottom. If done, the bread will make a hollow sound. Cool the bread on a cooling rack. Wrap the cooled bread in a large cotton towel. Do not refrigerate or store in plastic.

MAKES 1 LARGE LOAF

VARIATION: *Pane scuro*, dark Tuscan bread, can be made by substituting 2 cups (8 oz/250 g) of stone-ground whole wheat flour for an equal amount of all-purpose flour when making the dough. The 2 flours should be sifted together to blend thoroughly.

Using Terra-Cotta Tiles to Simulate a Brick Oven

Unglazed Italian terra-cotta tiles can be used to simulate a brick oven when baking bread, pizza, and focaccia. Soak the tiles in water overnight before using them for the first time. Let the tiles air-dry. It will not be necessary to soak the tiles again. Arrange the tiles side by side on the center shelf of the oven. The tiles should not cover the entire surface of the rack. Leave enough space for the hot air to circulate around the tile shelf. Bread, pizza, and focaccia can be baked directly on the tile shelf without sticking. A pizza stone can also be used in place of the terra-cotta tiles. If you are using a pizza stone, follow manufacturer's instructions.

Pane all'Anice e Alloro
Anise and Laurel Bread Shaped like a Laurel Leaf Crown

FOR THE BREAD DOUGH

1 TEASPOON ANISEED

1 CUP (8 FL OZ/250 ML) WATER

1 TABLESPOON HONEY

1 CUP (8 FL OZ/250 ML) WHOLE MILK

7½ TEASPOONS ACTIVE DRY YEAST

SEA SALT

4½ TO 5 CUPS (18 TO 20 OZ/540 TO 600 G) UNBLEACHED ALL-PURPOSE FLOUR

2 TABLESPOONS (1 FL OZ/30 ML) EXTRA VIRGIN OLIVE OIL

10 BAY LEAVES

FOR THE EGG WASH

1 LARGE EGG YOLK

1 TEASPOON WATER

1. To make the bread dough, combine the aniseed and water in a small saucepan and boil for 5 minutes. Pour the mixture into a large bowl. Stir in the honey and milk. Let the mixture cool to 105 to 115°F (40 to 46°C).

2. Sprinkle the yeast and 1 teaspoon salt over the warm liquid and stir until the yeast is completely dissolved. Add the flour, 1 cup (4 oz/120 g) at a time. Use only enough flour to make a soft dough. Turn out the dough onto a lightly floured pastry board or work surface. Knead for 10 minutes, incorporating more flour, if necessary, to keep the dough from sticking to the board. The dough should be smooth and tender.

3. Transfer the dough to a large bowl and drizzle the olive oil over the ball of dough. Rub the oil over the dough and cover the bowl with a cotton kitchen towel. Let the dough rest in a warm draftfree place for 1 hour, or until doubled in size.

4. Preheat the oven to 400°F (200°C). Oil a large baking sheet.

5. When the dough is ready, turn it out onto the pastry board. Knead the dough for 2 minutes to incorporate the olive oil and to force out any air bubbles. Flour the dough lightly, wrap it in the towel, and let it rest for 5 minutes.

6. Roll the dough into a 28-inch-long (70-cm-long) rope. Twist the rope several times and arrange it on the baking sheet in a ring. Pinch the ends together and tuck them under. Make 10 diagonal slashes on the surface, spacing them evenly apart. Tuck a bay leaf into each slash. Cover the dough with the towel and let it rest for 15 minutes.

7. Make the egg wash by beating the egg yolk and water in a small bowl. Brush the egg wash over the surface of the dough. Bake the bread on the center shelf of the oven for 30 to 35 minutes, or until golden brown and cooked through. Turn the bread on its side and knock on the bottom. If done, the bread will make a hollow sound. Cool the bread on a cooling rack. Remove bay leaves before slicing the bread.

MAKES 1 LOAF

Schiaccia con Ricotta
Tuscan Flatbread with Ricotta

When baking breads, Janet Hansen rests a long wooden spoon over the top of her bowl of rising dough. She then drapes a cotton dishtowel over the spoon, to cover the bowl and protect the dough from any drafts. The wooden spoon prevents the towel from falling into the bowl and sticking to the dough.

FOR THE BREAD DOUGH

7½ TEASPOONS ACTIVE DRY YEAST

1 CUP WARM WATER (105 TO 115°F/40 TO 46°C)

8 OUNCES (240 G) RICOTTA, ALLOWED TO SIT AT ROOM TEMPERATURE FOR 15 MINUTES

SEA SALT

PINCH OF GROUND FENNEL SEEDS

3½ TO 4 CUPS (14 TO 16 OZ/400 TO 450 G) UNBLEACHED ALL-PURPOSE FLOUR

2 TABLESPOONS (1 FL OZ/30 ML) EXTRA VIRGIN OLIVE OIL

FOR THE EGG WASH

1 LARGE EGG YOLK

1 TEASPOON WATER

1. To make the bread dough, sprinkle the yeast over the warm water in a large bowl. Stir in the ricotta, 1 teaspoon salt, and fennel seeds. Add the flour, 1 cup (4 oz/120 g) at a time. Use only enough flour to make a soft dough. Turn out the dough onto a lightly floured pastry board or work surface. Knead the dough for 10 minutes, incorporating more flour, if necessary, to keep the dough from sticking to the board. The dough should be smooth and tender.

2. Transfer dough to a large bowl and drizzle olive oil over the ball of dough. Rub the oil over the dough and cover the bowl with a cotton kitchen towel. Let rest in a warm draftfree place for 1 hour, or until doubled in size.

3. Preheat the oven to 400°F (200°C). Oil a large baking sheet.

4. When the dough is ready, turn it out onto the pastry board. Knead the dough for 2 minutes, to incorporate the olive oil and to force out any air bubbles. Flour the dough lightly, wrap it in the towel, and let it rest for 5 minutes.

5. Flatten the dough with a rolling pin and shape it into a 13 x 8-inch (33 x 20-cm) oval. Transfer the dough to the baking sheet. Cut a 7-inch-long (18-cm-long) slit lengthwise through the center of the dough. Cut completely through the dough to the baking sheet. Spread the slit open slightly. Cover the dough with the towel and let it rest 15 minutes more.

6. Make the egg wash by beating the egg yolk and water in a small bowl. Brush the egg wash over the surface of the dough. Bake the *schiaccia* on the center shelf of the oven for 25 to 30 minutes, or until rich brown in color and cooked through. Turn the bread on its side and knock on the bottom. If done, the bread will make a hollow sound. Cool the bread on a cooling rack.

MAKES 1 FLATBREAD

VARIATION: To make a *Schiaccia con Fricioli*, a flatbread with crispy bits of pancetta, finely dice 12 ounces (350 g) of pancetta and render it in a large skillet over medium heat until golden brown and crispy. Remove the pancetta with a slotted spoon and drain it on paper towels. Substitute the pancetta for the ricotta in Step 1 and reduce the salt to just a pinch. Prepare the dough and bake as described. Because the pancetta has less moisture than the ricotta, the dough will absorb less flour.

SECOND VARIATION: To make a *Pane dei Morti*, a flatbread with walnuts, raisins, and figs, prepare the dough through Step 2, letting it rest until doubled in size. Meanwhile soak 2½ ounces (50 g) golden raisins in hot water for 10 minutes. Drain and pat dry with paper towels. Chop 2½ ounces (50 g) walnuts and cut 2½ ounces (50 g) dried figs into ½-inch (1.25-cm) dice. Turn out the dough onto the pastry board. Knead the dough for 2 minutes and flatten it, by hand, to a 9-inch (22-cm) round. Sprinkle the round with half of the dried fruit and nuts, lightly pressing them into the dough, and fold the dough into thirds. Flatten the dough into a long strip, sprinkle with the remaining fruit and nuts, and roll up the dough like a jelly roll. Gently and briefly knead the dough to evenly distribute the fruit and nuts. Cover the dough with a cotton kitchen towel and let it rest for 5 minutes. Shape the dough, brush it with egg wash, and bake it as in Step 6.

FATTORIA DI MONTAGLIARI

O n the outskirts of the medieval village of Panzano, off the Via Chiantigiana, the picturesque road that winds through miles of vineyards and olive groves in the heart of Tuscany's Chianti zone, a rustic *trattoria*, or simple restaurant, occupies a stone farmhouse. The trattoria is part of the wine estate Fattoria di Montagliari. Giovanni Cappelli, a good-natured and lighthearted man, opened the trattoria in 1975, offering a comfortable place to eat the country food of Chianti and to drink the wines of the estate. The Cappelli family has upheld the tradition of wine making in Panzano for more than two centuries, and the wines of the Montagliari vineyards are highly regarded.

Giovanni Cappelli, ABOVE, produces an extensive range of wines at his wine estate in Tuscany's Chianti zone. The Chianti territory extends from the cities of Florence in the north to Siena in the south and is the official wine-growing zone for Chianti Classico. LEFT, the Trattoria di Montagliari offers an arugula sauce served over spinach filled ravioli, or handmade pasta ribbons, pappardelle or tagliatelle.

Trattoria di Montagliari has the air of a hunting lodge, and the handwritten *lista del giorno*, or menu of the day, reflects the simplicity of Tuscan cuisine. This is the food of hardworking, outdoor people. A meal at Montagliari could begin with a platter of local *salumi*, or cured meats, including *prosciutto crudo* and *finocchiona*, a salami seasoned with fennel seeds, or an assortment of *crostini*—thin slices of toasted bread topped with olive paste, spicy sausage, or a piquant tomato purée. As *primo piatto*, or first course, hand-rolled pappardelle and tagliatelle, wide and medium-width pasta ribbons, or spinach-stuffed ravioli are served with a choice of sauces—a hearty Tuscan ragù, a thick meat sauce made with aromatic vegetables, or a porcini mushroom sauce, or one of the two Montagliari specialties, a puréed walnut sauce or one made with fresh arugula.

Tuscany is known for its fine meats, and Montagliari offers an impressive list of meat and game. Early winter is still hunting season and the menu is likely to offer *cinghiale*, or wild boar. Each morning the kitchen staff trusses meat and small birds for roasting. A loin of pork, rabbit, and squab or guinea hen are well seasoned with salt, pepper, and garlic, then nestled together in a large pan. They are doused with olive oil and white wine; branches of fresh rosemary and sage are tucked here and there; then they are roasted in the large wood-burning oven. Thick slabs of Chianina beef are seared over a wood-burning grill and served charred on the outside and extremely rare

Panzano

*Opposite the Trattoria
di Montagliari, a small
shop is stocked with
products of the estate as
a convenience to guests.
Products range from a
full line of wines to
specialty oils, vinegars,
and fruit preserves,*
BELOW.

within, in the Tuscan style. Some of the finest beef
cattle in the world, Chianina, is raised in the nearby
Chiana Valley in the province of Arezzo. Signor
Cappelli buys the beef directly in the village of
Figline Valdarno. Most other meats are purchased
from a well-respected macelleria, or butcher shop,
in the neighboring market city of Greve. The
Antica Macelleria Falorni, established in the 1840s,
supplies many of the best restaurants of Chianti.

Tuscans are called *mangiafagioli*, or bean
eaters, beacause of their fondness for legumes. At
Montagliari, cannellini beans are often the side
dish of choice with roasted or grilled meats. They
are offered simply boiled and served with a
cruet of house olive oil for drizzling, or cooked
with tomatoes, garlic, and sage. Tuscans are also
particularly fond of fresh vegetables. Though
the offerings for winter are slim, Signor Cappelli's
orto, or small vegetable garden, will supply the
trattoria with cavolo nero, or Tuscan black cabbage, a kind of kale that becomes more flavorful
after a deep frost. *Cavolo nero* is essential in Tuscan
minestrone and when it is available, Montagliari
serves it with cannellini beans spooned over *pane
arrostito*, also called *fettunta*, a thick slice of toasted
or grilled Tuscan bread rubbed with garlic.

The trattoria offers a simple selection of
pecorino toscano cheese, which Signor Cappelli
buys in Pienza, a hill town known for its fine
sheep's milk cheese. Though Tuscans usually prefer
a wedge of cheese or piece of fresh fruit for
dessert, the specialty of Montagliari is difficult to
refuse, a thin slice of apple cake, baked in the
wood-burning oven until the apples develop a
caramelized glaze.

The wine list at the trattoria is extensive.
It features several vintages of both Montagliari
Chianti Classico and Chianti Classico Riserva in
addition to the Chianti Classico produced under
Giovanni Cappelli's La Quercia label. Montagliari
also offers Brunesco di San Lorenzo, a superb
wine produced from 100 percent Sangiovese
grapes, the dominant grape used in the production of Chianti wines.

Vin santo, literally holy wine, is usually

sipped as a dessert wine. Vin santo has been the
pride of the Cappelli family for centuries, and
Fattoria di Montagliari boasts of having the
largest *vin santeria* in Chianti. The vin santeria is
an attic room where the vin santo is produced
and aged. The grapes for the vin santo are hung
from the rafters to dry. The length of drying time
varies from producer to producer. After two
months the grapes shrivel like raisins, concen-
trating their sweetness and flavor. Only the best
are crushed. The sweet must of the grapes is
then transferred to *caratelli*, small barrels made of
Slavonian oak or local chestnut, containing the
remains of previous vintages. This thick yeasty
sludge, known as the *madre*, or mother, is what
gives the vin santo of Montagliari its particular
character. The madre in some of the Montagliari
caratelli is close to one hundred years old. While
escorting visitors on a tour of the vin santeria,
which holds nearly five hundred caratelli, Signor
Cappelli always points proudly to the original
family recipe for vin santo, dated 1769, that hangs
on the wall of the attic room.

The usual companion to a glass of vin santo
is *cantuccini di Prato*, a dry sweet biscuit studded
with almonds. The hard biscuit is softened by
dipping it into the vin santo. Signor Cappelli's
favorite accompaniment to vin santo, however,
is a thin cracker topped with creamy gorgonzola
cheese and a dab of fig preserves.

In a small shop opposite the trattoria Signor
Cappelli sells the products of the estate. These
include sauces made from olives, basil, walnuts, or
hot red chili peppers; chestnut honey; Chianti
wine vinegar; fine quality extra virgin olive oil and
a lemon-infused oil; and several fruit preserves,
including one made with figs and almonds. Signor
Cappelli also produces *salsa di mosto*, a syrupy
vinegar aged in the style of the traditional balsamic
vinegar of Modena. He offers one aged for nine-
teen years and another aged for twenty-seven years.

Fattoria di Montagliari continues as it has in
past generations to offer a true taste of Chianti in
the spirit of a family committed to quality and
the pleasure this quality brings to others.

LEFT, *the kitchen staff prepares the Torta di Mele di Fattoria,* an apple cake baked in a wood-burning oven. ABOVE, *fresh ribbons of pappardelle.* BELOW, *a table near the hearth at Trattoria di Montagliari.* BELOW LEFT, cavolo nero, *Tuscan black cabbage, grows in the* orto, *or vegetable garden.*

Cavolo Nero con le Fette calls for a drizzling

Cavolo Nero con le Fette

Toasted Bread with Tuscan Black Cabbage and Cannellini Beans

Cavolo nero, Tuscan black cabbage, is similar to American kale though somewhat more full-flavored. If unavailable, a substitute could be Russian red kale often found at farmers' markets. Trattoria di Montagliari serves cavolo nero over garlic-rubbed toasted bread and tops it with cannellini beans. It makes a satisfying antipasto for a winter meal.

SEA SALT

1 POUND (450 G) TUSCAN BLACK KALE, RUSSIAN KALE, OR AMERICAN KALE, STEMS REMOVED

8 SLIGHTLY DRY SLICES FIRM-TEXTURED COUNTRY-STYLE BREAD (PANE TOSCANO, PAGE 78), SLICED 1 INCH (2.5 CM) THICK

1 LARGE CLOVE OF GARLIC

2½ CUPS (20 FL OZ/625 ML) COOKED WHITE CANNELLINI BEANS (FOR HOMEMADE, SEE PAGE 187), DRAINED

EXTRA VIRGIN OLIVE OIL, FOR DRIZZLING

1. Fill a small pot with 1 quart (1 liter) of water and bring it to a boil. Add salt to taste. Cut the kale into 2-inch (5-cm) pieces and stir it into the boiling water. Cover and simmer 10 to 15 minutes or until tender. Let the kale remain in the water.

2. Preheat the oven to 400°F (200°C).

3. Arrange the bread slices in a single layer on a baking sheet and toast them in the oven for 10 minutes. Turn the slices and toast them for 6 to 8 minutes more, or until lightly browned on each side. The bread can also be toasted on a grill. While the bread is hot, rub one side with garlic. Arrange the bread, garlic side up, on individual plates or on a large serving platter.

4. Scoop the kale from the pot using a skimmer or large slotted spoon and arrange it on the bread slices. Reserve the cooking water. Spoon the beans over the kale and moisten with 1 or 2 spoonfuls of the reserved cooking water. Pass a cruet of extra virgin olive oil at the table for drizzling.

MAKES 8 SERVINGS

Cavolo Nero con le Fette, *OPPOSITE.*

Sugo di Rucola

Arugula Sauce

Arugula becomes more peppery in flavor after the first frost, though its spiciness is reduced if heated. This sauce, a smooth purée that combines arugula with walnuts and pine nuts, is similar to pesto. It is warmed when tossed with steaming pasta and mellows significantly.

Trattoria di Montagliari serves Sugo di Rucola *with medium or wide fresh pasta ribbons or with a spinach-stuffed ravioli similar to Ventagli di Ricotta e Spinaci (page 103), fan-shaped ravioli stuffed with ricotta and spinach.*

6 OUNCES (180 G) ARUGULA, TRIMMED, AND COARSELY CHOPPED

¼ CUP (1 OZ/30 G) WALNUTS

⅓ CUP (1½ OZ/45 G) PINE NUTS

1 SMALL CLOVE OF GARLIC

2 TABLESPOONS (1 OZ/30 G) UNSALTED BUTTER, SOFTENED

5 TABLESPOONS (2½ FL OZ/75 ML) EXTRA VIRGIN OLIVE OIL

½ CUP (2 OZ/60 G) GRATED PECORINO ROMANO

½ CUP (2 OZ/60 G) GRATED PARMIGIANO-REGGIANO

SEA SALT AND FRESHLY GROUND BLACK PEPPER

1. Combine the arugula, walnuts, pine nuts, and garlic in a food processor and process until the ingredients are finely chopped. Add the butter and olive oil and process until creamy.

2. Transfer the mixture to a large bowl and stir in the pecorino and Parmigiano. Season with salt and black pepper to taste. Refrigerate the sauce until needed. (This sauce will keep up to 1 week tightly covered in the refrigerator.)

MAKES ABOUT 1½ CUPS (14 OZ/400 G)

Note: To serve the sauce with pasta, spoon the desired amount into a small bowl while the pasta is boiling. Whisk 2 or 3 tablespoonfuls of the pasta water into the sauce. The consistency should be like soft whipped cream. When the pasta is ready, drain it and transfer it to a serving bowl. Pour the sauce over the pasta and toss until the pasta is well coated. Serve immediately.

of a very bold extra virgin olive oil.

Sugo di Noci

Walnut Sauce

This sauce is suitable to serve with any fresh egg pasta or tossed with green or white potato gnocchi (see page 42).

1½ CUPS (6 OZ/180 G) WALNUTS
1 SMALL CLOVE OF GARLIC
4 MEDIUM BASIL LEAVES, COARSELY CHOPPED
½ CUP (2 OZ/60 G) GRATED PECORINO ROMANO
½ CUP (2 OZ/60 G) GRATED PARMIGIANO-REGGIANO
2½ TABLESPOONS (1¼ OZ/40 G) UNSALTED BUTTER, SOFTENED
¼ CUP (2 FL OZ/60 ML) EXTRA VIRGIN OLIVE OIL
⅓ CUP (3 FL OZ/80 ML) HEAVY CREAM
SEA SALT AND FRESHLY GROUND BLACK PEPPER

l. Combine the walnuts, garlic, and basil in a food processor and process until the ingredients are very finely chopped. Add the pecorino, Parmigiano, butter, and olive oil and process until smooth.

2. Transfer the mixture to a large bowl and stir in the heavy cream. Season to taste with salt and black pepper and refrigerate. (This sauce will keep up to 1 week tightly covered in the refrigerator.)

MAKES 2 CUPS (16 FL OZ/500 ML)

Note: To serve the sauce with pasta, spoon the desired amount into a small bowl while the pasta is boiling. Whisk 2 or 3 tablespoonfuls of the pasta water into the sauce. The consistency should be like softly whipped cream. Drain the pasta and transfer it to a serving bowl. Pour the sauce over the pasta and toss until well coated. Serve immediately.

Sugo di Carne della Fiammetta

Chunky Meat Sauce with Vegetables

Giovanni Cappelli, an avid recipe collector for nearly fifty years, has amassed a collection of more than fifteen hundred recipes that fill eight large binders. Each of the recipes received from family members and local farmers of Chianti has been personally tested and documented. This thick meat and vegetable sauce, a specialty of his wife, Fiammetta, is a favorite. Heartier than a traditional Tuscan ragù, or meat sauce, this version uses onions, carrots, celery, beef, pork, and sausage, diced as they might be for a chunky soup.

This meat sauce is delicious when tossed with pappardelle, wide fresh egg pasta ribbons and freshly grated Parmigiano-Reggiano.

2 MEDIUM ONIONS
1 MEDIUM CARROT, PEELED
1½ CELERY STALKS
¼ CUP (2 FL OZ/60 ML) EXTRA VIRGIN OLIVE OIL
2 TABLESPOONS (1 FL OZ/30 ML) UNSALTED BUTTER
5 SPRIGS OF ITALIAN FLAT-LEAF PARSLEY, LEAVES ONLY, COARSELY CHOPPED
1 POUND (450 G) BONELESS BEEF SIRLOIN (SEE NOTE)
¾ POUND (350 G) BONELESS PORK SHOULDER (SEE NOTE)
8 OUNCES (225 G) SWEET ITALIAN SAUSAGE, WITHOUT FENNEL SEEDS, CASING REMOVED (SEE NOTE)
SEA SALT AND FRESHLY GROUND BLACK PEPPER
1 CUP (8 FL OZ/250 ML) DRY RED WINE, PREFERABLY CHIANTI
1 TABLESPOON TOMATO PASTE
2 TO 3 CUPS (8 TO 12 FL OZ/500 TO 750 ML) MEAT BROTH (FOR HOMEMADE, SEE PAGE 187)

1. Cut the onions, carrot, and celery into ½-inch (1.25-cm) dice.

2. Heat the olive oil and butter in a large heavy flame-proof casserole over medium-low heat. Add the vegetables and parsley. Cook slowly, tossing occasionally, until very tender, about 20 minutes.

3. Cut the beef, pork, and sausage into ½-inch (1.25-cm) dice. Add the meat to the casserole and increase the heat to medium. Cook, tossing frequently, just until the meat has lost its raw color. Season with salt and pepper to taste. Pour in the red wine and simmer the mixture briskly until the wine has reduced by half.

4. In a small bowl, blend the tomato paste with 1½ tablespoons of the broth. Stir this mixture into the casserole and add an additional ½ cup (4 fl oz/125 ml) broth. Simmer the sauce for 1½ hours, adding broth, ½ cup (4 fl oz/125 ml) at a time, to keep the sauce from becoming too thick and sticking to the bottom. It may not be necessary to use all of the broth. Taste the sauce for additional seasoning.

MAKES 6 SERVINGS

Note: Signor Cappelli suggests using the flavorful triangle-shaped morsel of beef cut from the sirloin section known as sirloin tip, loin tip, or top sirloin. If not available, use boneless sirloin. The pork shoulder can be cut from either the side called Boston butt or from the picnic ham. The Boston butt is slightly fatty with a soft membrane that surrounds the individual muscles. The fat and membrane, which melt when the meat is simmered, keeps the pork tender and moist. The picnic ham is a leaner cut and tends to be dryer, but if you prefer leaner meat, request shoulder from the picnic ham. Use an Italian sausage that is seasoned with just salt and black pepper, sometimes called luganega sausage. Avoid using sausage seasoned with fennel seeds, which are never used in Tuscan-style sausage.

Coniglio Imporchettato di Montagliari

Roast Boneless Rabbit with Rosemary and Fennel

Coniglio imporchettato, *which means rabbit roasted like Tuscan-style pork, is scented with rosemary, garlic, and fennel seeds. The boneless rabbit is rolled and wrapped in caul fat, a thin weblike membrane that lines the abdominal cavity of a pig. Caul fat resembles a lacy net, most of which melts away during the roasting. It keeps the meat moist and creates a golden crust.*

1   RABBIT LIVER

1   LARGE CLOVE OF GARLIC

1   SPRIG OF ROSEMARY, LEAVES ONLY

½   TEASPOON FENNEL SEEDS

SEA SALT AND FRESHLY GROUND BLACK PEPPER

1   RABBIT (3 POUNDS/1.4 K), BONED WHOLE

3   OUNCES (90 G) IMPORTED ITALIAN PROSCIUTTO, THINLY SLICED

2   OUNCES (60 G) CAUL FAT (OPTIONAL) (SEE NOTE)

2   TABLESPOONS (1 FL OZ/30 ML) EXTRA VIRGIN OLIVE OIL

1   CUP (8 FL OZ/250 ML) DRY WHITE WINE

1. Preheat the oven to 400°F (200°C).

2. Combine the liver, garlic, rosemary, fennel seeds, ¼ teaspoon salt and ⅛ teaspoon black pepper on a cutting board and chop them together until the mixture is pastelike.

3. Place the rabbit, skin side down, on a work surface. Spread the liver paste over the rabbit then cover with the prosciutto. Starting at the neck end, roll the rabbit toward the legs. Wrap the rabbit in caul fat and tie it like a roast using butcher's twine.

4. Heat the olive oil in a small roasting pan over medium-high heat, add the rabbit and brown it evenly on all sides. Pour the wine over the rabbit and bring it to a boil. Roast in the oven for 50 to 60 minutes, or until golden brown and a meat thermometer registers 160°F (71°C).

5. Transfer the rabbit to a carving board, cover it with aluminum foil, and let it rest for 10 minutes. Strain the pan juices through a sieve. If the juices have become thick, stir in 1 or 2 tablespoonfuls of boiling water. Season the juices with salt and pepper to taste. Slice the rabbit thin and serve it moistened with the juices.

MAKES 5 TO 6 SERVINGS

Note: Most butchers can supply caul fat if given advance notice. It is easier to work with if it is soaked for 10 minutes in warm water. If you cannot obtain the caul fat or prefer not to use it, baste the roast with the pan juices every 20 minutes.

Variation: A butterflied boneless loin of pork (2½ to 3 pounds/1.1 to 1.4 k) can be used in place of the boned rabbit. If you are wrapping the pork in caul fat, trim away the outer layer of fat. If not, leave a thin layer of fat, to keep the pork moist. The fat can be cut away after the pork has roasted. Finely chop the garlic, rosemary, and fennel seeds with the salt and black pepper. Transfer the mixture to a small bowl and add enough olive oil to make a paste. Arrange the pork, fat side down, on a work surface, spread with the paste, and cover with slices of prosciutto. Roll up the pork, wrap it in caul fat, if desired, and tie it like a roast. Roast the pork for 60 to 65 minutes or until a thermometer registers 160°F (71°C).

MAKES 4 SERVINGS

LEFT, a collection of Giovanni Cappelli's wines enjoyed over lunch at the Trattoria di Montagliari.

The wood-burning stove at the trattoria is fired up each morning, RIGHT, and is used for roasting meat and game, as well as for baking Montagliari's golden farmhouse apple cake.

Cacciucco di Pollo
Tuscan Chicken Stew

Cacciucco is a soupy stew ladled over toasted bread. The best-known cacciucco is made with fish and shellfish. The version at Montagliari uses chicken. Select a free-range chicken that is meaty and lean. Ask the butcher to cut the chicken into small pieces using a meat saw to avoid splintered bones.

- 5 TABLESPOONS (3 FL OZ/80 ML) EXTRA VIRGIN OLIVE OIL
- 1 FREE-RANGE CHICKEN (4 LBS/1.8 K), CUT INTO 18 PIECES
- 2 MEDIUM CLOVES OF GARLIC, THINLY SLICED, PLUS 1 WHOLE CLOVE OF GARLIC
- 30 SMALL FRESH SAGE LEAVES
- 2 SMALL HOT RED CHILI PEPPERS
- SEA SALT
- 1 CUP (8 FL OZ/250 ML) DRY RED WINE, PREFERABLY CHIANTI
- 2½ CUPS (20 FL OZ/600 ML) CHICKEN BROTH (FOR HOMEMADE, SEE PAGE 187)
- 2 CUPS (16 FL OZ/500 ML) CANNED TOMATOES, WITH THEIR JUICE
- 4 SLIGHTLY DRY SLICES FIRM-TEXTURED COUNTRY-STYLE BREAD (PANE TOSCANO, PAGE 78), SLICED 1 INCH (2.5 CM) THICK

1. Heat the olive oil over medium-high heat in a sauté pan large enough to comfortably hold the chicken in a single layer. Add half the chicken and cook until golden brown on all sides. Remove from the pan and brown the second half. Return all the chicken to the pan and add the garlic, sage, and chili peppers and cook until the garlic is golden. Season the chicken with salt to taste then pour in the red wine. Simmer briskly until the wine is reduced by half.

2. Heat the broth in a small saucepan until it is simmering. Add tomatoes to the chicken mixture and break them into small chunks with the back of a wooden spoon. Simmer for 5 minutes. Pour in the broth, cover, and simmer gently for 30 minutes, turning the chicken occasionally. Uncover the pan and simmer briskly for 5 minutes, or until the sauce thickens slightly.

3. Preheat the oven to 400°F (200°C).

4. Cut the bread slices in half. Arrange them in a single layer on a baking sheet and toast them in the oven for 10 minutes. Turn and toast them 6 to 8 minutes more, or until lightly browned on each side. While the bread is hot, rub 1 side with the whole clove of garlic.

5. Transfer the *cacciucco* to a rimmed platter. Spoon the pan juices over the chicken and arrange the toasted bread around the edge of the platter. Serve each portion of cacciucco spooned over toasted bread.

MAKES 4 SERVINGS

Fagioli all'Uccelletto
Cannellini Beans with Tomatoes and Sage

- 2 SMALL CLOVES OF GARLIC, THINLY SLICED
- 3 TABLESPOONS (1½ FL OZ/45 ML) EXTRA VIRGIN OLIVE OIL
- 2 CUPS (16 FL OZ/500 ML) CANNED TOMATOES, WITH THEIR JUICE
- 2 TEASPOONS COARSELY CHOPPED FRESH SAGE LEAVES OR ¾ TEASPOON DRIED SAGE
- SEA SALT AND FRESHLY GROUND BLACK PEPPER
- 4½ CUPS (36 FL OZ/1 LITER) COOKED CANNELLINI BEANS (FOR HOMEMADE, SEE PAGE 187)

1. Sauté the garlic with the olive oil in a large heavy flame-proof casserole over medium heat until golden. Add the tomatoes, sage, and salt and pepper to taste. Simmer rapidly for 5 minutes while breaking up the tomatoes into large chunks with the back of a wooden spoon.

2. Add the beans with 1½ cups (12 fl oz/375 ml) of the bean liquid. Simmer the mixture, uncovered, for 30 minutes, stirring occasionally. Add more bean liquid if the mixture becomes too thick.

MAKES 6 SERVINGS

Variation: 1½ pounds (675 g) luganega sausage, a sweet Italian-style sausage without fennel seeds, can be added to the casserole with the beans. Simmer until the sausage is cooked through.

Finocchi Montagliari
Fennel Braised with Tomatoes

- 2 FENNEL BULBS, TOPS AND BRUISED LEAVES TRIMMED
- 4 SPRIGS OF ITALIAN FLAT-LEAF PARSLEY LEAVES
- 2 SMALL CLOVES OF GARLIC
- ⅔ CUP (5½ FL OZ/165 ML) CANNED TOMATOES, DRAINED AND CHOPPED
- ¼ CUP (2 FL OZ/60 ML) EXTRA VIRGIN OLIVE OIL
- SEA SALT AND FRESHLY GROUND BLACK PEPPER

1. Cut each fennel bulb in half, from top to bottom, then slice each half lengthwise, ⅜ inch (1 cm) thick.

2. Combine parsley and garlic on a cutting board and chop fine. Place mixture in a medium-size heavy flame-proof casserole. Add the fennel, tomatoes, and olive oil. Season with salt and pepper to taste and pour in ½ cup (4 fl oz/125 ml) water. Cover and simmer over low heat for 25 to 30 minutes, stirring occasionally, until the fennel is tender.

MAKES 4 SERVINGS

Slow cooking brings out the sweetness in cipolline. *Stewed in olive oil,* Cipolline in Umido, RIGHT, *can be served alongside roasted pork, veal, or rabbit.*

The farmhouse apple cake at Montagliari, LEFT, *develops a golden caramelized glaze.*

1. Combine the cipolline and olive oil in a small heavy casserole. Dilute the tomato paste in ½ cup (4 fl oz/125 ml) warm water and add it to the casserole. Season with salt and pepper to taste. Cover the casserole and simmer slowly, stirring occasionally, for 45 minutes, or until the cipolline are tender and the sauce has thickened slightly. Serve hot or at room temperature.

MAKES 6 SERVINGS

Torta di Mele di Fattoria
Farmhouse Apple Cake

The vanilla-like essence and dry nature of a Golden Delicious apple makes it an excellent choice for baking in cakes and tarts. This apple cake has a moist pudding texture. Serve a thin wedge with either a dollop of whipped cream or a small scoop of vanilla gelato.

  5 GOLDEN DELICIOUS APPLES
  2 LARGE EGGS
1¼ CUPS (8 OZ/250 G) SUGAR
 ½ CUP (2 OZ/60 G) UNBLEACHED ALL-PURPOSE FLOUR
 ½ CUP (4 FL OZ/125 ML) WHOLE MILK
 7 TABLESPOONS (3½ OZ/100 G) UNSALTED BUTTER, MELTED
  1 TEASPOON VANILLA EXTRACT
  2 TEASPOONS BAKING POWDER
CONFECTIONERS' SUGAR, FOR DUSTING

1. Preheat the oven to 375°F (190°C). Butter and flour an 11-inch (28-cm) cake pan or deep dish pizza pan.
2. Peel, core, and quarter the apples. Slice the apple sections crosswise into very thin slivers. This can be done by hand or with the slicing blade of a food processor.
3. Beat the eggs and sugar in a very large bowl with a wire whisk until the sugar is dissolved. Stir in the flour, then add the milk, butter, and vanilla. Blend the mixture thoroughly. Quickly stir in the baking powder then fold in the sliced apples.
4. Pour the mixture into the cake pan or pizza pan and bake on the floor of the oven for 10 minutes. Transfer the pan to the center rack and bake for 50 to 55 minutes more, or until the cake is golden brown and cooked through. The cake is done when a small paring knife inserted into the center comes out clean. Cool the *torta* on a cooling rack and serve warm or at room temperature. Dust with confectioners' sugar before serving.

MAKES 8 SERVINGS

Cipolline in Umido
Small Italian Onions Stewed in Olive Oil

Cipolline *are small, squat onions with papery, golden skins, about 1½ inches in diameter. In the United States, they can be found in specialty produce markets, often sold in bulk or packaged in small net bags. Locally grown* cipolline *are sometimes available at farmers' markets. When gently stewed,* cipolline *become honey-sweet in flavor. To keep them from falling apart, be careful not to trim away too much of the root end. Serve the* cipolline *alongside roasted pork, veal, or rabbit.*

1½ POUNDS (675 G) CIPOLLINE, PEELED AND TRIMMED
 ¼ CUP EXTRA VIRGIN OLIVE OIL
  1 TABLESPOON (2 FL OZ/60 ML) TOMATO PASTE
SEA SALT AND FRESHLY GROUND BLACK PEPPER

BAFFO

The culinary traditions of an often overlooked mountain culture remain cradled within an Alpine valley deep in the northern reaches of Lombardy, the Valtellina. Extending east from the northern tip of Lake Como and bordering Switzerland, the Valtellina is a land of few resources but they have been creatively utilized. The cuisine reflects the needs of hard-working people who have learned to subsist in a rugged mountain terrain.

The survival of the Valtellinese people is based on their unique management of the land. The Valtellina lies between the Rhaetian Alps to the north and the Orobie Alps on the south. Terraced farming has made cultivation possible at even the steepest angles. The sunny position of the Rhaetian slopes, shielded from cold northern winds, has provided an environment suitable for vineyards, believed to have been originally planted by the Etruscans. This unlikely location, six hundred to eight hundred meters above sea level, is one of Italy's important wine-producing zones. The cultivation of the chiavennasca grape, the local name for the nebbiolo grape used for Barolo in Piedmont, yields superb wines—Grumello, Inferno, Valgella, Sassella, and Sfursàt.

Typical of many Alpine environments, the Valtellina has also been successful in the cultivation of cereals, though difficult and sometimes impossible to grow above certain heights. Buckwheat, rye, corn, millet, and barley make their way into the traditional rustic coarse-grained breads, pasta, polenta, and hearty soups. In parts of the terrain unsuited for cultivation, animal husbandry has always been important, with cows, sheep, and goats providing the Valtellina with milk, butter, and cheese of outstanding quality. Limited quantities of seasonal vegetables grow in small gardens while apples, pears, walnuts, wild berries, mushrooms, and chestnuts are plentiful.

Mario Gianni provides an authentic taste of the Valtellina in an austere mountain setting at a restaurant with the farcical name of Baffo, or moustache (named for father Emilio who sports a bushy moustache and exhibits a spirited sense of humor). While his brother Fabrizio mans the dining room, Mario prepares the traditional

Each morning Mario Gianni, ABOVE, works in his large kitchen at Baffo making a fresh batch of pizzoccheri, enough to feed sixty to seventy people. This buckwheat pasta is the pride of Valtellina. OPPOSITE, the majestic Orobie Alps make a stunning backdrop for the rugged mountain vineyards.

Valtellina

The fügascia, *or focaccia,* TOP, *that Mario enjoyed as a child bakes with sugar and chunks of butter on top that caramelize to form a hardened crust.* ABOVE, *farmers still use a twig backpack known as a* gierla *to transport hay in winter to farm animals in snow-covered fields.*

dishes of the Valtellina. The restaurant, originally established by their parents in the city of Sondrio, the heart of Valtellina, is situated on Via Stelvio, the main thoroughfare, which is a direct link to the nearby mountain villages and Valtellina's numerous ski resorts. Baffo has become a familiar stopover for locals as well as passing travelers, both business and recreational.

Mario begins most mornings caring for his barnyard animals—chickens, rabbits, turkeys, and geese—and tending to his *orto*, the vegetable garden that is tucked between the back of the restaurant and his house. There are no shortcuts at Baffo. Mario cultivates and raises most of what he uses in the kitchen; all other provisions come from small local sources. Baffo is best known for *pizzoccheri*, considered the pride of the Valtellina, a buckwheat pasta cooked together with potatoes and cabbage, then tossed with brown butter and cheese. Mario hand rolls enough pizzoccheri each morning to serve sixty to seventy, cutting the coarse-textured, ashen-toned dough into short, narrow ribbons. Without hand-rolled pizzoccheri made just as his mother Rosa did, "there would be no Baffo," Mario says. The potatoes and cabbage are, of course, from the orto and the cheese is delivered from a *caseficio*, or dairy, in the nearby village of Chiuro.

Cheese is a basic element in the cuisine of the Valtellina. Casera Valtellina, an aged cow's-milk cheese produced from partially skimmed milk, is used in both pizzoccheri and a traditional antipasto called *sciatt*, crispy fritters made with cubes of casera dipped into a buckwheat and white flour batter. Sciatt, or tails in local dialect, takes its name from the tail-like strands of batter that extend from the fritter. Mario serves sciatt with a salad made from greens grown in the orto, combining leaves that are tender and mild with those that are more assertive. Bresaola, a lean filet of beef, that is salt-cured and dried in the clear mountain air, is an important product of the

Valtellina, and it is often served as an antipasto. Mario highlights the delicate flavor of the bresaola by cutting it into silky thin slices and topping it with rounds of oranges or dressing it with shards of Grana Padano, an aged grating cheese with a nutty flavor similar to Parmigiano-Reggiano.

Polenta, soothing cold-weather fare and long important in the diet of the Valtellinese, is often made with a combination of cornmeal and buckwheat flour. Mario serves his *polenta mischiata*, which means mixed polenta, alongside poultry or meat braised in local wines. Polenta mischiata is also served on its own as a *primo piatto*, or first course, with a generous sprinkling of Grana Padano. When cubes of casera and a pat of butter are stirred into the polenta mischiata it is then called *polenta taragna*.

The evening meal in the Valtellina was traditionally the most important meal of the day. Farmers often carried a simple lunch to the fields; the steep slopes they had to maneuver made it difficult to return home during midday for something more comforting and substantial. A hearty dinner, called *cena*, would then be shared around the glow of the hearth that stood in the center of the main room of the house. As in all cultures, life for the Valtellinese has changed, and many of the traditional dishes are no longer prepared at home, but Mario Gianni prides himself in having preserved the essence of *la cucina valtellinese* at his family restaurant, Baffo.

Savoy cabbage, a real flavor-packed cabbage, is cooked with potatoes and buckwheat pasta in Mario's pizzoccheri, RIGHT.

Bresaola al Carpaccio
Bresaola with Grana Padano and Marinated Mushrooms

Mario Gianni thinly slices bresaola, a delicate cured filet of beef and a principal product of Valtellina, and arranges it on a platter dressed like carpaccio with shards of Grana Padano cheese and bits of marinated porcini mushrooms. As a variation, thinly sliced marinated artichokes can replace the mushrooms.

  6 OUNCES (180 G) BRESAOLA, VERY THINLY SLICED
  24 SMALL MARINATED, CULTIVATED OR WILD MUSHROOMS,
     COARSELY CHOPPED
  1 TABLESPOON FINELY CHOPPED ITALIAN FLAT-LEAF PARSLEY LEAVES
GRANA PADANO, FOR SHAVING
FRESHLY GROUND BLACK PEPPER
EXTRA VIRGIN OLIVE OIL, FOR DRIZZLING
  1 LEMON, CUT INTO WEDGES

Mario Gianni preparing sciatt, *RIGHT, crispy fritters made with Casera Valtellina cheese dipped in a nutty buckwheat batter.*

When Bresaola al Carpaccio, *LEFT, is served at Baffo it is accompanied by a basket of* pane di segole. *These flattened rings of rye bread were once baked in wood-burning ovens then hung from the rafters to dry. A crusty rye or whole grain bread would make an excellent accompaniment to this dish.*

1. Arrange the *bresaola* slices, slightly overlapping, on a large platter. Scatter the mushrooms over the *bresaola*, then sprinkle with parsley. Shave thin slivers of the Grana over the bresaola using a vegetable peeler, sprinkle with black pepper, and drizzle with olive oil.

2. Serve with wedges of lemon to squeeze over the bresaola.

MAKES 6 SERVINGS

Sciatt
Crispy Cheese Fritters

These morsels of melted cheese fried in a nutty buckwheat batter are served piping hot and can be accompanied by a refreshing garden salad as Mario does.

  ½ CUP (2 OZ/60 G) UNBLEACHED ALL-PURPOSE FLOUR
  ½ CUP (2 OZ/60 G) FINELY GROUND LIGHT BUCKWHEAT FLOUR
  1 TABLESPOON GRATED GRANA PADANO
  2 TABLESPOONS BREAD CRUMBS
PINCH OF SEA SALT
  1 CUP (8 FL OZ/250 ML) SPARKLING MINERAL WATER
  ¼ CUP (2 FL OZ/60 ML) GRAPPA
  1 POUND (450 G) CASERA VALTELLINA CHEESE, CUT INTO
     ¾-INCH (2-CM) CUBES
SUNFLOWER OIL, FOR FRYING
SEA SALT

1. To make the batter, combine the flours, Grana, bread crumbs, and salt in a large bowl. Add the mineral water and stir with a wire whisk until the mixture is smooth. Stir in the grappa, cover the bowl, and let the mixture rest for at least 1 hour.

2. Pour enough sunflower oil into a large skillet with high sides, to come at least 1 inch up the sides. Heat the oil over medium heat. When the oil is hot, dip the cheese, one piece at a time, into the batter and fry, several pieces at a time, until golden brown. Remove them from the skillet with a slotted spoon and drain on paper towels. Continue this procedure until all of the cheese has been fried.

3. Arrange the *sciatt* on a large platter and sprinkle lightly with salt. Serve immediately while the cheese is hot and melted.

MAKES 8 SERVINGS

Pizzoccheri alla Baffo

Buckwheat Pasta with Potatoes and Cabbage

Pizzoccheri, *ribbons of pasta made from a blend of white and buckwheat flour, are generally cooked with potatoes and cabbage. Dried* pizzoccheri*, made in Valtellina, is readily available and can be substituted for handmade.*

For the Buckwheat Pasta

2 CUPS (8 OZ/240 G) UNBLEACHED ALL-PURPOSE FLOUR

2 CUPS (8 OZ/240 G) FINELY GROUND LIGHT BUCKWHEAT FLOUR

PINCH OF SEA SALT

1¼ CUPS (5 OZ/150 G) GRATED GRANA PADANO

6 OUNCES (180 G) CASERA VALTELLINA CHEESE OR FONTINA D'AOSTA CHEESE, CUT INTO ½-INCH (1.25-CM) DICE

SEA SALT

¾ POUND (12 OZ/350 G) YUKON GOLD OR RUSSET POTATOES, PEELED, CUT INTO QUARTERS, THEN SLICED ⅜ INCH (1 CM) THICK

1 POUND (450 G) SAVOY CABBAGE, CORED, LARGE RIBS REMOVED, AND CUT INTO 1-INCH (2.5-CM) CHUNKS

8 TABLESPOONS (4 OZ/125 G) UNSALTED BUTTER

10 FRESH SAGE LEAVES

4 CLOVES OF GARLIC

1. Combine the all-purpose flour and the buckwheat flour in a large bowl and blend thoroughly. To make the pasta dough, use the flour mixture, 1 cup (8 fl oz/250 ml) tepid water, and salt as directed on page 188, the section entitled Making the Dough. Knead the dough entirely by hand until smooth and firm, about 10 minutes. It is not necessary to use all of the flour. Excess flour will make the dough tough and dry. The remaining flour will be used when stretching and cutting the pasta. Flour the dough lightly, wrap it in plastic wrap and let it rest for 10 minutes.

2. Spread 2 large cotton kitchen towels on a work surface and dust lightly with the flour mixture. Divide the dough in half. Work with 1 piece at a time, keeping the unused portion wrapped in plastic wrap. Lightly dust a pastry board or work surface with the flour mixture and roll out the dough to a ⅛-inch-thick (0.3-cm-thick) round. Arrange the round of dough on one of the towels. Dry the pasta slightly, turning it occassionally to dry evenly. The surface should be dry to the touch, but the pasta should remain flexible. Roll out the second piece of dough and let it dry the same way.

3. When the pasta has dried sufficiently, cut each sheet of dough into 4-inch-wide strips. Lightly flour both sides of each strip and stack the strips three at a time. Slice each stack into ½-inch-wide (1.25-cm-wide) strands and transfer them to the towels, dust with flour, and gently toss.

4. To prepare the *pizzoccheri* for serving, combine 1 cup of the Grana in a bowl with the casera or fontina cheese, and set aside. Fill a very large pot (at least 8 quarts) with water and bring it to a rapid boil. Add salt to taste. Stir in the potatoes and cabbage and cover the pot until the water returns to a boil. Uncover and boil for 5 minutes.

5. While the vegetables are cooking, combine the butter, sage, and garlic in a small heavy saucepan and cook over medium-low heat until the garlic is golden brown and the butter is nutty.

6. After the vegetables have boiled for 5 minutes, stir the pasta into the pot and cover until it returns to a boil. Uncover and boil the pasta with the vegetables for 5 minutes, or until the pasta is tender. Arrange alternate layers of cheese and pasta in a large serving bowl or rimmed platter, 3 layers of each, starting with cheese and finishing with pasta. Sprinkle the remaining ¼ cup (1 oz/30 g) Grana over the top. Pour the brown butter mixture over the pasta and let stand for 1 minute. Then toss the pizzoccheri until the pasta is evenly coated with the brown butter and all of the cheese has melted. Serve immediately.

MAKES 6 SERVINGS

Polenta Mischiata

Cornmeal and Buckwheat Polenta

Cornmeal and buckwheat flour are combined to make a dark-toned polenta commonly eaten in Valtellina.

1½ CUPS (7 OZ/225 G) COARSELY GROUND YELLOW CORNMEAL

1½ CUPS (6 OZ/180 G) FINELY GROUND LIGHT BUCKWHEAT FLOUR

SEA SALT

1. Blend the cornmeal and buckwheat together in a large bowl. Bring 2½ quarts (2.5 liters) of water to a rolling boil in a large heavy pot. Season with salt to taste. Hold a fistful of the cornmeal mixture over the pot. Stir constantly while the cornmeal mixture slips through your fingers in a slow steady stream into the boiling water. When all of the cornmeal mixture has been added, lower the heat. Simmer for 45 minutes, stirring occasionally, or until the polenta is thick and creamy. As the polenta thickens it will be necessary to stir more frequently.

2. Pour the polenta into a large dampened bowl or eight dampened 8-ounce (250-ml) ramekins. Smooth the top and let stand for 10 minutes, then unmold.

MAKES 8 SERVINGS

Tzigonier
Grilled Beef on a Stick

This grilled beef on a stick is an Alpine dish seldom seen today in Valtellina. Mario serves it with fried or roasted potatoes and a tossed garden salad.

EXTRA VIRGIN OLIVE OIL, FOR RUBBING DOWELS AND MEAT

18 OUNCES (500 G) BONELESS BEEF SIRLOIN, VERY THINLY SLICED

FRESHLY GROUND BLACK PEPPER

¾ TEASPOON CHOPPED FRESH ROSEMARY LEAVES

SEA SALT

1. Rub six ⅝-inch-thick (2-cm-thick) wooden dowels about 22 inches (55 cm) long with olive oil. Allow oil to soak into the wood. Do this 3 or 4 times several hours before grilling.

2. Wrap the slices of beef around the sticks, overlapping on each turn around the stick. Leave 2 to 3 inches (5 to 8 cm) of wood exposed at each end of the stick and cover the exposed portion with aluminum foil. Rub the beef lightly with olive oil and season generously with freshly ground black pepper. Sprinkle the beef with chopped rosemary and place the sticks on a hot grill or griddle. Brown the *tzigonier* lightly on all sides and sprinkle with salt to taste. Each stick will make 1 serving.

MAKES 6 SERVINGS

Mario shovels glowing embers under an iron grate that rests in the hearth then grills thin slices of beef wrapped around a wooden dowel to make a traditional Alpine dish called Tzigonier, LEFT.

Tacchino alla Cacciatore
Braised Morsels of Turkey with Vegetables

Mario oven braises white and dark meat boneless turkey with vegetables in a white wine and tomato sauce. He serves it with Patate Arrosto *(recipe follows) and a timbale of* Polenta Mischiata *(page 95).*

¾ OUNCE (25 G) DRIED PORCINI MUSHROOMS

2½ POUNDS (1.2 K) SKINLESS, BONELESS TURKEY BREAST AND THIGHS

3 TABLESPOONS (1½ OZ/45 G) UNSALTED BUTTER

2 TABLESPOONS (1 FL OZ/30 ML) EXTRA VIRGIN OLIVE OIL

1 SMALL SPRIG OF ROSEMARY

1 CLOVE OF GARLIC, THINLY SLICED

1 BAY LEAF

2 MEDIUM ONIONS, CUT INTO 1-INCH (2.5-CM) CHUNKS

4 MEDIUM CARROTS, CUT INTO 1-INCH (2.5-CM) CHUNKS

2 CELERY STALKS, CUT INTO 1-INCH (2.5-CM) CHUNKS

¼ TEASPOON DRIED MARJORAM

¼ TEASPOON DRIED SAGE

¼ TEASPOON DRIED THYME

SEA SALT AND FRESHLY GROUND BLACK PEPPER

2 TABLESPOONS UNBLEACHED ALL-PURPOSE FLOUR

1 CUP (8 FL OZ/250 ML) DRY WHITE WINE

1½ CUPS (12 FL OZ/375 ML) CANNED TOMATOES, COARSELY CHOPPED

1 CUP (8 FL OZ/250 ML) MEAT BROTH (FOR HOMEMADE, SEE PAGE 187)

1. Preheat the oven to 400°F (200°C). Soak the porcini in ⅔ cup (5½ fl oz/165 ml) warm water for 15 minutes. Lift them out of the soaking liquid, and strain the liquid through a double layer of cheesecloth. Scrape off any sand left on the porcini and coarsely chop them.

2. Cut the turkey into 2 x 3-inch (5 x 7.5-cm) pieces. Melt the butter and oil in a large, heavy, ovenproof sauté pan over medium-high heat. Add the turkey and the sprig of rosemary. Brown the turkey on all sides. Add the garlic and bay leaf and cook until the garlic is golden. Stir in the onions, carrots, and celery. Sprinkle with marjoram, sage, and thyme. Season with salt and pepper to taste. Sprinkle with flour and stir until dissolved. Stir in the wine, tomatoes, porcini mushrooms, mushroom liquid, and half of the broth. Bring to a boil and transfer the pan to the oven. Bake, uncovered, 35 to 40 minutes, or just until the turkey is cooked through. If the sauce becomes too thick, stir in some of the remaining broth. Remove the bay leaf and the rosemary sprig before serving.

MAKES 6 SERVINGS

Patate Arrosto

Crispy Roasted Potatoes

These crunchy roasted potatoes employ three cooking methods: boiling, sautéing, and roasting.

2 POUNDS (900 G) YUKON GOLD OR RUSSET POTATOES, PEELED
    AND CUT INTO 1 X 1½-INCH (2.5 X 4-CM) CHUNKS
SEA SALT AND FRESHLY GROUND BLACK PEPPER
2 TABLESPOONS (1 OZ/30 G) UNSALTED BUTTER
2 TABLESPOONS (1 FL OZ/30 ML) EXTRA VIRGIN OLIVE OIL
1 SPRIG OF ROSEMARY
1 TABLESPOON FINE DRY BREAD CRUMBS

1. Preheat the oven to 400°F (200°C).

2. Place the potatoes in a large pot and fill it with cold water to cover by 2 inches (5 cm). Bring the water to a boil, add salt to taste, and boil for 2 minutes. Drain the potatoes in a large colander.

3. Combine the butter, olive oil, and rosemary in a large, heavy, ovenproof skillet that will hold the potatoes comfortably in a single layer. Heat the skillet over medium-high heat. When the butter has melted, add the potatoes and sauté them, tossing frequently, just until they begin to brown. Season the potatoes with salt and pepper to taste, sprinkle with bread crumbs, and toss. Transfer the pan to the center shelf of the oven and roast for 35 to 40 minutes, tossing occasionally, until crusty on the outside, and creamy on the inside. Serve immediately.

MAKES 4 SERVINGS

Fügascia

Sweet Caramelized Focaccia

Mario fondly remembers the caramelized focaccia brought by his aunt on visits from Ponte Valtellina. The fügascia, still made at the same panetteria, or bread shop, in a wood-burning oven, uses rye and white flour.

2 TEASPOONS ACTIVE DRY YEAST
1 CUP (8 FL OZ/250 ML) WARM WATER (105 TO 115°F/40 TO 46°C)
1½ CUPS (6 OZ/180 G) UNBLEACHED ALL-PURPOSE FLOUR
1½ CUPS (6½ OZ/200 G) RYE FLOUR
SEA SALT
3 TABLESPOONS (1½ OZ/45 G) UNSALTED COLD BUTTER,
    CUT INTO SMALL CHUNKS
⅓ CUP (2½ OZ/75 G) SUGAR

1. Sprinkle the yeast over ¼ cup (2 fl oz/60 ml) of the warm water in a small bowl. Stir until the yeast is dissolved. Sift the white and rye flour together 3 times to combine thoroughly. Set aside ¾ cup (6 oz/180 g) and transfer the rest to a large bowl.

2. Make a well in the center of the bowl and add the remaining ¾ cup (6 oz/180 g) of warm water, ¼ teaspoon salt, and the dissolved yeast. Blend the ingredients in the well with a wooden spoon and gradually incorporate the flour. The mixture will be very coarse and sticky. Turn the dough out onto a lightly floured pastry board or work surface. Knead for 5 to 10 minutes, or until the dough is smooth and tender. Incorporate just enough flour to keep the dough from being sticky. Transfer the dough to a large well-oiled bowl. Rub the dough against the bowl to coat it with oil. Cover the bowl with a cotton kitchen towel and let the dough rest in a warm draftfree place for 1 hour, or until doubled in size.

3. When the dough is ready, turn it out onto the lightly floured pastry board. Knead the dough for 2 minutes to force out any air bubbles, then let the dough rest for 5 minutes, covered with the towel.

4. Place a 10-inch (25-cm) flan ring or springform ring on a flat baking sheet, preferably black steel. Oil both the ring and the baking sheet. Transfer the dough to the ring and stretch it to evenly line the bottom. Cover the dough with the towel and let it rest for 30 minutes, or until it has risen by half.

5. While the dough is rising, arrange terra-cotta tiles or a pizza stone on the center shelf of the oven as directed on page 78. Preheat the oven to 425°F (215°C). Allow 30 minutes for the oven and the tiles to preheat.

6. When the dough is ready, use your fingertips or knuckles to make dimples, or deep impressions, all over the surface. Scatter the butter on top. Sprinkle with sugar and place the baking sheet directly on the hot tiles. Bake for 30 minutes, or until the *fügascia* is golden and the butter is bubbling.

7. Remove the fügascia from the oven and turn on the broiler. If you are using an electric oven, place a shelf as close to the broiler unit as possible. Place the fügascia directly under the broiler to melt and caramelize the sugar on top, 20 to 30 seconds. Watch carefully. Rotate the pan when necessary to caramelize the sugar evenly. When the sugar is completely caramelized, remove the pan from the broiler unit, lift off the ring, and slide the fügascia onto a cooling rack. Serve warm or at room temperature.

MAKES 6 TO 8 SERVINGS

The cypress-lined road that leads to La Suvera in the small peaceful village of Pievescola di Casole d'Elsa, ABOVE. *The Marchese and the Marchesa gaze from a window above the Ristorante Oliviera,* OPPOSITE. *The building, once the olive mill of the estate, now houses the restaurant, as well as several guest suites.*

Pievescola di Casole d'Elsa

LA SUVERA

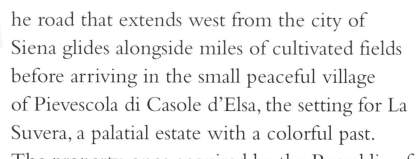

The road that extends west from the city of Siena glides alongside miles of cultivated fields before arriving in the small peaceful village of Pievescola di Casole d'Elsa, the setting for La Suvera, a palatial estate with a colorful past.

The property, once acquired by the Republic of Siena from the Chigi family, a prominent Sienese banking family, was bestowed upon Pope Julius II della Rovere in 1507 to consolidate the alliance between Siena and the papacy. In 1970 the estate became the country residence of the Marchese Ricci Paracciani Bergamini and his wife, the Marchesa Eleonora Maria, Principessa Massimo, who have unlocked the stately doors of La Suvera for all to enjoy.

The iron gates, crowned with the regal crest of La Suvera, open into the courtyard where the villa stands near a small church, a farmhouse, and the former stables. After painstaking restoration the estate has been rejuvenated to reflect the distinguished ancestry of the Ricci family and has attained the status of a five-star hotel. The buildings have been transformed into guest quarters and the estate now includes a formal Italian garden, an olive grove, and nearly twenty acres of vineyards that produce organic wines—Rango Rosso, an aged red typical of Tuscany; Vino Bianco La Suvera, a full-bodied white; and a crisp sparkling wine called Cuvée Italienne Brut.

Beyond the gates is the former *frantoio*, or olive mill. A restaurant, called Oliviera, now occupies the first floor of the structure and Gigliola Papa, a native of the village, is the restaurant's chef. The cuisine, which is pure Tuscan in flavor, has been reinterpreted in Gigliola's clever way. Having been raised on a farm, Gigliola's closeness to nature is reflected in her seasonal cooking. Just outside the kitchen door is a small garden where she finds most of the fresh herbs and many of the vegetables she uses, often filling in with wild herbs and field greens she brings from home. Olive oil is produced from the fruit of La Suvera's trees and all other ingredients are purchased from local suppliers.

Gigliola's menus, which change daily, underscore high-quality Tuscan products and reflect the fine taste of the Ricci family who dine at and visit La Suvera often.

Cooking at home *has been a lifelong practice for Gigliola. While she was working as an assistant at Oliviera her innate talent and flair, combined with enthusiasm and determination, were recognized by the Ricci family, and after a short stint at Le Cordon Bleu in Florence she was prepared to take charge of the restaurant kitchen. Working with five assistants of her own, Gigliola now prepares dinner for fifty guests each night.* RIGHT, *Gigliola uses a dumpling press to make* Ventagli, *fan-shaped ravioli. The* Ristorante Oliviera, TOP RIGHT, *occupies the old olive mill.* BELOW RIGHT, Canestrini, *potato baskets filled with porcini mushrooms.* BELOW, Minestra di Ceci, *a Tuscan chickpea soup with small squares of pasta.* OPPOSITE, *a meat stuffing redolent with the flavors of thyme, marjoram, rosemary, and sage fills the cavity of Gigliola's boneless roast chicken.*

Canestrini

Potato Baskets Filled with Porcini Mushrooms

Gigliola prepares this antipasto in the early part of winter when she can still find fresh porcini mushrooms.

1½ POUNDS (657 G) YUKON GOLD OR RUSSET POTATOES, PEELED
SEA SALT
1½ TABLESPOONS UNSALTED BUTTER, SOFTENED
4 LARGE EGG YOLKS
¼ TEASPOON FRESHLY GRATED NUTMEG
¼ CUP (1 OZ/30 G) UNBLEACHED ALL-PURPOSE FLOUR, FOR DREDGING

For the Mushroom Filling
6 OUNCES (180 G) FRESH PORCINI MUSHROOMS (SEE NOTE)
2 TABLESPOONS (1 FL OZ/30 ML) EXTRA VIRGIN OLIVE OIL
1 CLOVE OF GARLIC, CRUSHED
SEA SALT AND FRESHLY GROUND BLACK PEPPER

2 LARGE EGGS, LIGHTLY BEATEN
¾ CUP (2½ OZ/75 G) FINE DRY BREAD CRUMBS
SUNFLOWER OIL, FOR FRYING

1. Place the potatoes in a large pot and fill it with cold water to cover the potatoes by 2 inches (5 cm). Bring the water to a boil and add salt to taste. Boil the potatoes for 20 to 30 minutes, or until tender when tested with a small paring knife. Drain and purée the potatoes using a food mill fitted with the medium disk or a potato ricer.

2. Return the potatoes to the pot and stir them over medium heat to evaporate any moisture. The potatoes are dry when they begin to coat the bottom of the pot. Add the butter and stir until it is melted. Transfer the potatoes to a large bowl and let them cool.

3. When the potatoes are cool, stir in the egg yolks and the nutmeg. Divide the potatoes into 8 equal portions. Roll each portion into a ball. Dredge the balls in flour and shake off the excess. Gently press the bottom of a shot glass into the center of each potato ball, to flatten it and make a well in the center. Refrigerate the potato baskets until chilled and firm, at least 1 hour.

4. To prepare the mushroom filling, clean the mushrooms. Trim away the dried end of the stems and brush away any soil or grit. Wipe the mushrooms clean with a damp cloth and coarsely chop them. Heat the olive oil in a skillet over medium heat. Add the garlic and cook until it is golden brown. Stir in the mushrooms and sauté until

they are cooked through and any liquid in the pan has evaporated. Season to taste with salt and pepper and remove the clove of garlic.

5. When the potato baskets are firm, dip them, one at a time, into the lightly beaten eggs, then coat them with bread crumbs. Refrigerate until ready to fry.

6. Heat 1½ inches (3.8 cm) of sunflower oil in a large heavy skillet with high sides over medium heat. When the oil is hot, add half of the potato baskets, hollow side up. Fry, turning the baskets once, until they are golden brown. Using a slotted spoon or skimmer remove the baskets from the skillet and drain on paper towels. Fry the remaining potato baskets in the same way. While they are frying, reheat the mushroom filling. Sprinkle the potato baskets with salt and fill the hollows with equal portions of filling. Serve immediately.

MAKES 8 SERVINGS

Note: When fresh porcini mushrooms are not available the mushroom filling can be made with 5 ounces (150 g) of any fresh cultivated or wild mushrooms purchased in specialty markets (see page 19) and ½ ounce (15 g) of dried porcini mushrooms. Clean the fresh mushrooms as directed in Step 4 and coarsely chop them. Soak the dried porcini mushrooms in ⅓ cup (3 fl oz/80 ml) of warm water for 15 minutes. Lift them out of the soaking liquid, reserving the liquid. Scrape off any grit left on the porcini and coarsely chop them. Strain the liquid through a double layer of cheesecloth. Use the fresh cultivated or wild mushrooms for the fresh porcini mushrooms as directed. When the mushrooms have cooked through stir in the dried porcini and their liquid. Cook until the liquid has evaporated and continue as directed.

The path through the formal Italian gardens of La Suvera, BELOW, leads to an olive grove, and nearly twenty acres of vineyards that produce organic wines.

Ventagli di Ricotta e Spinaci
Fan-shaped Ravioli Filled with Ricotta and Spinach

Gigliola was delighted with the Asian dumpling press she received as a gift from a friend returning from a visit to the United States. Gigliola uses the press to create ravioli with a classic spinach filling. She calls them ventagli, *for their fan shape. You will probably recognize the shape as pot stickers.*

For the Ricotta and Spinach Filling

- 1 CUP (8 OZ/225 G) RICOTTA
- 2 POUNDS (900 G) SPINACH, STEMS REMOVED AND WELL WASHED (SEE PAGE 141)
- SEA SALT AND FRESHLY GROUND BLACK PEPPER
- ½ CUP (2 OZ/60 G) GRATED PARMIGIANO-REGGIANO
- ¼ TEASPOON FRESHLY GRATED NUTMEG
- 2 LARGE EGG YOLKS, LIGHTLY BEATEN

For the Pasta

- 5½ CUPS (24 OZ/660 G) UNBLEACHED ALL-PURPOSE FLOUR
- 4 LARGE EGGS
- 4 LARGE EGG YOLKS

- 8 TABLESPOONS (4 OZ/120 G) UNSALTED BUTTER
- 12 SMALL FRESH SAGE LEAVES
- 1 CUP (4 OZ/120 G) GRATED PARMIGIANO-REGGIANO

1. To make the filling, drain the ricotta if moist. Place it in a strainer resting over a bowl and refrigerate it for 2 to 3 hours or overnight.

2. Place the spinach, with only the water that clings to its leaves, in a large heavy pot. Sprinkle with ½ teaspoon salt, cover the pot, and cook over medium heat, stirring, until it is wilted, 8 to 10 minutes. Drain the spinach, refresh it under cold water, and drain again. Squeeze out all of the water. Pat the spinach dry with paper towels and finely chop it.

3. Transfer the chopped spinach to a large bowl and combine with the ricotta, Parmigiano, and nutmeg. Blend the mixture thoroughly, then season with salt and black pepper to taste. Stir in the egg yolks and refrigerate the filling while making the pasta.

4. To make the pasta dough for the *ventagli*, use the flour, eggs, and egg yolks as directed on page 188, the section entitled Making the Dough. The dough will be kneaded and stretched in a manual pasta machine. Line 2 trays or baking sheets with cotton kitchen towels and dust lightly with flour.

5. Divide the dough into 4 equal portions and knead as directed in the section entitled Kneading the Dough in a Pasta Machine.

6. Stretch the dough as directed in the section entitled Stretching the Dough in a Pasta Machine. Stretch the dough 1 piece at a time, as thin as possible, taking it to the last setting on the dial. The ventagli must be stuffed as soon as each piece of dough has been stretched. Using a fluted pastry wheel cut each sheet of dough into 5-inch-long (12-cm-long) pieces.

7. To make the ventagli, use an Asian dumpling press. Open the press and lightly dust it with flour. Place a piece of pasta over the press and spoon a rounded teaspoon of the filling into the center. Be careful not to overstuff the ventagli, or they will not seal properly. Dip a small brush into water and lightly moisten the dough around the filling. Close the press and squeeze firmly to seal the dough. Trim away the excess dough with a small paring knife, reserving the scraps to serve in broth. Open the press and transfer the ventagli to one of the towel-lined trays. Continue to make the ventagli using the remaining pasta dough. Cover the ventagli with towels until they are ready to be cooked.

8. To cook the ventagli, fill a very large pot (at least 8 quarts/ 8 liters) with water and bring it to a rapid boil. Add salt to taste. Stir in the ventagli and cover the pot, just until the water returns to a boil. Uncover and boil, stirring occasionally, for 4 to 5 minutes, or until tender.

9. Meanwhile, melt the butter with the sage leaves in a large sauté pan or Dutch oven large enough to hold the ventagli. Do not allow the butter to brown. When the ventagli are ready, remove them from the pot with a large skimmer or strainer. Being sure to drain them well. Add the ventagli to the sauté pan. Sprinkle with Parmigiano and carefully toss over low heat until the ventagli are evenly coated with butter and the cheese has melted. Transfer the ventagli to a large serving platter and serve immediately.

MAKES 6 SERVINGS

Variation: Gigliola also serves the ventagli with a sauce she makes from nettles, a wild herb she finds in her garden in early spring. Nettles become available after the last winter frost. Always wear gloves when handling raw nettles to avoid being stung by their prickly needles, which are destroyed when cooked. Cook 10 ounces of well-washed nettle leaves in a large pot of salted boiling water until tender, about 10 minutes. Drain and purée through a food mill fitted with the medium disk or in a food processor until coarsely puréed. Melt 4 tablespoons unsalted butter in a medium saucepan over low heat. Add 1 clove of chopped garlic and cook until golden. Stir in the purée and ⅔ cup (5½ fl oz/185 ml) heavy cream. Season with salt to taste and simmer gently for 5 minutes. Pour the nettle sauce over the cooked ventagli and serve immediately.

Minestra di Ceci
Chickpea Soup with Handmade Pasta Squares

Gigliola's Tuscan chickpea soup is ideal to serve during cold-weather months. She adds tiny quadretti, *handmade pasta squares, which cook in the soup and thicken the broth. You can substitute any tiny tubular dry pasta for the* quadretti. *Always buy chickpeas from a source that can assure you they were harvested within one year (see Mail Order Sources page 189).*

For the Chickpea Soup

2¼ CUPS (18 FL OZ/550 ML) COOKED CHICKPEAS (FOR HOMEMADE, SEE PAGE 187), DRAINED AND LIQUID RESERVED

3 TABLESPOONS (1½ FL OZ/45 ML) EXTRA VIRGIN OLIVE OIL PLUS ADDITIONAL FOR DRIZZLING

3 MEDIUM CLOVES OF GARLIC, CRUSHED

1 LARGE SPRIG OF ROSEMARY

⅓ CUP (3 FL OZ/80 ML) TOMATO PURÉE

6 TO 7 CUPS (48 TO 56 FL OZ/1500 TO 1725 ML) VEGETABLE OR MEAT BROTH (FOR HOMEMADE, SEE PAGE 187), PLUS ADDITIONAL IF NEEDED

SEA SALT AND FRESHLY GROUND BLACK PEPPER

For the Pasta Squares

¾ CUP (3 OZ/90 G) UNBLEACHED ALL-PURPOSE FLOUR

1 LARGE EGG

¾ TEASPOON EXTRA VIRGIN OLIVE OIL

PINCH OF SEA SALT

1. To make the soup, coarsely purée half of the chickpeas in a blender or food processor. Add a little of the chickpea liquid to the purée and process again until it is thick and smooth.

2. Heat 3 tablespoons (1½ fl oz/45 ml) olive oil over medium heat in a large heavy flameproof casserole or Dutch oven. Add the crushed garlic and the rosemary and cook until the garlic is golden. Add the tomato purée and cook the mixture for 2 to 3 minutes. Stir in 6 cups (48 fl oz/1500 ml) of the broth, the whole chickpeas, and the chickpea purée. Season with salt and black pepper to taste. Simmer the soup, uncovered, for 1 hour. If the soup becomes too thick, add more broth.

3. To make the pasta dough for the quadretti, use the flour, egg, olive oil, and salt as directed on page 188, the section entitled Making the Dough. The dough will be kneaded and stretched in a manual pasta machine. Line a tray or baking sheet with a cotton kitchen towel and dust lightly with flour.

4. Knead the whole piece of dough in the pasta machine as directed in the section entitled Kneading the Dough in a Pasta Machine.

5. Stretch the dough as directed in the section entitled Stretching the Dough in a Pasta Machine. Stretch the dough as thin as possible, taking it to the last setting on the dial. Using a fluted pastry wheel, cut the sheet of dough into 6-inch (15-cm) lengths and arrange them side by side, on the towel-lined tray. Dry the pasta slightly, turning the sheets occasionally to dry them evenly. The surface should be dry to the touch but the pasta should remain flexible.

6. When the pasta has dried sufficiently, attach the cutting blades to the pasta machine. Pass each sheet of dough through the wide cutting blade used for tagliatelle or fettuccine. After each piece has been cut, line up the long strands, side by side, on a cutting board. Using a large chef's knife, cut the strands crosswise into small squares. Transfer the pasta squares to the towel-lined tray, dust with flour, and toss.

7. When ready to serve the soup, remove the garlic cloves and the sprig of rosemary and bring the soup to a boil. Add the pasta squares, reduce the heat and simmer, stirring often, until the squares are tender, 15 to 20 seconds, and the soup has thickened. Ladle the soup into shallow bowls and let it rest for 2 minutes. Drizzle about 2 teaspoons of olive oil into each bowl or pass a cruet of olive oil at the table.

MAKES 4 SERVINGS

Pollo Ripieno alla Suvera
Boneless Roast Chicken with Savory Meat Stuffing

Begin this dish by marinating the boneless chicken, which is turned inside out, with salt and fresh lemon juice the night before. The marinade tenderizes and adds flavor to the flesh. The chicken is stuffed the following day with a meat stuffing seasoned with a blend of aromatic fresh herbs. It is sewn, tied, and roasted until crisp and walnut brown in color.

For the Marinade

1 FREE-RANGE CHICKEN (2½ TO 3 POUNDS/1.2 TO 1.4 K), BONED WITH DRUMSTICKS AND WINGS LEFT INTACT (SEE NOTE)

SEA SALT

JUICE OF 3 LEMONS

For the Stuffing

    2   SLIGHTLY DRY SLICES FIRM-TEXTURED COUNTRY-STYLE
        BREAD (FOR PANE TOSCANO SEE PAGE 78) SLICED ½ INCH
        (1.25 CM) THICK
    1   CUP (8 FL OZ/250 ML) WHOLE MILK
    1   SHALLOT, COARSELY CHOPPED
    1   MEDIUM CLOVE OF GARLIC, COARSELY CHOPPED
    1   LARGE SPRIG OF THYME, LEAVES ONLY
    1   SPRIG OF MARJORAM, LEAVES ONLY
    1   SPRIG OF ROSEMARY, LEAVES ONLY
    1   SPRIG OF SAGE, LEAVES ONLY
    1   POUND (450 G) LEAN GROUND BEEF
    ¾   POUND (350 G) PORK LOIN, FAT TRIMMED AND CUT INTO
        ⅜-INCH (1-CM) DICE
    ¾   CUP (3 OZ/90 G) GRATED PARMIGIANO-REGGIANO
        SEA SALT AND FRESHLY GROUND BLACK PEPPER
    ¼   CUP (1½ OZ/45 G) BLACK OLIVES IN BRINE, PITTED AND SLICED

    2   SPRIGS OF ROSEMARY
    2   SPRIGS OF SAGE
    3   TABLESPOONS (1½ FL OZ/45 ML) EXTRA VIRGIN OLIVE OIL
    ½   CUP (4 FL OZ/125 ML) DRY WHITE WINE

1. Marinate the chicken the day before cooking. Turn the chicken inside out and place it in a glass or crockery bowl. Sprinkle the flesh with salt and pour the lemon juice over it. Toss the chicken several times in the lemon juice, cover the bowl, and refrigerate overnight. Turn the chicken at least once while it marinates.

2. The next day, preheat the oven to 475°F (245°C).

3. To prepare the stuffing, tear the bread into small pieces and soak them in the milk until softened. Drain the milk and squeeze the bread dry. Combine the shallot and garlic with the thyme, marjoram, rosemary, and sage leaves on a cutting board and chop them together until very fine. Place the ground beef and diced pork in a large bowl. Add the bread, chopped herb mixture, and the Parmigiano. Season with salt and pepper and blend the ingredients thoroughly. Add the olives and toss.

4. Remove the chicken from the marinade and dry it with paper towels. Turn the chicken so that the skin is once again on the outside. Dry the skin with paper towels. Fill the cavity with the stuffing mixture. Sew both the cavity opening and the neck opening with a needle and strong button thread. Using butcher's twine, tie the chicken, like a roast, every 1½ inches (3.8 cm). Tuck the sprigs of rosemary and sage under the twine.

5. Place the chicken, breast side up, in an oiled roasting pan.

Drizzle the olive oil over the chicken and roast it for 30 minutes. Turn the chicken over so it is breast side down and baste it with the pan juices. Return the chicken to the oven for 15 minutes. Remove the chicken from the oven and turn it so it is breast side up. Degrease the juices at the bottom of the pan with a large spoon or turkey baster. Pour the white wine over the chicken and return it to the oven for 15 minutes more. Lower the oven temperature to 425°F (215°C). Baste the chicken and roast it for 10 minutes more, or until a meat thermometer inserted into the center reads 160°F (71°C).

6. Transfer the chicken to a serving platter and remove the twine. Strain and degrease the pan juices and season with salt and pepper to taste. Slice and serve the chicken moistened with the pan juices.

MAKES 6 SERVINGS

Note: Boning a chicken takes skill and practice. Most butchers can handle the task. Make the request a few days ahead.

Radicchi Grigliati

Grilled Radicchio

Radicchio, a vegetable that is plentiful in winter, can be grilled and served alongside roasted meat or poultry as Gigliola often does.

    3   MEDIUM (1 POUND/450 G) RADICCHIO DI TREVISO OR
        DI VERONA, WELL WASHED, DRIED, AND HALVED LENGTHWISE
        EXTRA VIRGIN OLIVE OIL, FOR DRIZZLING
        SEA SALT

1. Preheat the broiler or barbecue grill 15 minutes ahead.

2. If broiling, place the radicchio, cut side down, on a broiler pan or wire rack resting over a shallow baking pan. Drizzle lightly with olive oil. Broil the radicchio 4 to 5 inches (10 to 13 cm) from the heat source until lightly browned, about 5 minutes. Turn, drizzle with additional oil, and broil, cut side up, until lightly browned, 5 minutes more. If grilling, lightly drizzle olive oil over the cut side of the radicchio, then grill oiled side down on the grill rack 4 to 5 inches (10 to 13 cm) from the heat source. Drizzle the top side of the radicchio lightly with oil, then turn and grill until lightly browned, 5 minutes more.

3. Transfer the radicchio to a large platter, sprinkle with salt, and serve immediately.

MAKES 6 SERVINGS

Torta di Cioccolata con la Spuma d'Arancia

Flourless Chocolate Cake with Orange Sauce

Gigliola smiles proudly as she confesses her Torta di Cioccolata, a flourless chocolate cake made with ground almonds and flavored with orange zest, is the favorite dessert of the Marchese.

For the Chocolate Cake

2½ CUPS (10 OZ/300 G) SLIVERED ALMONDS

12 OUNCES (360 G) SEMISWEET CHOCOLATE, CHOPPED

10 OUNCES (300 G) UNSALTED BUTTER

8 LARGE EGGS, SEPARATED

2⅓ CUPS (8½ OZ/250 G) CONFECTIONERS' SUGAR

GRATED ZEST OF 2 ORANGES

PINCH OF SEA SALT

For the Orange Sauce

1¼ CUPS (10 FL OZ/300 ML) WHOLE MILK

1 STRIP LEMON ZEST

1 STRIP ORANGE ZEST, PLUS THE GRATED ZEST OF 1 ORANGE

4 LARGE EGG YOLKS

¼ CUP (1¾ OZ/50 G) SUGAR

3 TABLESPOONS UNBLEACHED ALL-PURPOSE FLOUR

2 TABLESPOONS (1 FL OZ/30 ML) GRAND MARNIER

1 CUP (8 FL OZ/250 ML) HEAVY CREAM

For the Orange Syrup

¼ CUP (1¾ OZ/50 G) SUGAR

ZEST OF ½ ORANGE, CUT INTO JULIENNE STRIPS

1. To prepare the cake, preheat the oven to 400°F (200°C). Line a 10-inch (2.5-cm) cake pan with heavy-duty aluminum foil. Fold the excess foil over the sides of the pan and butter the foil.

2. Grind the almonds in a food processor. Combine the chocolate and butter in the top of a double boiler over simmering water; stir until melted. Cool the mixture to room temperature.

3. Transfer the chocolate mixture to a large bowl. Blend in the egg yolks, one at a time, with an electric mixer on low speed. Sift the confectioners' sugar into the bowl and blend. Blend in the ground almonds and orange zest. The mixture will become very stiff. Rinse off the beaters and dry them thoroughly.

4. In a separate bowl, beat the egg whites and salt until stiff peaks form. Stir one quarter of the beaten whites into the chocolate mixture to lighten it, then fold in the rest. Pour the mixture into the cake pan and bake for 40 minutes. Cool on a cooling rack, then refrigerate.

5. To prepare the orange sauce, heat the milk with the strips of lemon and orange zest in a small heavy saucepan over medium-low heat until scalded. Meanwhile, blend the egg yolks and the sugar in a large bowl with a wire whisk. Add the flour and stir until it is completely dissolved. Slowly whisk one third of the scalded milk into the egg yolk mixture. Add the remaining milk all at once and blend thoroughly. Pour the mixture back into the saucepan and return it to the heat. Stir constantly until the mixture has thickened, about 5 minutes. Turn off the heat, remove and discard the lemon and orange zest strips, and stir in the Grand Marnier and the grated orange zest. Pour the mixture into a bowl and smooth the top with a rubber spatula. Place a buttered round of wax paper on the surface. When cool, cover and chill the mixture in the refrigerator.

6. To prepare the orange syrup, melt the sugar in a small heavy saucepan over medium heat. Do not stir until the sugar is almost melted, then stir until the syrup is smooth and walnut brown in color. Remove the pan from the heat and pour in 2½ tablespoons water. The syrup will sputter rapidly when the water is added. Be sure to wear oven mitts, to prevent burns. Stir rapidly to dissolve the syrup. Add the julienned orange peel and return the pan to the heat. Simmer for 1 minute, or until the syrup has thickened slightly. Remove from the heat and cool completely. The syrup should remain pourable; if it becomes too thick when cool, thin it with a few drops of water.

7. Remove the chilled cake from the refrigerator. Grasp the foil overhang and carefully lift the cake out of the pan. Fold back the foil and use a large cake spatula to transfer it to a cake plate. Let the *torta* come to room temperature before serving.

8. Meanwhile, beat the heavy cream until stiff and fold it into the chilled sauce. Serve each slice of *torta* with a spoonful of the sauce and a drizzle of orange syrup with strips of zest alongside.

MAKES 12 SERVINGS

Within the courtyard of the estate, LEFT, stands the old church, the farmhouse, and an iron aviary.

Insalata di Gallina

Chicken Salad

Thin strips of celery root add a surprise element to this Piedmontese chicken salad with ground walnuts. If celery root is not available use julienned strips of celery.

1   LARGE WHOLE CHICKEN BREAST
     (1½ POUNDS/675 G)

SEA SALT

1   SMALL CELERY ROOT, PEELED
     AND CUT INTO ¼-INCH
     (0.6-CM) JULIENNE STRIPS

4   TEASPOONS FRESH LEMON
     JUICE

½   CUP (3 OZ/90 G) GROUND
     WALNUTS

6   TABLESPOONS (3 FL OZ/90 ML)
     EXTRA VIRGIN OLIVE OIL

12   OUNCES (350 G) ARUGULA,
     TRIMMED, WELL WASHED,
     DRIED, AND SHREDDED

1. Place the chicken breast in a large saucepan. Fill the pan with cold water to cover the chicken by 1 inch (2.5 cm). Add salt to taste. Bring the water to a boil, then simmer until the chicken is cooked through, 15 to 20 minutes. Transfer to a plate to cool.

2. Toss the julienned celery root in a large bowl with 2 teaspoons of the lemon juice.

3. Skin and debone the chicken. Cut it into ¼-inch (0.6-cm) julienne strips and add them to the bowl with the celery root. Add the ground walnuts and 3 tablespoons (1½ fl oz/45 ml) of the olive oil. Season with salt to taste and toss.

4. Place the arugula in a large bowl. Pour the remaining 3 tablespoons (1½ fl oz/45 ml) of olive oil and the remaining 2 teaspoons of the lemon juice over the arugula. Season with salt to taste and toss. Arrange the arugula salad on 6 individual salad plates. Top it with the chicken salad and serve.

MAKES 6 SERVINGS

Risotto alla Contadina

Veal and Vegetable Risotto

This substantial Tuscan risotto can be served as a one-dish meal.

1   MEDIUM ONION, CHOPPED

1   MEDIUM CARROT, CHOPPED

1   CELERY STALK, CHOPPED

1   MEDIUM LEEK, TRIMMED,
     WASHED, AND CHOPPED

8   CUPS (2 QUARTS/2 LITERS)
     CHICKEN OR MEAT BROTH (FOR
     HOMEMADE, SEE PAGE 187)

¼   CUP (2 FL OZ/60 ML) EXTRA
     VIRGIN OLIVE OIL

½   POUND (250 G) GROUND VEAL

1½   CUPS (7½ OZ/225 G) ITALIAN
     CARNAROLI OR ARBORIO RICE

SEA SALT

⅔   CUP (2½ OZ/80 G) GRATED
     PARMIGIANO-REGGIANO, PLUS
     ADDITIONAL FOR SERVING

1. Combine the onion, carrot, celery, and leek on a cutting board. Chop them together very fine. Heat the broth in a large saucepan and simmer gently.

2. Heat the olive oil in a medium-size flameproof casserole over medium-low heat. Add the vegetables and cook until they are tender, about 15 minutes. Add the ground veal and increase the heat to medium. Crumble and stir the veal with a fork as it cooks. When the veal has lost its raw color, add the rice. Stir constantly until the rice becomes translucent. Add a ladleful of the broth and stir until it is completely absorbed by the rice. Continue adding the broth, a ladleful at a time, until the rice is almost tender, about 25 to 30 minutes. Season with salt to taste. Turn off the heat and stir in the Parmigiano. Serve immediately, passing a small bowl of Parmigiano at the table.

MAKES 4 SERVINGS

Zuppa di Zucca

Winter Squash Soup

One type of *zucca*, or winter squash, used by Ester Carnero at La Luna e i Falò in the Piedmontese village of Canelli (see page 37), is similar in taste and texture to butternut or buttercup squash. Ester uses the zucca for this chunky soup based on an old Piedmontese recipe.

6   TABLESPOONS (3 OZ/90 G)
     UNSALTED BUTTER

4   CUPS (24 OZ/650 G)
     BUTTERNUT OR BUTTERCUP
     SQUASH, CUT INTO ½-INCH
     (1.25-CM) DICE

2   MEDIUM CARROTS, PEELED AND
     CUT INTO ½-INCH (1.25-CM)
     DICE

1   MEDIUM ONION, CUT INTO
     ½-INCH (1.25-CM) DICE

1   LARGE CELERY STALK, CUT
     INTO ½-INCH (1.25-CM) DICE

4   CUPS (1 QUART/1 LITER)
     CHICKEN BROTH (FOR
     HOMEMADE, SEE PAGE 187)

SEA SALT

½   CUP SWISS EMMENTAL CHEESE,
     CUT INTO ⅜-INCH (1-CM) DICE

4   TEASPOONS GRATED
     PARMIGIANO-REGGIANO

1. Melt the butter in a small pot. Add the squash, carrots, onion, and celery and cook over medium-high heat, stirring often, until the onions are lightly golden, about 7 to 8 minutes. Add the broth and season with salt to taste. Bring the mixture to a boil, reduce the heat, and simmer, uncovered, for 1 hour.

2. Ladle the hot soup into 4 individual soup bowls. Sprinkle each with 2 tablespoons of the Swiss cheese and 1 teaspoon of Parmigiano. Let the soup rest 5 minutes before serving.

MAKES 4 SERVINGS

VARIATION: Ester sometimes serves the *zuppa* with homemade croutons. To make croutons, cut a slightly dry firm-textured country-style bread into cubes and fry them in sunflower oil until golden brown. Drain on paper towels.

Spring market days are filled with the anticipation of asparagus tied up in bundles, spring onions fresh from the garden, and long-stemmed artichokes piled high in wooden crates.

Vegetables
verdure

Artichokes, *carciofi,* are the edible buds of a garden thistle. The fleshy base of the bud, called the heart or bottom, is surrounded by tough petal-shaped leaves that are edible only at their base. Within the bud are an inedible fuzzy choke, which must be discarded, and tender pale yellow leaves. The large round globe artichoke, most commonly available in the United States, is only one of nearly fifty varieties grown around the world. Artichokes should be deeply colored, firm, and heavy for their size and have stiff, tightly closed leaves with no brown discoloration. During the secondary season in fall, freezing temperatures can cause blistering and a darkening or bronzing of the leaves, as well as a deepening of the flavor. Artichokes should be covered and stored unwashed in the refrigerator for no longer than 2 days. Artichokes are widely available in spring and again in early fall.

Arugula, *rucola,* is a member of the cabbage family, related to watercress and radishes. It has dark green leaves with deeply notched edges and firm stems. When arugula is young and tender it has an aromatic nutty flavor, while older, larger arugula is more assertive and peppery. Arugula should be firm and fresh-looking, never wilted or yellowing. To store arugula trim the stems of their roots and place the unwashed bunch upright in a glass of water like a bouquet of flowers, cover tightly with a plastic bag and refrigerate up to 2 days. Arugula has a tendency to be sandy. Wash it well just before using. Arugula has a long growing season that spans from early spring to early winter. The freshest and best quality arugula is that which is locally grown as it does not travel well. Look for it at farmers' markets and farm stands.

Asparagus, *asparagi,* are edible shoots commonly called spears. They can be slender as a pencil or as thick as a thumb. Size is not a sign of age or quality but rather an indication of the age of the asparagus beds. Though asparagus are available in green, white, and purple, the most common ones in the United States are green. Asparagus spears should be firm and crisp with a smooth skin and tightly closed tips. Avoid spears with tips that have started to elongate. Selecting asparagus that are similar in size will ensure even cooking. To store asparagus, stand the stalks upright in 1 inch of water. Cover and refrigerate for up to 2 days. Most asparagus are harvested from April to late June. Look for local asparagus at farmers' markets and farm stands.

Fava beans, *fave,* also called broad beans, grow in long green pods and are similar in size and shape to fresh lima beans. After shelling, the beans—except for very young ones—must be peeled to remove the thick skin (called the pericarp), which develops undesirable bitter tannins. When selecting fava beans, choose medium-size pods; they contain smaller, more delicately flavored beans than large pods. The pods should be bright green, thick and firm, and slightly shiny. Avoid pods that are dull, shriveled, or blackened at the ends. Cover and refrigerate fava beans in their pods for up to 2 days. Fresh fava beans are available from late spring through early summer and can be found at Italian or Middle Eastern markets, specialty markets, and farmers' markets.

Peas, *piselli,* also known as English peas or garden peas, are a herald of spring. Look for firm medium-size pods that are vibrant green, risp, and shiny with the shape of the peas visible through the pods. Avoid bulging pods with very large peas. Pods should never be shriveled, pale, or show signs of yellowing. Peas should be eaten as soon after they have been picked as is possible because the natural sugars convert into starch quickly, a process retarded by chilling. If you must, cover and store unshelled peas in the refrigerator for 1 day. Fresh sweet peas are available from spring to early summer and the best are found at farmers' markets and farm stands.

Spring onions, *cipollotti,* are small, immature onion bulbs with long green tops. These pleasantly sweet onions have a moist, thin skin and a soft, juicy flesh, which is considerably milder in flavor than mature onions. The bulbs are either round or elongated in shape and either white or pink in color. Spring onions may be served raw, lightly grilled, or used in place of mature onions when a more delicate flavor is desired. The bulbs should be firm with green, crisp tops. Loosely cover spring onions and store in the refrigerator for up to 2 weeks. They are available only from mid-spring through early summer.

Fruit
frutta

Strawberries, *fragole,* have a sweet, intense flavor and aroma. Small local strawberries, generally sold when fully ripe, are of a higher eating quality than large cottony berries produced for shipping and storing. Select strawberries that are uniformly red with fresh green leafy tops. Berries should be firm, shiny, and fragrant. Reject strawberries with green tips or those that are partially white, indications of underripeness. Strawberries are fragile, and they should be eaten the day of purchase, but can be refrigerated for 1 day unwashed, loosely covered, and arranged in a single layer. The best are found at farmers' markets and farm stands from late spring to late summer.

PECORINO TOSCANO

Pecorino Toscano e Miele al Forno

Roasted Tuscan Pecorino with Honey

Select a pecorino toscano that is young and creamy with a rich full flavor. Choose a honey that is delicate yet fragrant.

Slice the pecorino ⅜ inch (1 cm) thick and arrange a single layer of slices, slightly overlapping, in a gratin pan. Drizzle with the honey and bake the cheese in a preheated 450°F(230°C) oven for 6 to 7 minutes or until the cheese is soft and bubbly but not browned. Serve immediately as a cheese course at the end of the meal with a crusty firm-textured, country style bread, such as Tuscan Bread (page 78), and a glass of Chianti Classico.

When Till Gelpke was six years of age a Sardinian shepherd brought a small flock of sheep to graze on the fields of the farming complex where the boy lived. His father had purchased two neighboring farms in San Casciano in Val di Pesa in the Chianti zone, not far from Florence. He had moved the family from their native Switzerland after falling in love with the beauty and rich culture of Chianti. Till enjoyed working with the *contadini*, or farmworkers, in the fields; he pruned olive trees, helped in the vineyards, and developed a particular kinship with the shepherd, learning to milk the sheep by the age of eight. Till was hardly more than twelve when the shepherd departed, leaving him a gift of several sheep, which he continued to care for. At sixteen, certain of his destiny, he traveled to Sardinia and returned home with one hundred and fifty pedigreed sheep.

Till now maintains a flock that numbers five hundred. They are bred and raised for the milk he uses in his small but exclusive production of *pecorino toscano*. Until recently he sold the sheep's milk to cheese makers in nearby villages. One cheese maker in particular, a master of his craft, willingly shared his expertise and techniques. Till began by producing the classic *pecorino fresco* (fresh cheese), and *stagionato* (aged cheese) and a *ricotta di pecora* (sheep's milk ricotta). He increasingly perfected his skills and expanded his line. He created less traditional cheeses made with rosemary and garlic and two spicy versions—one with chili pepper and another with chili pepper, parsley, and garlic. One of Till's most popular cheeses, called *buccia di rospo*, literally toad skin, is appropriately named for its craggy texture. This pecorino was the result of an error during production. In order to dispose of these curious cheeses he offered them at a discounted price. After they were sold, numerous requests obliged him to add the new cheese to his line. Till supplies several fine restaurants and *enoteche*, or wine bars, in Florence. He has also become a consultant to chefs and restaurateurs on the attributes of pecorino toscano and its outstanding by-product, ricotta di pecora.

Pecorino toscano
is a cheese of rare quality made throughout Tuscany and becoming more widely available in the United States. It is made from sheep's milk and takes its name from the Italian word for sheep, pecora. Sheep's milk, which is high in butterfat, produces a cheese that is rich and nutty in flavor. Young pecorino has a medium-soft texture with a flavor reminiscent of fresh cream. Slightly older cheeses are more firm-textured with fuller, nuttier flavors. Many Italian specialty markets and cheese shops carry several types and ages of pecorino toscano. Request a taste before selecting. Pecorino toscano should not be confused with pecorino romano, an aged pecorino, slightly salty and most often used as a grating cheese. Always serve pecorino toscano, as you would all cheeses, at room temperature.

LA CASCINA POMERA

Gabriella and Eugenio,
ABOVE, *who run their*
agriturismo *in the small*
village of Vignale Monferrato,
both come from families
of farmers. Guests can watch
Gabriella working,
OPPOSITE, *from an open*
window in the dining room.

Though Gabriella Trisoglio might be expecting fifty for dinner in two hours in her contemporary farmhouse restaurant, she is more likely to be in the fields behind the house operating a back hoe or chopping firewood than in her kitchen. This present day-renaissance woman is capable of juggling several arduous tasks simultaneously and performing each with remarkable skill and confidence. Her reputation as a fine cook led her to expand her restaurant from a single table for twelve to seating for more than sixty in two large dining rooms.

Gabriella and her husband, Eugenio Baiano, built their farmhouse in Vignale Monferrato, the small village where they met and spent most of their lives. The village is in a wine-growing zone of Piedmont known as Basso Monferrato, just northeast of Asti. They transformed their home into an *agriturismo*, an Italian-style farmhouse bed and breakfast, which they call La Cascina Pomera. An agriturismo provides comfortable lodging in a rural agricultural setting—a more casual and cordial setting than an urban hotel. It offers insight into the culture and the day-to-day life of those who work and live on farms and vineyards throughout Italy. Guests can sometimes participate in farm or kitchen chores, such as harvesting olives or grapes, jarring homemade preserves, or caring for barnyard animals. Most *agriturismi* offer a simple Italian-style breakfast; others also provide casual home-cooked meals served family style, seated around a large table with the hosting family and other guests. Some offer meals served in the style of a small country restaurant.

Vignale
Monferrato

La Cascina Pomera has afforded Gabriella the opportunity to unleash her culinary prowess. Like most Italian women, Gabriella's cooking skills developed at home guided by her mother. The food was purely regional in flavor, the traditional home-cooking of the Monferrato. Though her experience was limited to serving just her large family and friends, the notion of preparing meals for others appealed to Gabriella.

There are no menus at La Cascina Pomera. Meals begin at a leisurely pace with antipasti and a carafe of local Barbera. Spring offerings might include a small ramekin

A cherry tree in Monferrato,
TOP. Torta di Asparagi,
ABOVE. OPPOSITE
CLOCKWISE FROM TOP,
Gabriella's collection of
crockery. Gabriella snips fresh
chives for her Polenta con
Formaggio alla Cipollina.
Marriages, births, and deaths in
the family are recorded on a
door of the old dish cupboard.
Upon a guest's request,
Gabriella will pack a picnic
lunch complete with a bottle
of local wine and a large
woolly blanket.

of anchovy butter served with thin toasted rounds of bread or sliced *fior di latte*, cow's milk mozzarella, topped with a verdant purée made from lettuce just pulled from the *orto*, the vegetable garden behind the house. The pace then quickens as several more plates arrive—Gabriella occasionally turns out as many as ten antipasti. She often includes a seasonal vegetable tart with a crisp buttery crust featuring asparagus, spinach, or sweet garden peas; a light and airy cheese mousse mounded alongside wedges of polenta fried until golden and crispy; or tender Swiss chard croquettes that she calls *fricciolini*. She may also include one or two cold salads and a wedge of her *torta*, a tall stack of crepes layered with béchamel sauce, melted cheese, and small bits of cooked ham.

Guests can observe Gabriella at work in the kitchen through a large open window. It gives her a bird's-eye view of most tables and enables her to time the meal accordingly. She relishes her center-stage position and enjoys performing her culinary maneuvers for an attentive audience—rolling out long sheets of pasta, filling ravioli, or assembling a tart on the spot. Gabriella glides through the kitchen with all the grace and confidence of a high-wire performer as plate after tempting plate spills into the dining room.

There is always handmade pasta and Gabriella's choice for the day reflects the best of the season. Fresh asparagus are a spring favorite whether sliced in a sauce or blended in a stuffing for ravioli. Braised meat usually follows as a traditional *secondo piatto*, or meat course, served with a refreshing garden salad tossed with the standard Italian dressing. The greens are impeccably fresh and ingredients for the dressing are applied and tossed just before serving—a drizzle of extra virgin olive oil; a splash of wine vinegar, white or red; and a sprinkle of natural sea salt.

Gabriella's teenage son, Lorenzo, who has developed first-rate baking skills, prepares many of the desserts for his mother, consulting a personal notebook of recorded recipes. A particular favorite of guests is a golden cornmeal cake, *Torta di Mais*, that can be served alongside a pile of fresh strawberries in spring or a warm apple compote in fall.

Between kitchen preparations Gabriella, who has been operating heavy farm equipment since she was a child, assists Eugenio with the chores on their sixty-acre farm. They now rent several rooms and small apartments in a newly renovated farmhouse next to a barn that Gabriella has filled with vintage objects once used on local farms. She intends to establish a museum and has amassed a collection of equipment, tools, furniture, kitchen implements, and clothing.

With an eye on the future, Gabriella recently established an apple orchard. She has planted more than three hundred trees comprised of forty-nine heirloom varieties that once grew in the Monferrato district, most befitting for La Cascina Pomera, which means the apple farm in the Monferrato dialect. Each tree bears the name of a contributing friend, family, or guest, invited back to reap the fruits of the harvest. The trees will be ready for picking in 1999 and Gabriella aptly refers to them as "apples of the millennium." In anticipation she has already begun a collection of apple recipes. It would be safe to predict that Gabriella will be welcoming the year 2000 at La Cascina Pomera with a fully stocked pantry of apple preserves.

The Monday following Easter, called *Pasquetta*, or Little Easter, is a traditional day for picnics in Italy.

Pane di Rosmarino
Braided Rosemary Bread

Gabriella mixes up large batches of bread dough several times a week. She uses it to make a cheese-topped focaccia and a long braided bread scented with fresh rosemary. This is a sturdy dough that requires long, slow risings.

- 1½ TEASPOONS ACTIVE DRY YEAST
- 1 CUP (8 FL OZ/250 ML) WARM WATER (105 TO 115°F/40 TO 46°C)
- 4 CUPS (17 OZ/480 G) UNBLEACHED ALL-PURPOSE FLOUR
- 1½ TEASPOONS SEA SALT
- ¼ CUP (2 FL OZ/60 ML) EXTRA VIRGIN OLIVE OIL
- 1 TABLESPOON COARSELY CHOPPED FRESH ROSEMARY LEAVES

1. Sprinkle the yeast over ¼ cup (2 fl oz/60 ml) of the warm water in a small bowl. Stir until the yeast is dissolved.

2. To make the dough by hand, place 2 cups (8 oz/240 g) of the flour in a large mixing bowl. Make a well in the center and add the remaining ¾ cup (6 fl oz/185 ml) water, the salt, olive oil, and dissolved yeast. Blend the ingredients in the well with a wooden spoon. Incorporate the flour gradually, until the mixture becomes very thick. Turn the dough out onto a pastry board or work surface and knead for 10 minutes incorporating additional flour until the dough is smooth and tender and no longer sticky.

To make the dough in a heavy-duty mixer, place 3 cups (12 oz/ 360 g) of the flour in the mixer bowl. Add the remaining ¾ cup (6 oz/185 ml) warm water, the salt, olive oil, and dissolved yeast. Blend the ingredients with the paddle attachment on low speed. Replace the paddle with the dough hook. Knead the dough on low speed, while gradually adding flour until it is no longer sticky. Continue to knead for 8 minutes more, or until the dough is very smooth.

3. Transfer the dough to a large well-oiled bowl. Rub the dough against the bowl to coat it with oil. Cover the bowl with a cotton kitchen towel and let it rest in a warm draftfree place for 2 hours, or until doubled in size.

4. When the dough is ready, turn it out onto the lightly floured pastry board. Flatten it slightly and sprinkle the surface with half of the rosemary. Press the rosemary into the dough, then fold it into thirds, like a business letter. Repeat the procedure using the remaining rosemary. Gently knead the dough until the rosemary is evenly distributed. Flour the dough lightly, wrap it in the towel, and let it rest for 10 minutes.

5. Oil a large baking sheet. Divide the dough into 3 equal pieces. Roll each piece into a 22-inch-long (55-cm-long) rope. Arrange the ropes, side by side, on the pastry board. Starting from the center, braid the ropes together, working in one direction, then the other. Press the ends together. Transfer the braid to the baking sheet and tuck the ends under. Cover the braid with the towel and let it rest for 1 to 1½ hours, or until doubled in size.

6. Thirty minutes before baking, preheat the oven to 375°F (190°C).

7. Bake the braid on the center shelf of the oven for 25 to 30 minutes, or until lightly golden. Turn the bread on its side and knock on its bottom. If done, it will make a hollow sound. Cool the bread on a cooling rack.

MAKES 1 LOAF

Variation: To make *Panini di Rosmarino*, or individual rosemary twists, follow the recipe for the bread through Steps 4. Divide the dough into 8 equal pieces. Roll each piece into a 16-inch-long (40-cm-long) rope. Fold each rope in half and give it 2 twists. Arrange the twists on a large oiled baking sheet, allowing 2 inches (5 cm) of space between them. Cover with a cotton kitchen towel and let the twists rest for 1 hour, or until doubled in size. Preheat the oven and bake for 20 to 25 minutes as in Steps 6 and 7.

Focaccia al Formaggio
Cheese Focaccia

Gabriella prepares a focaccia topped with cheese, a specialty of the coastal village of Recco in the region of Liguria. She makes it ahead and serves it at room temperature. Stracchino, the cheese used in Recco, is a soft cow's milk cheese from Lombardy that remains soft after the focaccia has cooled. If stracchino is not available you can substitute taleggio. If you plan to serve the focaccia hot from the oven, the choices are limitless—fresh mozzarella, Fontina d'Aosta, or Swiss emmental; if you prefer, sprinkle with Parmigiano-Reggiano and drizzle lightly with olive oil.

- 1 RECIPE PANE DI ROSMARINO (BRAIDED ROSEMARY BREAD, PRECEDING RECIPE), WITHOUT THE ROSEMARY
- UNBLEACHED ALL-PURPOSE FLOUR, FOR KNEADING
- 1½ POUNDS (675 G) STRACCHINO CHEESE, THINLY SLICED

1. Follow the recipe for the bread through Step 3.

2. Preheat the oven to 500°F (260°C). Oil two 14-inch (35-cm) round pizza pans.

3. Place the dough on a lightly floured pastry board or work surface and knead for 2 minutes to force out any air bubbles. Lightly flour the dough, wrap it in a cotton kitchen towel, and let it rest in a warm draftfree place for 10 minutes.

4. Cut the dough in half. Roll 1 half into a 14-inch (35-cm) round. Keep the remaining piece of dough covered with the towel until it is ready to be rolled out. Transfer the round to one of the pizza pans. Top the dough with half of the sliced stracchino. Bake the focaccia for 10 to 12 minutes, or until the cheese is bubbly and the bottom crust is golden. Meanwhile, make the second focaccia in the same way. Serve hot or at room temperature.

MAKES 2 FOCACCE

Note: If the 2 *focacce* are baked together in the same oven, place them on separate racks. Stagger them by several inches, so they are not sitting one over the other. Reverse positions after 8 minutes to ensure even baking.

Salsa di Lattuga
Green Sauce Made with Lettuce

Tender Boston or leaf lettuce is used in this mildly seasoned green sauce that Gabriella spoons over sliced cheese for an antipasto. She usually selects a freshly made fior di latte, *a cow's milk mozzarella, but also serves it with a mild goat cheese such as caprini or fagottini, both made in Piedmont. Be sure to have plenty of crusty bread on hand.*

    1   MEDIUM HEAD BOSTON OR LEAF LETTUCE, WELL WASHED
        AND TORN
    3   TABLESPOONS CHOPPED ONION
    2   TEASPOONS BALSAMIC VINEGAR
   SEA SALT
   ¾   CUP (6 FL OZ/185 ML) EXTRA VIRGIN OLIVE OIL

1. Combine the lettuce and onion in a food processor. Process until the mixture is finely chopped. Add the vinegar, 1½ teaspoons salt, and olive oil. Process until the sauce is smooth.

2. Prepare the sauce at least 1 hour before serving. The sauce will keep, tightly covered, in the refrigerator up to 1 week.

MAKES 2 CUPS (16 FL OZ/500 ML)

Torta di Asparagi
Asparagus Tart

Asparagus spears begin poking out of the ground in early spring. Gabriella blends them in a ricotta filling that puffs up golden brown inside a crisp pastry crust. The Torta di Asparagi *can be served warm or at room temperature as an antipasto or as a light meal with a salad.*

For the Pastry Dough
   1⅓   CUPS (5½ OZ/160 G) UNBLEACHED ALL–PURPOSE FLOUR
    4   TABLESPOONS (2 OZ/60 G) UNSALTED BUTTER, SOFTENED
    1   LARGE EGG, LIGHTLY BEATEN
    3   TABLESPOONS WHOLE MILK
   SEA SALT

For the Asparagus Filling
   ¾   POUND (375 G) ASPARAGUS, TRIMMED AND WELL WASHED
   SEA SALT
    2   TABLESPOONS (1 OZ/30 G) UNSALTED BUTTER
    2   TABLESPOONS UNBLEACHED ALL–PURPOSE FLOUR
    8   OUNCES (240 G) RICOTTA
   ¼   TEASPOON FRESHLY GRATED NUTMEG
    3   LARGE EGGS, LIGHTLY BEATEN

1. To make the pastry dough, place the flour in a large bowl. Make a well in the center and add the butter, egg, milk, and a pinch of salt. Blend the ingredients in the well with a fork; the butter will remain slightly lumpy. Gradually incorporate the flour. Turn the mixture out onto a pastry board or work surface. Gently knead just until the mixture forms a ball of dough. Flatten the dough slightly, wrap it in wax paper, and refrigerate it for at least 1 hour.

2. Preheat the oven to 400°F (200°C).

3. To make the filling, bring a large pot of water to a rapid boil. Add salt to taste. Lower the asparagus into the water and cook just until tender, 3 to 6 minutes. Using a large skimmer, transfer the asparagus to a bowl of cold water. When cool, drain on a cotton kitchen towel.

4. Make a roux by melting the butter in a small heavy saucepan over medium heat. Add the flour and stir until dissolved and foamy. Remove from the heat and let the roux cool.

5. Cut off the asparagus tips and set them aside. Cut the stems into ¾-inch (2-cm) pieces and combine them in a bowl with the ricotta, roux, and nutmeg. Season with salt to taste, then blend in the eggs.

6. On the lightly floured pastry board, roll out two thirds of the chilled dough into an 11-inch (28-cm) round, ⅛ inch (0.3 cm) thick. Line a 9-inch (23-cm) tart tin with the round. Trim off the excess dough, and prick the bottom with a fork. Spread the filling evenly over the dough and top with the asparagus tips. Roll out the remaining piece of dough into a smaller round, also ⅛ inch (0.3 cm) thick. Cut the dough into ¾-inch-wide (2-cm-wide) strips using a fluted pastry wheel. Arrange the strips over the filling in a lattice pattern. Bake for 25 to 30 minutes, or until puffed and golden. Transfer to a cooling rack to cool for 10 minutes before serving.

MAKES 6 SERVINGS

Polenta con Formaggio alla Cipollina
Polenta and Cheese Mousse with Chives

This light-as-air cheese mousse is made from robiola piemonte and the blue-veined gorgonzola dolce, both excellent cheeses produced in Piedmont. The mousse is delicately flavored with snipped fresh chives and can be served in a multitude of ways for antipasti. Use it as a filling for celery or spoon a dab into a leaf of endive. Gabriella often serves the mousse with fried polenta. In winter she substitutes toasted walnuts for the fresh chives. Both robiola piemonte and gorgonzola dolce are available in Italian markets and cheese shops, as is imported or domestic mascarpone.

For the Polenta

1   CUP (5 OZ/150 G) COARSELY GROUND YELLOW CORNMEAL

SEA SALT

For the Cheese Mousse

8   OUNCES (240 G) MASCARPONE

10 OUNCES (300 G) ROBIOLA PIEMONTE

4   OUNCES (120 G) GORGONZOLA DOLCE

SEA SALT AND FRESHLY GROUND BLACK PEPPER

4   TEASPOONS SNIPPED FRESH CHIVES

SUNFLOWER OIL, FOR FRYING

1. The polenta must be made the day before or several hours ahead. Bring 3¾ cups (31 fl oz/930 ml) of water to a rolling boil in a large heavy saucepan. Hold a fistful of cornmeal over the pot. Stir constantly while the cornmeal slips through your fingers in a slow steady stream into the boiling water. When all of the cornmeal has been added, lower the heat and simmer, stirring constantly, for 25 to 30 minutes, or until the polenta is very thick and starts to pull away from the sides of the pan. Season with salt to taste and turn off the heat. Spoon the polenta into a wet 9 x 5-inch (23 x 13-cm) loaf pan and smooth with a rubber spatula. Cool completely. Cover and refrigerate overnight, or until firm.

2. To make the cheese mousse, combine the mascarpone, robiola, and gorgonzola in a large bowl. Whip with an electric mixer until the mixture becomes light and fluffy. Season with salt and black pepper to taste. Stir in the chives and refrigerate. (Remove the mousse from the refrigerator 15 minutes before serving.)

3. Pour 1 inch (2.5 cm) of sunflower oil into a heavy skillet with

Pollo in Carpione, OPPOSITE.

high sides. Heat the oil over medium heat. Turn the polenta out of the loaf pan and slice it about ⅝ inch (1.6 cm) thick. Cut each slice in half diagonally. When the oil is hot, add several pieces of polenta. Fry until golden and crisp on each side. Drain on paper towels. Transfer to a large serving platter and serve with a bowl of the cheese mousse.

MAKES 8 SERVINGS

Pollo in Carpione
Marinated Fried Chicken Breasts

Gabriella thinly slices chicken breasts, breads and fries each piece, and marinates them. She serves the marinated chicken as antipasto. In carpione is an old way of preserving that is also applied to fish and zucchini. In times before refrigeration the finished dish would be kept in a cool cellar or in a small compartment inside a well.

2   WHOLE SKINLESS, BONELESS CHICKEN BREASTS
    (1 POUND/450 G), SPLIT

3   LARGE EGGS, LIGHTLY BEATEN

1¼ CUPS (5 OZ/150 G) FINE DRY BREAD CRUMBS

SUNFLOWER OIL, FOR FRYING

SEA SALT

3   MEDIUM CLOVES OF GARLIC, CHOPPED

1   TABLESPOON COARSELY CHOPPED SAGE LEAVES, OR MORE TO TASTE

1   SMALL CARROT, SHREDDED

⅓   CUP (3 FL OZ/85 ML) RED OR WHITE WINE VINEGAR

1. Thinly slice the chicken breasts crosswise. Dip the slices into the beaten eggs, then coat with bread crumbs.

2. Heat 1 inch (2.5 cm) of oil in a heavy skillet with high sides over medium heat. When the oil is hot, add the chicken, several pieces at a time. Fry, without turning, until completely golden. Remove the chicken from the oil using a slotted spoon or skimmer and drain on paper towels. Sprinkle with salt to taste. Fry the remaining pieces in the same way. When all of the chicken has been fried, let the oil cool. Transfer the chicken to a large porcelain, glass, or crockery bowl.

3. To make the marinade, pour 1 cup (8 fl oz/250 ml) of the oil from the sauté pan into a small saucepan and heat over medium heat. Stir in the garlic, sage, carrot, and salt. When the garlic is lightly golden, pour in the vinegar and cook for 10 seconds. Pour the marinade over the chicken and toss. Marinate the chicken for at least 1 hour before serving, tossing occasionally. The chicken will keep tightly covered in the refrigerator up to 4 days.

MAKES 6 SERVINGS

Ravioli con Asparagi
Asparagus-filled Ravioli

The full flavor of newly harvested asparagus is emphasized in Gabriella's fresh ravioli made with two tones of pasta, green spinach pasta and white egg pasta. The asparagus are blended into a light ricotta filling; additional asparagus are sautéed with a hint of garlic and tossed with the ravioli.

Prepare the filling and all of the pasta before you begin to stretch the dough. When making a stuffed pasta like ravioli the dough must be filled as soon as it is stretched; if the dough dries it may not hold together. Gabriella uses a handy implement called a raviolatore, *a small tray useful in filling, shaping, and cutting ravioli. Italian imported ravioli trays are widely available in cookware shops.*

For the Filling

8 OUNCES (240 G) RICOTTA

SEA SALT AND FRESHLY GROUND BLACK PEPPER

½ POUND (240 G) PLUS ¾ POUND (375 G) ASPARAGUS, TRIMMED
   AND WELL WASHED

½ CUP (2 OZ/60 G) GRATED GRANA PADANO

¼ TEASPOON FRESHLY GRATED NUTMEG

1 LARGE EGG, LIGHTLY BEATEN

For the Egg Pasta

2½ CUPS (10 OZ/300 G) UNBLEACHED ALL-PURPOSE FLOUR

3 LARGE EGGS

1½ TEASPOONS WATER

PINCH OF SEA SALT

For the Spinach Pasta

2 CUPS (8 OZ/240 G) UNBLEACHED ALL-PURPOSE FLOUR

2 LARGE EGGS

1 TEASPOON WATER

PINCH OF SEA SALT

1 TABLESPOON CHOPPED COOKED SPINACH, DRAINED AND
   SQUEEZED DRY

8 TABLESPOONS (4 OZ/125 G) UNSALTED BUTTER

¼ TEASPOON FINELY CHOPPED GARLIC

1 CUP (4 OZ/125 G) GRATED GRANA PADANO

ABOVE, Gabriella fills the ravioli by piping the filling through a pastry bag. RIGHT, trimming the ravioli. BELOW LEFT, drying the ravioli. BELOW RIGHT, the completed Ravioli con Asparagi.

1. To make the filling, drain the ricotta if moist. Place it in a strainer resting over a bowl and refrigerate it for 2 to 3 hours or overnight. Meanwhile bring a large pot of water to a rapid boil. Add salt to taste. Lower ½ pound (8 ounces/240 g) of the asparagus into the boiling water and cook until tender, 3 to 6 minutes depending on their thickness. If the asparagus are not tender, they could possibly poke holes in the pasta dough. Transfer the asparagus with a large skimmer to a bowl of cold water. Reserve the cooking water. When cool, drain the asparagus on a cotton kitchen towel. Finely chop the asparagus and blend them in a large bowl with the ricotta, grana, and nutmeg. Season with salt and pepper to taste, then blend in the egg. Refrigerate the filling for at least 1 hour.

2. Return the asparagus water to a boil. Cook the remaining
¾ pound (12 ounces/360 g) of asparagus in the boiling water until
al dente, 3 to 6 minutes. Transfer with a large skimmer to a bowl
of cold water. When cool, drain on a cotton towel, then slice them
½ inch (1.25 cm) thick. Set aside for serving with the ravioli.

3. Make the egg and spinach pasta dough for the ravioli separately,
using the ingredients listed for each as directed on page 188, the
section entitled Making the Dough. The dough will be kneaded and
stretched in a manual pasta machine. Line 3 trays or baking sheets
with cotton kitchen towels and dust lightly with flour.

4. Divide the egg pasta dough into three equal portions and the
spinach pasta dough in two. Knead as directed in the section entitled
Kneading the Dough in a Pasta Machine.

5. Stretch the dough as directed in the section entitled Stretching
the Dough in a Pasta Machine. Stretch the dough one piece at a time
as thin as possible, taking it to the last setting on the dial. The ravioli
must be stuffed as soon as each piece of dough has been stretched.

6. Drape 1 end of the long sheet of dough over a lightly floured
ravioli tray. Let the excess dough hang over the edge; it should be long
enough to fold over the tray to enclose the fillings. Gently press the
dough against the tray. Fill each of the small pockets with ¾ teaspoon
of the asparagus filling. When all of the pockets have been filled,
dip a small brush in water and lightly moisten the dough around the
fillings and fold the excess dough over the tray to enclose the fillings.
Using a rolling pin, roll back and forth over the tray to seal the ravioli.
Trim away the excess dough. Reserve the scraps of dough to serve
in broth. Remove the ravioli from the tray. Gently press the edges to
seal and transfer to one of the towel-lined trays. Continue to make
ravioli with the remaining pieces of egg and spinach pasta dough. Cover
the ravioli with towels until they are ready to be cooked.

7. Fill a very large pot (at least 8 quarts/8 liters) with water and
bring it to a rapid boil. Add salt to taste. Stir in the ravioli and
cover the pot, just until the water returns to a boil. Uncover and boil,
stirring occasionally, for 4 to 5 minutes, or until tender.

8. Meanwhile, melt the butter over medium heat in a sauté pan or
Dutch oven large enough to hold the ravioli. Add the garlic and sauté
until golden. Stir in the sliced asparagus and cook until heated through.

9. When the ravioli are ready, remove them from the pot with
a large skimmer or strainer, being sure to drain well. Add the ravioli to
the pan, sprinkle with grana, and carefully toss over low heat until
the ravioli and asparagus are evenly coated with butter and the cheese
has melted. Transfer to a large serving platter and serve immediately.

MAKES 8 SERVINGS

Maiale al Latte

Savory Pork Roast Braised with Milk and Fresh Herbs

*Gabriella often serves a braised pork roast similar to this one, a Piedmontese
classic, that slow-cooks with milk and white wine.*

1   BONELESS PORK LOIN (3 TO 3½ POUNDS/1.4 TO 1.6 K)
¼   CUP (2 FL OZ/60 ML) EXTRA VIRGIN OLIVE OIL
1   SPRIG OF ROSEMARY
1   SPRIG OF SAGE
1   BAY LEAF
2   JUNIPER BERRIES, CRUSHED
1   CLOVE OF GARLIC, CHOPPED
SEA SALT AND FRESHLY GROUND BLACK PEPPER
½   CUP (4 FL OZ/125 ML) DRY WHITE WINE
3   CUPS (24 FL OZ/750 ML) WHOLE MILK

1. Preheat the oven to 350°F (175°C).

2. Tie the pork loin like a roast with heavy butcher's twine, if not
already done by the butcher. Heat the olive oil in a large heavy
flameproof casserole over medium heat. Add the roast, the sprigs of
rosemary and sage, the bay leaf, and juniper berries. Brown the roast
on all sides, then add the chopped garlic and season the roast with salt
and pepper to taste. When the garlic is golden, pour the white wine
over the roast and simmer briskly until it is reduced by half. Pour
the milk over the roast and heat just until scalded. Cover the casserole
and place it on the center shelf of the oven. Braise, turning every
20 minutes, for 1½ to 2 hours, or until tender and the roast and pan
juices are nutty brown.

3. Remove the roast from the casserole and transfer it to a carving
board. Cover with aluminum foil. Strain the juices in the casserole and
skim off the fat. Return the juices to the casserole and reduce them
over medium-high heat to thicken slightly. Taste for additional seasoning. Slice the roast and serve moistened with a spoonful of the juices.

MAKES 4 SERVINGS

Torta di Mais
Golden Polenta Cake

A coarse stone-ground cornmeal, one you would use for making polenta, lends a nutty texture and flavor to Gabriella's Torta di Mais, *a golden yellow cornmeal cake. The cake takes only minutes to assemble. Don't even butter and flour the pan; Gabriella lines it with parchment paper. She makes the* torta *in various baking pans, round or square cake pans, loaf pans, or a Rehrücken mold, a long rectangular pan with a rounded grooved bottom that is often nonstick.*

Sweet berries are a perfect accompaniment in spring and summer. In fall Gabriella serves a warm apple compote. She simmers peeled, chopped apples in a covered saucepan with one or two tablespoons of water and a strip of lemon peel, just until the apples are soft. Then she stirs in a touch of sugar and simmers until dissolved.

1½ CUPS (6 OZ/180 G) UNBLEACHED ALL-PURPOSE FLOUR
1¼ CUPS (6 OZ/180 G) COARSELY GROUND YELLOW CORNMEAL
¾ CUP (5 OZ/150 G) SUGAR
2 TEASPOONS BAKING POWDER
1 LARGE EGG, LIGHTLY BEATEN
¾ CUP (6 FL OZ/185 ML) WHOLE MILK
6 TABLESPOONS (3 FL OZ/90 ML) SUNFLOWER OIL

1. Preheat the oven to 400°F (200°C). Line a 9 x 5-inch (23 x 13-cm) loaf pan with parchment paper. Allow the paper to extend over the edges of the pan by at least 1 inch.

2. Combine the flour, cornmeal, sugar, and baking powder in a large mixing bowl and blend thoroughly. Combine the egg, milk, and oil and add them to the dry ingredients. Stir with a rubber spatula just until the dry ingredients have become moistened. Do not overwork the batter. Pour the batter into the loaf pan.

3. Bake on the center shelf of the oven for 50 to 55 minutes, or until the cake is golden and a toothpick inserted into the center comes out clean. Transfer to a cooling rack for 10 minutes. Use the parchment paper as a handle and lift the cake out of the pan. Continue to cool it on the rack. Remove the parchment paper just before serving.

MAKES 6 SERVINGS

Variation: Gabriella sometimes adds a handful of raisins to the batter. To do this, soak ⅓ cup (1½ oz/45 g) of dark or golden raisins in a small bowl of hot water for 10 minutes. Drain the raisins and dry them with paper towels. After all the dry and wet ingredients have been blended, gently fold in the raisins and bake as directed.

Gabriellini
Delicate Butter Cookies

White flour blended with potato starch and confectioners' sugar creates a cookie that simply melts in your mouth.

4 LARGE EGGS, AT ROOM TEMPERATURE
1⅔ CUPS (6½ OZ/200 G) UNBLEACHED ALL-PURPOSE FLOUR
1¼ CUPS (5 OZ/150 G) POTATO STARCH
¾ CUP (2½ OZ/75 G) CONFECTIONERS' SUGAR PLUS ADDITIONAL FOR DUSTING (OPTIONAL)
8 OUNCES (125 G) UNSALTED BUTTER, SOFTENED

1. Place the eggs in a medium saucepan. Cover with cold water by 2 inches (5 cm). Bring the water to a boil, then lower the heat and simmer the eggs for 9 minutes. Using a slotted spoon or skimmer, transfer the eggs to a bowl of ice water. When the eggs have cooled, peel and cut them in half. Scoop out the yolks and reserve the whites for another use. Press the yolks through a sieve.

2. Sift the flour, potato starch, and confectioners' sugar together 3 times. Place the sifted ingredients in a large bowl and make a well in the center. Cut the butter into chunks and add them to the well. Add the egg yolks. Blend the butter and egg yolks with your fingertips, then incorporate the sifted ingredients. Turn the mixture onto a pastry board or work surface and gather it together to form a mass of dough. Knead gently until the dough is very smooth. Flatten the dough slightly and wrap it in wax paper. Refrigerate for 1 hour.

3. Preheat the oven to 350°F (175°C). Line 3 baking sheets with parchment paper.

4. Lightly dust a pastry board or flat work surface with flour. Divide the dough into 4 portions. Roll out 1 portion at a time into a round ¼ inch (0.6 cm) thick. Cut out cookies using a 2-inch (5-cm) decorative cookie cutter. Using a metal spatula, transfer the cookies to the baking sheets. Space them at least 1 inch (2.5 cm) apart. Gather together the scraps to reroll later. Bake 1 sheet at a time on the center shelf of the oven for 13 to 15 minutes, or until the edges of the cookies are golden. Transfer the baking sheets to cooling racks. When the cookies are cool, dust them with confectioners' sugar, if desired.

MAKES 4 DOZEN COOKIES

Torta di Mais, *OPPOSITE.*

CASTELLO IL CORNO

The Contessa Maria Giulia, ABOVE, slices green tomatoes for her Marmellata di Pomodori Verdi, OPPOSITE, which she serves with pecorino toscano.

The Contessa Maria Giulia Frova characterizes today's young Italian woman—career-minded, independent, and energetic. But this modern-day Contessa, who prefers to be called Giulia, always keeps one foot firmly planted in the past—cherishing and upholding her family's traditions. Giulia lives and works on her family estate, Castello il Corno, in the fairy-tale setting of San Casciano in Val di Pesa in the Chianti zone of Tuscany. The family home is a noble fifty-room Renaissance-style manor house encompassing the tower of a castle once belonging to the del Corno family who lived there in the thirteenth century.

San Casciano in Val di Pesa

The property was acquired by the Frova family in 1911 and left to Giulia's grandmother, the Contessa Paula Aroni di Arona, after her husband's untimely death. The Contessa bravely took charge of the large farming complex that was then operating under a system of tenant farming known as *la mezzadria* while at the same time she established and ran a private medical clinic in the city of Florence. Giulia's fond memory of her grandmother, who was a maverick in her day, has been her inspiration.

Today Castello il Corno, which spans over five hundred acres, functions as a wine estate under the direction of Giulia's father and aunt, the Conte Antonio and Contessa Maria Teresa Frova. Giulia handles the commercial business for the estate, which produces wines of the Chianti zone. Il Corno has nearly ten thousand olive trees which are hand picked for an estate-bottled olive oil produced in the traditional Tuscan manner. An agriturismo, a rural bed and breakfast, has been developed on the grounds.

Despite her busy schedule, Giulia often entertains for family and friends, in keeping with the tradition of her grandmother who hosted many social gatherings at Castello il Corno. She warmly recalls her grandmother's penchant for entertaining and her appreciation for fine food and wine, with which she hastens to identify. Giulia's gatherings are always planned around a theme—she might prepare a dinner to celebrate the wine harvest, to indulge in recently pressed olive oil, or to usher in a season and pay tribute to *primizie*, the first harvesting of the season's vegetables and fruit.

LEFT, *a winding road on the estate.*
ABOVE, Salvia Fritta, *fried sage leaves
stuffed with anchovies.* OPPOSITE, *mixed
grain and bean soup with shrimp,* Zuppa
alla Giulia. *Maria Giulia and friends
making spring pizzas,* BELOW. *A slice of*
Pizza di Stagione, BELOW LEFT.

The estate is clearly marked by signs that limit access for hunting, LEFT.

Castello il Corno, RIGHT, has a long and proud history.

Salvia Fritta

Fried Stuffed Sage Leaves

Generally, when flavoring with fresh sage, use the smallest, most intensely flavored leaves; the larger leaves can then be used to prepare this palate-pleasing antipasto.

> 36 LARGE SAGE LEAVES
> 9 SALT-PACKED ANCHOVIES, FILLETED (SEE PAGE 12)
> 1 LARGE EGG
> EXTRA VIRGIN OLIVE OIL, FOR FRYING
> SEA SALT

1. Place eighteen of the sage leaves, face up, on a tray or baking sheet. Cut the anchovy fillets lengthwise in half. Top each leaf with a piece of anchovy. Cover each anchovy with a sage leaf, face down. Press the leaves together, place a second tray over the leaves, and top it with heavy weights. Let stand for about 15 minutes.

2. Lightly beat the egg in a shallow bowl or glass pie plate and add the stuffed sage leaves.

3. Heat ½ inch (1.25 cm) olive oil in a large heavy skillet over medium heat. When hot, lift the stuffed sage out of the bowl, one at a time. Let the excess egg drip back into the bowl. Add several stuffed leaves to the hot oil. Fry until golden and crisp, turning just once. Drain the leaves on paper towels and cook the others in the same way. Sprinkle with sea salt, if desired, and serve immediately.

MAKES 6 SERVINGS

Insalata di Fave

Fava Bean Salad with Pecorino Toscano

When the first fava beans are ready for harvesting, Giulia considers it a treat worth celebrating. As most Tuscans agree, the best way to savor young fava beans is raw with pecorino toscano, sheep's milk cheese made in Tuscany.

> 6 CUPS (10 OZ/300 G) (LOOSELY PACKED) TORN ARUGULA
> 6 CUPS (10 OZ/300 G) (LOOSELY PACKED) TORN LETTUCE SUCH AS GREEN OR RED LEAF LETTUCE, BOSTON, OR OAK LEAF
> 4 OUNCES (125 G) YOUNG PECORINO TOSCANO, THINLY SLICED
> 1½ POUNDS (675 G) FRESH YOUNG FAVA BEANS, SHELLED
> SEA SALT AND FRESHLY GROUND BLACK PEPPER
> ¼ CUP (2 FL OZ/60 ML) EXTRA VIRGIN OLIVE OIL

1. Combine the arugula and lettuce in a large shallow bowl. Refrigerate until just before you are ready to serve the salad.

2. Place the cheese on top of the salad greens. Scatter with the fava beans and sprinkle with salt to taste and a generous grinding of black pepper. Drizzle with olive oil, toss, and serve immediately.

MAKES 4 SERVINGS

Variation: In fall and winter this salad can be made with thin slivers of apple in place of the fava beans. Choose an apple that is very crisp and mildly tart and a pecorino that is aged about six months. Its sharp nutty flavor will complement the tartness of the apple. Serve the salad as soon as the apple has been sliced.

Pizza di Stagione

Pizza with Seasonal Toppings

After running into an old friend in Florence, Alessandro Masini, Giulia was inspired to organize a luncheon the following day. Alessandro, who runs a pizza shop in the city, offered to come by and prepare his version of spring pizza for a small group of Giulia's friends. Giulia supplied Il Corno wine and olive oil. Alessandro brought all the other ingredients with him. It was nearing summer and juicy vine-ripened tomatoes were at last ready, the small round type used for slicing. He baked all of the pizza crusts and allowed them to cool. Creamy sheep's milk ricotta, chunks of tomatoes, and a handful of fresh basil was used as a topping on one. Another was stacked with fresh mozzarella, tomatoes, and thin slices of speck, a lean smoked pork product from the region of Alto Adige that has become a popular topping for pizza throughout Italy. Lots of coarsely chopped arugula was piled on top. All of the pizzas were drizzled with extra virgin olive oil and cut into wedges. Everyone helped to assemble, which inspired many creative ideas for new toppings. Giulia's party was a success.

For the Pizza Dough

4   TEASPOONS ACTIVE DRY YEAST

3   TEASPOONS SUGAR

2   CUPS (16 FL OZ/500 ML) WARM WATER (105 TO 115°F/40 TO 46°C)

6   CUPS (24 OZ/725 G) UNBLEACHED ALL-PURPOSE FLOUR

2   TEASPOONS SEA SALT

¼   CUP (2 OZ/60 G) SOLID SHORTENING

1   TEASPOON EXTRA VIRGIN OLIVE OIL

For Topping with Tomatoes and Ricotta

4   MEDIUM TOMATOES, CORED AND CUT INTO ¾-INCH
     (2-CM) CHUNKS

10   OUNCES (300 G) RICOTTA

SEA SALT AND FRESHLY GROUND BLACK PEPPER

¼   CUP (½ OZ/15 G) COARSELY CHOPPED BASIL LEAVES

EXTRA VIRGIN OLIVE OIL, FOR DRIZZLING

For Topping with Speck and Arugula

1   POUND (450 G) FRESH MOZZARELLA, THINLY SLICED

3   MEDIUM TOMATOES, CORED AND THINLY SLICED

SEA SALT AND FRESHLY GROUND BLACK PEPPER

2   TEASPOONS FINELY CHOPPED FRESH OREGANO OR
     1 TEASPOON DRIED OREGANO

3   OUNCES (90 G) SPECK, VERY THINLY SLICED

3   CUPS (5 OZ/150 G) (LOOSELY PACKED) TORN ARUGULA

EXTRA VIRGIN OLIVE OIL, FOR DRIZZLING

1. Preheat the oven to 425°F (215°C). Oil two 14-inch (35-cm) round pizza pans, preferably black steel.

2. To make the pizza dough, sprinkle the yeast and the sugar over ½ cup (4 fl oz/125 ml) of the warm water in a small bowl. Stir until the yeast is dissolved. Mound 5 cups of the flour on a pastry board or work surface. Make a well in the center and add the remaining 1½ cups (12 fl oz/375 ml) of water, salt, shortening, olive oil, and the dissolved yeast. Blend the ingredients in the well with your fingertips. The shortening will remain slightly lumpy. Incorporate enough of the flour to make a soft ball of dough. Reserve the remaining flour. Knead the dough for 5 minutes, or until the dough is smooth and tender. Incorporate some of the reserved flour if the dough feels sticky.

3. Transfer the dough to a well-oiled large bowl. Rub the dough against the bowl to coat it with oil. Cover the bowl with a cotton kitchen towel and let it rest in a warm draftfree place for 15 minutes.

Punch down the dough and turn it out onto the lightly floured pastry board. Knead the dough for 1 minute, to ease out any air bubbles. Wrap the dough in the towel and let it rest for 5 minutes.

4. Divide the dough in half. Roll 1 half into a 14-inch (35-cm) round. Keep the remaining piece of dough covered with the towel until it is ready to be rolled out. Transfer the round to one of the pizza pans and prick the entire surface with a fork. Bake the pizza for 15 minutes, or until lightly golden, then transfer to a cooling rack. Cool thoroughly. Meanwhile make a second pizza with the remaining dough. The pizza should be topped just before serving.

5. For the topping with tomatoes and ricotta, scatter the tomato chunks over the pizza. Crumble the ricotta and spoon it over the tomatoes. Season with salt and pepper to taste. Sprinkle with chopped basil and drizzle with olive oil.

6. For the topping with *speck* and arugula, arrange mozzarella slices, slightly overlapping, on the pizza. Top with tomato slices. Season with salt and pepper to taste. Sprinkle with oregano. Arrange the speck over the tomatoes and top with arugula. Drizzle with olive oil.

MAKES 2 PIZZAS

A salad made with fresh young fava beans and pecorino toscano, BELOW.

Zuppa alla Giulia
Mixed Grain and Bean Soup with Shrimp

Giulia adds unshelled shrimp in varying sizes to this mixed grain and bean soup made with farro. *Farro, also known as emmer, is an ancient grain similar to barley. The shrimp shells render additional flavor to the soup and protect the shrimp from becoming dry. Italians appreciate the benefit and don't mind peeling them at the table.*

⅓ CUP (2½ OZ/75 G) EACH DRIED CANNELLINI BEANS, DRIED BORLOTTI BEANS, DRIED CHICKPEAS, LENTILS, AND FARRO, EACH SOAKED OVERNIGHT IN COLD WATER TO COVER BY 1 INCH (2.5 CM)

¼ CUP (2 OZ/60 G) PEARL BARLEY, SOAKED OVERNIGHT IN COLD WATER TO COVER BY 1 INCH (2.5 CM)

⅓ CUP (3 FL OZ/85 ML) EXTRA VIRGIN OLIVE OIL PLUS ADDITIONAL FOR DRIZZLING

2 SMALL SPRING ONIONS, TRIMMED, BULBS PEELED AND COARSELY CHOPPED

2 MEDIUM CLOVES OF GARLIC, SLICED

1 SMALL HOT RED CHILI PEPPER

3 TABLESPOONS DRY WHITE WINE

3 LARGE CANNED TOMATOES, COARSELY CHOPPED

5 CUPS (40 FL OZ/1200 ML) MEAT OR VEGETABLE BROTH (FOR HOMEMADE, SEE PAGE 187)

SEA SALT AND FRESHLY GROUND BLACK PEPPER

½ POUND (250 G) YUKON GOLD POTATOES, PEELED AND CUT INTO ½-INCH (1.25-CM) DICE

2 MEDIUM CARROTS, CUT INTO ⅜-INCH (1-CM) DICE

1 POUND VERY SMALL, SMALL, AND MEDIUM-SIZE SHRIMP WITH SHELLS AND HEADS IF AVAILABLE

1 TABLESPOON CHOPPED ITALIAN FLAT-LEAF PARSLEY LEAVES

1. Drain the beans and grains all together in a large colander. Heat the olive oil in a large pot over low heat. Add the onions, garlic, and chili pepper. Cook until the onions are translucent. Pour in the white wine, increase the heat to medium, and simmer until the wine has almost evaporated. Add the tomatoes and cook for 2 minutes. Add the beans and grains, the broth, 5 cups (40 oz/1200 ml) of water, a pinch of salt and black pepper to taste. Bring to a boil and simmer, uncovered, for 1 hour, stirring occasionally. Add the potatoes and carrots, and simmer for 1 hour more, or until the grains, beans, and vegetables are very tender and the soup has thickened. Remove the chili pepper and season with salt to taste.

2. Just before serving, bring the soup back to a boil and add the medium shrimp. Cover the pot and simmer for 2 minutes. Add the small shrimp, cover and simmer for 2 minutes more. Add the smallest shrimp, cover, and simmer for 2 minutes more, or until all of the shrimp are cooked through. Stir in the parsley and serve immediately, passing a cruet of olive oil to drizzle over each serving.

MAKES 8 SERVINGS

Baccalà alla Livornese
Salt-Dried Cod with Tomatoes and Basil

Don't underestimate the quality and outstanding flavor of baccalà, salt-dried cod. Giulia prepares it in a customary Tuscan style. Be sure to purchase the baccalà well in advance so that it has plenty of time to soak.

1½ POUNDS (675 G) SALT-DRIED COD, SOAKED IN FREQUENT CHANGES OF COLD WATER FOR 24 HOURS

EXTRA VIRGIN OLIVE OIL, FOR FRYING

UNBLEACHED ALL-PURPOSE FLOUR, FOR DREDGING

3 TABLESPOONS (1½ FL OZ/45 ML) EXTRA VIRGIN OLIVE OIL

3 MEDIUM CLOVES OF GARLIC

3 CUPS (24 FL OZ/750 ML) CANNED TOMATOES, DRAINED AND JUICES RESERVED

8 MEDIUM BASIL LEAVES, TORN IN HALF PLUS WHOLE BASIL LEAVES, FOR GARNISH (OPTIONAL)

1 SMALL HOT RED CHILI PEPPER

SEA SALT AND FRESHLY GROUND BLACK PEPPER

1. Dry the cod with paper towels and cut into 3 x 2½-inch (8 x 6-cm) pieces. Heat ½ inch (1.2 cm) olive oil in a large skillet over medium heat. When hot, dredge the salt cod, 1 piece at a time, in the flour. Add several pieces to the hot oil. Fry until golden and crisp on each side. Remove from the oil using a slotted spoon or skimmer and drain on paper towels. Dredge and fry the remaining pieces in the same way.

2. Preheat the oven to 400°F (200°C).

3. Heat the olive oil in a large sauté pan. Add the garlic and cook until golden. Stir in the tomatoes, the torn basil leaves, chili pepper, and salt and pepper to taste. Simmer for 15 minutes, breaking up the tomatoes with the back of a wooden spoon. If the sauce becomes too thick and sticks to the bottom of the pan, add some of the reserved tomato juice.

4. Arrange the fried salt cod in a single layer, in a 13 x 9-inch (32 x 23-cm) baking pan. Pour the sauce over the cod and bake for 25 minutes. Serve immediately. Garnish with basil, if desired.

MAKES 6 SERVINGS

Spring peas
flowering in the
garden, LEFT,
of Castello
il Corno.

Marmellata di Pomodori Verdi

Green Tomato Preserves

The hauntingly sweet-tart flavor of Giulia's green tomato preserves complements a young pecorino toscano as well as one that is more mature. Marmellata di Pomodori Verdi is in fact pleasing as an accompaniment to most cheeses or with toasted bread at breakfast. Green tomatoes begin to appear in farmers' markets mid- or late spring. Select firm, unripe tomatoes and use them quickly—before they begin to turn red.

1   LEMON
4   POUNDS (1.8 K) UNRIPE GREEN TOMATOES, CORED, HALVED, AND
    SLICED ⅜ INCH (1 CM) THICK
4½ CUPS (32 OZ/900 G) SUGAR
¼   CUP (2 FL OZ/60 ML) HONEY

1. Rinse six 8-ounce jelly jars with screw-top lids in warm soapy water. Place a rack at the bottom of a large pot. Open the jars and rest them on the rack with the lids. Fill the pot with boiling water to cover the jars by 1 inch (2.5 cm). Boil for 10 minutes. Remove the jars and lids with a jar lifter or tongs with heat-resistant handles. Invert the jars onto a cooling rack to cool and dry completely.

2. Peel the zest of the lemon in long sections and cut into julienne strips. Cut the lemon lengthwise in half, remove the seeds, and slice ¼ inch (0.6 cm) thick.

3. Combine the green tomatoes, sliced lemon, lemon zest, sugar, honey, and 1 cup (8 fl oz/250 ml) of water in a large, heavy, nonreactive pot. Bring to a boil and simmer gently for 1¼ to 1½ hours, stirring often, or until the preserves have thickened. Reduce the heat if the mixture begins sticking to the bottom of the pan. To test for density, place a spoonful of preserves on a small saucer and freeze it for 5 minutes. When cold, the preserves should be thick, like marmalade. Continue cooking and testing as necessary.

4. When ready, spoon the preserves into the jelly jars, leaving ½ inch (1.25 cm) of headspace. Use a clean, damp cloth to wipe away any drips from the headspace of the jars. Cool the jars completely. When cool, cover the jars tightly and store them in the refrigerator for up to 2 months.

Note: All of your utensils and work surfaces should be meticulously clean when preparing foods to be preserved.

MAKES SIX 8-OUNCE JARS

Piselli in Padella

Sweet Peas with Spring Onions and Pancetta

Giulia's aunt, Contessa Maria Teresa Frova, cooks sweet peas immediately after harvesting in a padella, *or large skillet, with spring onion, garlic, pancetta, and olive oil. For optimum sweetness purchase sweet peas from a local grower and use them immediately, before their natural sugars turn to starch.*

1   MEDIUM SPRING ONION, TRIMMED AND CHOPPED
½   OUNCE (15 G) PANCETTA, CHOPPED
1   MEDIUM CLOVE OF GARLIC, THINLY SLICED
¼   CUP (2 FL OZ/60 ML) EXTRA VIRGIN OLIVE OIL
3   POUNDS (1.4 K) SWEET PEAS, SHELLED
    (3 TO 3½ CUPS /16 TO 20 OZ/500 TO 600 G AFTER SHELLING)
¼   TEASPOON SUGAR
SEA SALT

1. Combine the onion, pancetta, garlic, and olive oil in a medium skillet. Cook over low heat until the onion is tender. Add the peas, ⅓ cup (3 oz/85 ml) water, the sugar, and salt to taste. Simmer, uncovered, stirring often, just until peas are tender, about 10 minutes.

MAKES 6 SERVINGS

DRÉ CASTÉ

very spring, city dwellers are lured to the Italian countryside by the debut of *primizie*, the first harvest of each new crop of the season. Country restaurants in small farming villages feature primizie prepared in the most simple manner. Dré Casté, a cozy restaurant housed in an eighteenth-century villa in the village of Vignale Monferrato in the Piedmont region, highlights primizie in menus that change daily. Carlo Santopietro, co-owner with his brother Roberto, offers the food served in homes throughout this farming community. Many of the dishes served at Dré Casté were inspired by their mother, who initially lent a hand in the kitchen.

Carlo Santopietro, ABOVE, *affirms that the food at Dré Casté reflects the good homecooking of his mother, grandmother, and aunts.* OPPOSITE CLOCKWISE FROM TOP, *the countryside of Vignale. Antipasti made on the family farm. A selection of grappa at Dré Casté. First of the season artichokes in the kitchen garden behind Dré Casté.*

The Santopietro brothers run a farm nearby, where their business was first launched producing two red wines characteristic of the region, Barbera and Grignolino. They then developed a line of food products based on family and regional farmhouse recipes, labeled under the name of their farm, Il Mongetto. The products are made from only the best local ingredients and are produced on a small scale with personal care.

Dré Casté, an easy jaunt for city dwellers of Milan or Turin, serves as a pleasant weekend escape from the rigors of cosmopolitan life. The setting is relaxed and informal. Country antiques, vases filled with fragrant cabbage roses from the garden, and soft lighting establish a casual dinner mood. The rhythms of a strummed guitar drift through the house as the third brother, Fabio, who serves at the restaurant on weekends, serenades arriving guests.

Rustic tables in each of the two small dining rooms are arranged with baskets of crusty bread along with small bowls of marinated vegetables jarred on the family farm. In spring, antipasti often include primizie gathered from the restaurant vegetable garden. For the *primo piatto*, or first course, handmade pasta may be tossed with fresh herbs or a sauce also made with primizie. Spring vegetables will emerge again as side dishes. Dré Casté celebrates the season's first sweet strawberries with a strawberry Bavarian cream served with a gin-spiked sauce. Wines produced by Il Mongetto, which now also include two refreshing whites, Cortese and Chardonnay, give good cause to linger late into the night.

Vignale Monferrato

Torta di Patate
Potato Tart

At Dré Casté a small wedge of this potato tart packed with big flavor is served as one of many antipasti. A local pecorino, a sheep's milk cheese, is blended with Parmigiano-Reggiano and gorgonzola. Use an aged gorgonzola that is firm and sharp and a pecorino toscano (page 112) that is slightly aged and can stand up to the more pronounced flavor of the gorgonzola.

1½ POUNDS (675 G) YUKON GOLD OR RUSSET POTATOES, PEELED
    AND CUT INTO 1-INCH (2.5-CM) CHUNKS
SEA SALT AND FRESHLY GROUND BLACK PEPPER
3 LARGE EGGS, LIGHTLY BEATEN
2 TABLESPOONS UNBLEACHED ALL-PURPOSE FLOUR
1 TEASPOON FINELY CHOPPED MIXED FRESH HERB LEAVES, SUCH AS
    BASIL, CHIVES, MINT, PARSLEY, TARRAGON, AND THYME
¼ CUP (1 OZ/30 G) GRATED PARMIGIANO-REGGIANO
4 OUNCES (120 G) PECORINO TOSCANO, CUT INTO SMALL DICE
3 OUNCES (90 G) AGED GORGONZOLA, CUT INTO SMALL DICE

1. Preheat the oven to 400°F (200°C). Butter a 10-inch (25-cm) pie plate or porcelain quiche pan.

2. Place the potatoes in a large saucepan. Fill it with enough cold water to cover the potatoes by 2 inches (5 cm). Add salt to taste and bring the water to a boil. Boil the potatoes, uncovered, for 15 to 20 minutes, or until tender when pierced with a paring knife. Drain in a colander.

3. Purée the potatoes through the medium disk of a food mill or in a potato ricer. Blend them with the eggs, flour, herbs, black pepper to taste, and the Parmigiano. Fold in the pecorino and gorgonzola. Spoon the mixture into the pie plate and spread it evenly. Bake for 35 to 40 minutes, or until puffed and golden brown. Let the torta rest for 5 minutes before serving.

MAKES 6 SERVINGS

Variation: During the fall and winter the *Torta di Patate* can be made with minced salami in place of the herbs. Substitute 2 tablespoons minced hard salami for the herbs.

Carciofi Ripieni
Artichokes Stuffed with Three Cheeses

Only the tenderest portion of the leaves and heart is used in this antipasto. It is served straight from the oven while the cheese filling is still melted and tangy.

For the Stuffing
½ CUP (2 OZ/60 G) GRATED PARMIGIANO-REGGIANO
⅓ CUP (1½ OZ/45 G) SHREDDED FONTINA D'AOSTA CHEESE
¼ CUP (1 OZ/30 G) FINELY DICED TALEGGIO CHEESE
¼ TEASPOON FINELY CHOPPED GARLIC
4 MEDIUM BASIL LEAVES, TORN INTO SMALL PIECES
2 TABLESPOONS (1 FL OZ/30 ML) EXTRA VIRGIN OLIVE OIL

4 LARGE ARTICHOKES
1 LEMON, HALVED
3 TABLESPOONS (1½ FL OZ/45 ML) EXTRA VIRGIN OLIVE OIL
¼ TEASPOON FINELY CHOPPED GARLIC
2 TABLESPOONS CHOPPED ITALIAN FLAT-LEAF PARSLEY LEAVES
⅔ CUP (5½ FL OZ/165 ML) MEAT OR VEGETABLE BROTH (FOR
    HOMEMADE, SEE PAGE 187)

1. Preheat the oven to 350°F (175°C).

2. To make the stuffing, combine the 3 cheeses, garlic, basil, and olive oil in a small bowl. Set aside.

3. Trim the artichokes, using the lemon, as described in note below.

4. Remove the stems from the trimmed artichoke, coarsely chop them, and set aside. Spoon the stuffing into the cavity of each artichoke, dividing the mixture evenly.

5. Heat the olive oil in a medium flameproof casserole over low heat. Add the garlic and sauté until golden. Add the parsley, the broth, and the chopped artichoke stems. Simmer for 15 minutes. Arrange the artichokes in the casserole and cover the pan. Bake for 50 to 60 minutes, or until the artichokes are tender. When tender, a small paring knife should easily slip in and out when inserted into the thickest part of the artichoke bottom. Serve immediately.

MAKES 4 SERVINGS

Note: To trim an artichoke of all its tough inedible parts, begin by soaking it for 20 minutes in a large bowl of cold water acidulated with the juice of ½ lemon. To prevent discoloration, use the other half of the lemon to rub the artichoke as the inner flesh is exposed. Begin at the base and snap off the dark green leaves. As the leaves become lighter in color, remove only the green portion leaving the tender yellow part closest to the base. Stop when the leaves are completely yellow. Cut off and discard one inch from the top of the artichoke. Open it carefully, remove the prickly inner leaves, and scrape out the fuzzy choke with the tip of a teaspoon. Rinse the artichoke under cold water then dip it into the acidulated water. Most of the stem is edible. Trim off the dry end then remove the outer green portion leaving only the tender white core. Trim away any additional dark green that remains on the artichoke and return it to the lemon water.

Primizie, the first harvest of each new crop of the season, are gathered from the kitchen garden at Dré Casté.

Tagliarini con Sugo di Erbe

Fresh Pasta with Mixed Herbs and Tomatoes

Fresh pasta is made each Friday at Dré Casté and served throughout the weekend with ingredients that reflect the season. Tagliarini, long, thin ribbons of pasta, are tossed with an herbal blend and served as a primo piatto, *or first course. Tomatoes can be stirred into the skillet and sautéed with the herbs.*

For the Tagliarini

4½ CUPS (19 OZ/540 G) UNBLEACHED ALL-PURPOSE FLOUR

5 LARGE EGGS

2½ TEASPOONS EXTRA VIRGIN OLIVE OIL

PINCH OF SEA SALT

½ CUP (4 FL OZ/125 ML) EXTRA VIRGIN OLIVE OIL

1 MEDIUM CLOVE OF GARLIC, FINELY CHOPPED

⅓ CUP (½ OZ/15 G) FINELY CHOPPED MIXED FRESH HERB LEAVES,
SUCH AS BASIL, OREGANO, PARSLEY, ROSEMARY, SAGE, AND THYME

5 MEDIUM PLUM TOMATOES, CORED AND CUT INTO ½-INCH
(1.25-CM) CHUNKS (OPTIONAL)

¾ CUP (3 OZ/90 G) GRATED PECORINO ROMANO

1. To make the pasta dough, use the flour, eggs, olive oil, and salt as directed on page 188, the section entitled Making the Dough. The dough will be kneaded and stretched in a manual pasta machine. Line 2 trays or baking sheets with cotton kitchen towels and dust lightly with flour.

2. Divide the dough into 5 equal portions and knead in the pasta machine as directed in the section entitled Kneading the Dough in a Pasta Machine.

3. Stretch the dough as directed in the section entitled Stretching the Dough in a Pasta Machine, stopping 2 notches before reaching the last position on the dial. Using a fluted pastry wheel, cut each sheet of pasta in half and arrange the sheets, side by side, on the towel-lined trays. Dry the pasta slightly, turning the sheets occasionally to dry them evenly. The surface should be dry to the touch but the pasta should remain flexible.

4. Attach the cutting blades to the pasta machine. Pass each sheet of dough through the narrow cutting blade. If the dough cannot be inserted easily, flatten the edge with your fingertips. Transfer the tagliarini to the towel-lined trays, dust with flour, and gently toss.

5. Fill a very large pot (at least 8 quarts/8 liters) with water and bring it to a rapid boil. Add salt to taste. Stir in the tagliarini and cover

Tagliarini con Sugo di Erbe, OPPOSITE.

the pot just until the water returns to the boil. Uncover and boil the tagliarini, stirring occasionally, for 8 to 10 minutes, or until al dente.

6. While the tagliarini are cooking, heat the olive oil in a sauté pan large enough to hold the tagliarini over medium heat. Add the garlic and sauté until it is lightly golden. Stir in the herbs and the tomatoes, if using, and cook for 1 minute, just until the tomatoes are heated through.

7. Drain the tagliarini, reserving some of the cooking water. Transfer the tagliarini to the sauté pan. Sprinkle with the pecorino and toss over low heat until the pasta is well coated with the herbs and the cheese has melted. If the pasta seems dry, add some of the reserved cooking water. Serve immediately.

MAKES 8 SERVINGS

Il Pollo al Limone

Braised Lemon Chicken

When this lemony chicken develops a rich brown glaze and begins to fall apart, it has achieved perfection.

3 TABLESPOONS (1½ FL OZ/45 ML) EXTRA VIRGIN OLIVE OIL

1 FREE-RANGE CHICKEN (3 TO 3½ POUNDS/1.4 TO 1.6 K), CUT
INTO 8 PIECES

3 TABLESPOONS UNBLEACHED ALL-PURPOSE FLOUR, FOR DREDGING

SEA SALT AND FRESHLY GROUND BLACK PEPPER

ZEST OF 1 LEMON, VERY FINELY CHOPPED

1 SMALL ONION, CHOPPED

2 SPRIGS OF SAGE, LEAVES ONLY, OR ¾ TEASPOON DRIED SAGE

1½ CUPS (12 FL OZ/375 ML) DRY WHITE WINE

1. Heat the olive oil in a large heavy sauté pan over medium-high heat. Pat the chicken pieces dry with paper towels, lightly dredge in flour, and add to the pan. Brown well on all sides, transfer to a platter, and season with salt and pepper to taste. Lower heat to medium-low.

2. Add the lemon zest, onion, and sage to the pan. Sauté until the onion is golden and tender, about 10 minutes. Return the chicken to the pan along with the juices that have accumulated on the platter. Pour the wine over the chicken, partially cover the pan, and simmer for 50 to 55 minutes, or until the chicken is very tender and most of the wine has evaporated. The chicken should be nutty brown in color and glazed with the pan juices. Taste for additional seasoning. Arrange the chicken pieces on a serving platter. Skim the fat from the pan juices. If too thick, stir in 1 or 2 tablespoons water. Pour the juices over the chicken and serve immediately.

MAKES 4 SERVINGS

Carote Arrosto con Salvia

Carrots Roasted with Sage

The sweet flavor of carrots becomes intensified when roasted in a hot oven. This easy side dish can be served alongside chicken, veal, or pork.

2 POUNDS (900 G) CARROTS, SLICED ⅜ INCH (1 CM) THICK
3 TABLESPOONS EXTRA VIRGIN OLIVE OIL
1 SPRIG OF SAGE, LEAVES ONLY
SEA SALT

1. Preheat the oven to 450°F (230°C). Oil a rimmed baking sheet that can hold the carrots in a single layer.

2. Toss the carrots in a large bowl with the olive oil and sage. Season with salt to taste. Transfer the carrots to the pan. Roast, without tossing, for 30 to 35 minutes, or just until tender. Transfer to a serving bowl and serve immediately.

MAKES 4 TO 6 SERVINGS

La Bavarese alle Fragole

Strawberry Bavarian Cream

This delicate bavarian cream is served at Dré Casté when strawberries are at their peak. Fresh lemon juice is added to strawberry purée to heighten the berry flavor. A slice of the chilled bavarian is served with a strawberry sauce that is enlivened with the unexpected flavor of gin. Giant berries grown for shipping can be dull and tasteless. Look for local strawberries beginning in late June.

For the Bavarian Cream
1 PINT (12OZ/360 G) STRAWBERRIES, WASHED AND HULLED,
   AT ROOM TEMPERATURE
JUICE OF 1 LEMON, STRAINED
1½ CUPS (5½ OZ/165 G) CONFECTIONERS' SUGAR
1 PACKET PLUS 1 TEASPOON UNFLAVORED GELATIN
2 CUPS (16 FL OZ/500 ML) HEAVY CREAM

For the Strawberry Sauce
1 PINT (12 OZ/360 G) STRAWBERRIES, WASHED AND HULLED
¾ TO 1 CUP (2½ TO 3½ OZ/80 TO 110 G) CONFECTIONERS' SUGAR
JUICE OF ½ LEMON, STRAINED
3 TABLESPOONS (1½ FL OZ/45 G) GIN

1. To make the bavarian cream, purée the strawberries in a food processor or blender. Strain the purée through a sieve into a large bowl and discard the seeds remaining in the sieve. Stir the lemon juice into the purée. Add the confectioners' sugar through a sifter and stir until the sugar is completely dissolved.

2. Sprinkle the gelatin over ¼ cup (2 fl oz/60 g) of cold water in a small saucepan and set aside until the mixture becomes firm and spongy. When it is ready, place the saucepan over very low heat and stir constantly until the gelatin is completely dissolved. Do not allow the gelatin to come to a boil. Stir the gelatin into the strawberry purée.

3. Refrigerate the purée, stirring often, until it cools slightly and begins to thicken. Whip the heavy cream with an electric mixer until stiff. Stir one fourth of the whipped cream into the strawberry mixture, then fold in the rest. When thoroughly blended, spoon the mixture into a 2-quart ring mold. Refrigerate until set, at least 2 hours.

4. While the bavarian cream is setting, make the sauce. Purée the strawberries in a food processor or blender. Strain the purée through a sieve into a large bowl and discard the seeds remaining in the sieve. Sift the confectioners' sugar, to taste, into the purée. Stir until the sugar is completely dissolved. Stir in the lemon juice and gin. Refrigerate the sauce until ready to serve.

5. To unmold the bavarian cream, invert the ring mold onto a flat serving platter. Dampen a kitchen towel with hot water. Drape the hot towel over the ring mold. When the towel cools, repeat the procedure. Do this several times, until the bavarian releases from the mold. If it does not release easily, slip a small paring knife around the edges to loosen the mold. Serve with the strawberry sauce.

MAKES 10 SERVINGS

Look for local strawberries that are ruby red inside and out and dripping with sugary juices. This kind of perfection goes into La Bavarese alle Fragole, BELOW, *served in spring at Dré Casté.*

Risotto Verde
Green Risotto for Spring

Celebrate spring with this green risotto from Piedmont, using a combination of spring green vegetables.

8   CUPS (2 LITERS) CHICKEN OR
    VEGETABLE BROTH (FOR
    HOMEMADE, SEE PAGE 187)
1   CUP (6 OZ/180 G) ASSORTED
    GREEN SPRING VEGETABLES,
    SUCH AS ASPARAGUS, BABY
    ZUCCHINI, SWEET PEAS, GREEN
    BEANS, OR SHELLED AND
    SKINNED FAVA BEANS
2   TABLESPOONS (1 FL OZ/30 ML)
    EXTRA VIRGIN OLIVE OIL
4   TABLESPOONS (2 OZ/60 G)
    UNSALTED BUTTER
2   SLENDER YOUNG LEEKS, WHITE
    PARTS ONLY, TRIMMED, WELL
    WASHED, AND FINELY CHOPPED
1   TABLESPOON FINELY CHOPPED
    IMPORTED ITALIAN PROSCIUTTO
2   CUPS (10 OZ/300 G) ITALIAN
    CARNAROLI OR ARBORIO RICE
1/3 CUP (1 OZ/30 G) FINELY CHOPPED
    ASSORTED LEAFY GREENS, SUCH
    AS SPINACH (SEE BOX AT RIGHT),
    SWISS CHARD, WATERCRESS,
    ARUGULA, OR ESCAROLE
1/2 CUP (2 OZ/60 G) GRATED
    PARMIGIANO-REGGIANO PLUS
    ADDITIONAL FOR SERVING
1   SMALL SCALLION, WHITE PART
    ONLY, FINELY CHOPPED
1   TEASPOON CHOPPED FRESH SAGE
    LEAVES
1   TABLESPOON CHOPPED ITALIAN
    FLAT-LEAF PARSLEY LEAVES
SEA SALT

1. Bring the broth to a boil in a large saucepan. Leave peas and fava beans whole. Dice the other vegetables the size of peas. Cook the vegetables in the broth for 3 minutes. Transfer them with a skimmer or a slotted spoon to a small bowl. Remove the broth from the heat and reserve.

2. Heat the olive oil with 2 tablespoons (1 oz/30 g) of the butter in a large heavy saucepan over medium-low heat. When the butter is melted, add the leeks and cook until tender. Add the prosciutto and cook for 2 minutes, stirring often. Reheat the broth to a simmer. Add the rice to the leeks and prosciutto and increase the heat to medium. Stir constantly until the rice becomes translucent.

3. Add a ladleful of the simmering broth and stir constantly until it is completely absorbed by the rice. Continue adding broth, 1 ladleful at a time, until the rice is almost tender, about 25 to 30 minutes. Stir in 1 last ladleful of broth. When it is almost absorbed, stir in the cooked vegetables and the chopped greens. Simmer for 2 minutes more. Add the remaining 2 tablespoons (1 oz/30 g) butter and the Parmigiano.

4. Remove the pan from the heat. Stir until the butter and cheese have melted. Stir in the scallion, sage, and parsley and season with salt to taste. Serve immediately, passing a small bowl of Parmigiano at the table for sprinkling over.

MAKES 6 SERVINGS

Buglione
*Lamb Braised with
Red Wine and Tomatoes*

Janet Hansen, a cooking teacher from the Maremma in southern Tuscany (see page 77) offers her version of Buglione, a saucy lamb stew created by local shepherds. The name is believed to come from the French word bouillon. The stew simmers for two hours, or until the meat falls from the bones.

3   POUNDS (1.4 K) SHOULDER LAMB
     CHOPS, EACH CUT INTO 3 PIECES
1/4 CUP (2 FL OZ/60 ML) EXTRA
     VIRGIN OLIVE OIL
4   CLOVES OF GARLIC, FINELY
     CHOPPED
1   TABLESPOON CHOPPED FRESH
     ROSEMARY LEAVES
1   CUP (8 FL OZ/250 ML) DRY RED
     WINE
1¾   CUPS (7 FL OZ/210 ML) CANNED
     TOMATOES WITH THEIR JUICE,
     CHOPPED
1   SMALL HOT RED CHILI PEPPER,
     CHOPPED
SEA SALT

1. Heat a large heavy sauté pan over medium-high heat. Add the lamb and cook, turning, until lightly browned on all sides and the juices have evaporated, about 10 minutes.

2. Add the olive oil, garlic and rosemary and cook for 2 to 3 minutes more, or until the garlic is lightly browned. Pour the red wine over the meat and simmer briskly, turning occasionally, until the wine has evaporated. Stir in the tomatoes and continue to simmer briskly for 5 minutes more. Pour in 1 cup (8 fl oz/250 ml) water, add the chili pepper, and season with salt to taste. Cover the pan, reduce the heat to very low, and simmer the lamb for 2 to 2½ hours, or until very tender. If the sauce becomes thick and sticks to the bottom of the pan, add some water. Taste for additional seasoning and serve.

MAKES 4 SERVINGS

How to Wash Spinach

Fresh spinach demands extra care and attention to eliminate all traces of sand and grit trapped in its crinkly leaves. To clean spinach, fill a large basin with cold water. Break off and discard the stems and add the spinach leaves to the water. Swirl the spinach to loosen the sand and grit then soak for 10 minutes. Lift the spinach out of the water and transfer it to a large bowl. Drain off the water, and refill the basin. Soak the spinach as many times as necessary, until there are no longer traces of sand left in the bottom of the basin.

SUM

MER

The assemblage of vegetables in the

Italian summer market is dazzling

in shades of red, yellow, orange, purple,

and green with succulently juicy

flavors from sweet to savory to sublime.

Vegetables
verdure

Eggplants, *melanzane,* can be small and round or large and pear-shaped. Besides the familiar dark purple, eggplants come in white, light violet, and green. They should be firm and not too large for their variety. The skin should be taut, evenly colored, and shiny; the stem and blossom cap should be bright green, moist, and fresh. Avoid eggplants that are shriveled, soft or with tan patches or bruises. Refrigerate eggplant loosely covered for up to 3 days. Eggplants peak in August and September and can be found at farmers' markets and farm stands.

Green beans, *fagiolini,* were once commonly known as stringbeans. They are in the same family as yellow wax beans; *haricots verts,* very slender beans, hardly ¼ inch thick; and Romano beans, sometimes called Italian green beans or flat beans. All beans should be firm and crisp except for haricots verts, which are more flexible. Select small beans with bright color (yellow beans with a slight tinge of green will have the best flavor). Refrigerate beans loosely covered for 1 or 2 days. Green beans and others in the family are best from early summer through early fall purchased at farmers' markets or farm stands.

Herbs, *erbe,* should be freshly picked for maximum flavor. The intensity of their flavor can vary, so use discretion—more can always be added later. Fresh herbs are used in larger quantities than dried, about 2 to 3 times the amount. Fresh basil is quite perishable and must be used within 2 or 3 days of picking. Chives add a delicate accent, which dried chives cannot duplicate. Likewise, dried mint cannot capture the vibrancy of fresh mint. Though oregano is used as a fresh herb, it is often preferred as a dried herb in Italy's southern regions. Fresh parsley, the flat-leaf variety, should always be on hand. Fresh rosemary adds character to grilled, roasted, or slow cooked foods. Mediterranean sage has a sweet bold flavor unlike American sage. Dried whole sage leaves from Italy, France, or Greece work better than fresh American sage but may be difficult to find. When using fresh sage, use the smaller, more flavorful leaves. Thyme, an herb that blends well with many other herbs, adds personality to sauces, stews, and soups. Rinse fresh herbs just before using. To store herbs, place stems in a glass of water, cover tightly with a plastic bag, and refrigerate.

Peppers, *peperoni,* come in both sweet and hot varieties. Sweet bell peppers are available in several colors. Green ones are mature but underripe with a mildly sweet flavor. As they ripen they become increasingly sweeter and turn red, yellow, and orange. Italian frying peppers are long, skinny, thin-walled peppers. Two sweet varieties are the Italianelle and Cubanelle. The Italian long hot is a fiery hot frying pepper that is bumpy-skinned and curved. Another type, the *nardello,* can be either sweet or hot. Each is available green or red. The hot red chili peppers often referred to by their Italian name, *peperoncini,* add fire to many Italian sauces and sautés. They are small and slender with a slight curve and pointy tip. When selecting peppers look for those that are firm with shiny skin. Avoid peppers that are shriveled, pliable, or those with soft spots. Cover peppers and store them in the refrigerator for up to 4 days. Peppers are best harvested between midsummer and mid-fall and are widely available.

Squash blossoms, *fiori di zucca,* are edible flowers of summer and winter squash. They have a delicate flavor with a hint of cucumber. Select blossoms that look fresh and alive. They should be used the day they are purchased. If they must be stored, immerse the stem ends in water, cover them loosely with a plastic bag and refrigerate for 1 day. Squash blossoms can usually be found at farmers' markets and specialty produce markets from mid-spring through early fall.

Swiss chard, *bietola* or *coste,* also known simply as chard, is a leafy green with dark crinkly leaves and red, silvery white, or golden ribs. Both the leaves and ribs are edible. Leaves should have a fresh appearance with crisp ribs that are free from browning. Cover and store unwashed Swiss chard in the refrigerator for up to 3 days. Swiss chard is widely available from late spring through winter.

Tomatoes, *pomodori,* are basically of two types, plum tomatoes and slicing tomatoes. In addition there are cherry tomatoes and such novelties as the tiny currant tomatoes. Plum tomatoes are thick skinned and meaty with relatively few seeds and juice; they are considered a cooking tomato. Slicing tomatoes are juicy and fragrant; they are best eaten raw. Cherry tomatoes are small bite-size tomatoes; currant tomatoes, developed from a wild tomato of South America, are sometimes as small as a pea. Succulent, juicy, full-flavored tomatoes are available only during the warm sunny months of summer. For a tomato to reach its full potential it must ripen on the vine. Ripe tomatoes are fragile and unsuitable for traveling long distances, so most tomatoes we see throughout the year have been picked green and hard, then ripened with ethylene gas. The finest quality tomatoes are those which have been locally grown. Select tomatoes that are firm and plump. Tomatoes should never be stored in the refrigerator; cold temperatures significantly dull their flavor and aroma and cause them to become mealy. Store tomatoes up to 1 week, stem end up, at room temperature, shielded from sunlight. Local tomatoes can sometimes be seen as early as late June. They reach their peak in August and can remain on the vines until the first frost of autumn; many will continue to ripen for several weeks after they have been harvested.

Zucchini, *zucchini,* is a summer squash that should be harvested young when they are thin skinned with small underdeveloped seeds. Select small zucchini that are heavy for their size. They should be firm and glossy with a fresh, moist stem end. Avoid zucchini that are spongy or those with gouges or soft spots. Store unwashed zucchini in the refrigerator for up to 5 days. Though widely available throughout the year, zucchini is a warm weather vegetable with a season that runs from late spring through summer. Locally grown zucchini can be found from late spring through early fall.

Fruit
frutta

Apricots, *albicocche,* are a small stone fruit related to the peach. The edible downy skin can range in color from pale orange to a red-orange and may have a rosy blush. Apricots must be tree-ripened to be superlative in terms of eating quality. Commercially grown varieties are picked underripe, and as a result, their flesh is often dry, mealy and devoid of flavor and aroma. Choose locally grown apricots that are firm but not hard, with an intense aroma and smooth, unblemished skin. Apricots bruise easily and should be handled with care. Store them at room temperature away from direct sunlight if they require softening; otherwise loosely cover and store them, unwashed, in the refrigerator for up to 5 days. Apricots are in season from June through early August when local varieties can be found at farmers' markets and farm stands.

Cantaloupe, *cantalupo,* is a summer melon that belongs to the same family as cucumber and squash. Cantaloupe should have raised netting covering a cream-colored skin with only a slight green tinge; skin that is mostly green indicates the melon is underripe. Since cantaloupe will not ripen off the vine, it is important to purchase one that is fully ripened. Look for a melon that is symmetrical and heavy for its size; avoid bruises or soft spots. The blossom end should feel resilient when pressed. A firm cantaloupe can be softened at room temperature in a cool, well-ventilated location for up to 3 days. Otherwise, store melon in the refrigerator for up to 5 days wrapped in plastic to prevent transferring its aroma to other foods. Melons are at their peak from June through August.

Cherries, *ciliege,* are a stone fruit that are cultivated in two types, sweet and sour. Sweet cherries are most often eaten out of hand. They come in shades of red or white and are plump and round or heart-shaped. Sour cherries, because of their tartness and astringency, are usually cooked in syrup, baked, or preserved in jams and jellies. All cherries must be picked ripe as they do not continue to ripen off the tree. When selecting sweet cherries, look for those with stems still attached. They should be firm, crisp, and deeply colored with a nice sheen. Avoid cherries that are undersized, soft, bruised, or those that have splits. Cover and refrigerate unwashed cherries with their stems still attached for up to 4 days. Cherries are at their best and are widely available during a very brief season in June and July.

Lemons, *limoni,* can range in size from a large egg to that of a small grapefruit, with either thin or very thick skins. Choose brightly colored lemons with fine-grained skin, free of green tinges, an indication of underripeness. Lemons should be firm, plump, and feel heavy for their size. Store lemons at room temperature for 1 week or in the refrigerator for 2 or 3 weeks. Lemons can be found year round with seasonal peaks in the warm weather months of May, June, and August.

Nectarines, *nettarine,* are related to peaches but have slightly firmer denser flesh with smoothly textured skin. Ripe nectarines are golden yellow or white blushed with a dark rosy red. Locally grown nectarines in season are superior to those commercially grown. When selecting nectarines, look for those that are fragrant with flesh that yields slightly when pressed. Avoid nectarines that are hard, bruised, or blemished. Nectarines can be softened at room temperature away from direct sunlight. Ripe nectarines can be refrigerated, unwashed, for up to 5 days. Locally grown nectarines are available from July through early September at farmers' markets and farm stands.

Peaches, *pesche,* are either freestone or clingstone, depending on the ease with which the stone is removed from the flesh. Freestone peaches, the type more commonly found in markets, are softer and juicier than clingstones. Skin colors range from golden yellow to creamy white, usually with a rosy blush. For best eating quality choose locally grown peaches. Select peaches with a delicate fragrance that yield slightly to pressure. Avoid dark colored peaches or those that are hard, bruised, or wrinkled. Firm peaches can be left at room temperature to soften. Cover and store unwashed peaches in the refrigerator for up to 5 days. Locally grown peaches are available from July through early September at farmers' markets and farm stands.

CLOCKWISE FROM ABOVE,
*freshly picked squash blossoms at
Hotel Santa Caterina. The lemons of
Amalfi grow in terraced gardens high
above the sea. Freshly harvested garlic
with the green tops still attached.
Fishing for dinner in Amalfi. Rows
of garden beans growing in the rich,
red Apulian soil.* PAGE 144
CLOCKWISE FROM LEFT, *Swiss
chard. Cherries and assorted summer
fruit from Apulia. Sweet bell peppers
in the Asti market.*

MOZZARELLA DI BUFALA

Caponata
Bread and Mozzarella Salad

Unlike Sicilian caponata, this Caponata is a Neopolitan bread and mozzarella salad.

1 POUND (450 G) SLIGHTLY
DRY, FIRM-TEXTURED
COUNTRY-STYLE BREAD
(FOR PANE TOSCANO, SEE
PAGE 78), SLICED

2 MEDIUM TOMATOES, CORED,
SEEDED, AND CUT INTO
½-INCH (1.25-CM) DICE

1 POUND (450 G) FRESH
MOZZARELLA, CUT INTO
½-INCH (1.25-CM) DICE

2 SPRIGS BASIL LEAVES, TORN

1 TEASPOON DRIED OREGANO

SEA SALT

½ CUP (4 FL OZ/125 ML)
EXTRA VIRGIN OLIVE OIL

1. Tear the bread into small chunks, briefly dip it in cold water, and squeeze dry.

2. Crumble the bread and combine with the tomatoes, mozzarella, basil, oregano, and salt to taste in a large bowl. Drizzle with olive oil and toss well.

MAKES 8 SERVINGS

Purists agree the consummate mozzarella is that made from the milk of water buffalo—*mozzarella di bufala*—produced by artisans in Italy's sunny region of Campania within the provinces of Salerno and Caserta where the massive, docile buffalo can be seen grazing. The Italian species of buffalo are said to be direct descendants of those bred in India, but how and when they made their way onto Italian shores and exactly at what point this cheese was first produced are difficult to say. With scarcely 100,000 buffalo in all of Italy, supplies are limited and most mozzarella di bufala remains close to home.

Mozzarella is classified as a *pasta filata*, a spun- or pulled-curd cheese composed of many delicate layers. Thick chunks of curd are crumbled, then allowed to drain and ferment for several hours. The curd is cut into strips and transferred to a vat where it is doused with boiling water. As it is stirred with a paddle, the curd melts into a soft taffylike substance. When the mixture approaches the proper texture, which the cheesemaker can determine only through experience, he begins a pulling and stretching action, which results in the layering. He then tears off a thick wad, manipulates it, and shapes it. The action of tearing, known as *mozzare* in Italian, gives the cheese its name. The cheese is then cooled and refreshed in pure water and later transferred to a salty brine where it remains stored under refrigeration until consumed.

Mozzarella di bufala has a mellow, milky flavor with a subtle tang. The texture is soft and cushiony though slightly firmer on the outside. Cow's milk mozzarella, known in Italy as *fior di latte*, literally the flower of milk, is also an excellent cheese and even preferred by some over mozzarella di bufala. It is moist and buttery with a spongy texture. Three liters of milk are required to produce one kilo of mozzarella (slightly more than two pounds). A buffalo provides merely ten liters of milk per day as compared to a cow's twenty-five to thirty; this is the basis for the steeper price of mozzarella di bufala. Mozzarella di bufala is shipped to the United States within twenty-four hours of production, sealed in plastic and floating in its original brine.

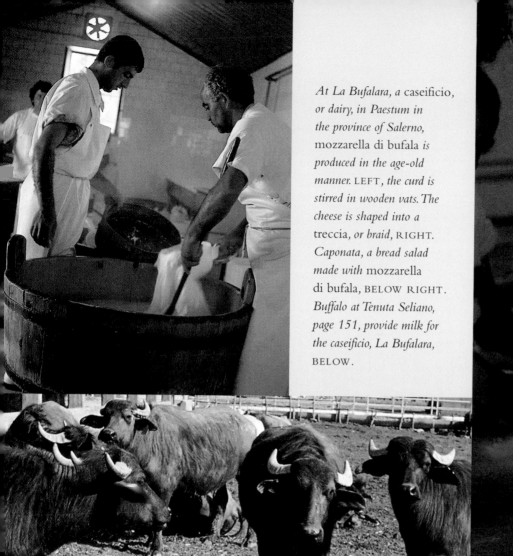

At La Bufalara, a caseificio, or dairy, in Paestum in the province of Salerno, mozzarella di bufala *is produced in the age-old manner.* LEFT, *the curd is stirred in wooden vats. The cheese is shaped into a treccia, or braid,* RIGHT. *Caponata, a bread salad made with* mozzarella di bufala, BELOW RIGHT. *Buffalo at Tenuta Seliano, page 151, provide milk for the caseificio, La Bufalara,* BELOW.

TENUTA SELIANO

The ancient Greek city of Paestum, founded about 600 B.C., lies south of Naples in Italy's southern region of Campania. It is noted for the archaeological remnants of its past. The impressive remains of ancient Doric temples, including those of the very well-preserved *Tempio di Nettuno*, or Temple of Neptune, stand within the city the Greeks referred to as Poseidonia. But upon entering Paestum it is clearly evident the city is known for something more than its archaeology. Along the main thoroughfare leading toward the ruins is a string of *salumerie*, or grocery shops, each one distinguished by its own colorful and graphically designed signboard announcing the sale of genuine *mozzarella di bufala*, a buttery soft cheese made from the milk of water buffalo. The giant beasts, descendants of the water buffalo of India, graze on the plains of Campania in both the Sele Valley, where Paestum lies, and in the northern valley of Volturno near the city of Caserta. Mozzarella di bufala is uniquely different from that made from cow's milk, and its influence on the cuisine of the region is significant.

The Baronessa Cecilia Bellelli and her two sons, Ettore and Massimo, manage a 250-acre farm in Paestum, where they raise more than two hundred head of water buffalo, a thriving family business that was established near the close of the eighteenth century. The buffaloes yield milk used for the production of mozzarella di bufala. Just a short drive from where these imposing creatures are housed, the Baronessa features the mozzarella in meals she prepares in the kitchen of her farmhouse, which serves as an *agriturismo*, or agricultural guesthouse. The unique retreat, which she calls Tenuta Seliano, provides her guests the opportunity to explore the gastronomic pleasures of Campania between excursions into antiquity. The large nineteenth-century farmhouse was impeccably restored with attention to fine detail and furnished to reflect the Baronessa's appreciation of fine art and antiques, many inherited from family collections and others acquired through travel.

Meals, served most of the year on an outdoor patio, are always festive gatherings.

The beautiful sundrenched countryside of Paestum in Campania is the setting of Tenuta Seliano, owned by the Baronessa Cecilia Bellelli, OPPOSITE TOP. Water buffalo produce the milk for authentic mozzarella di bufala and other regional cheeses, OPPOSITE BOTTOM LEFT AND RIGHT.

Paestum

Two long rectangular tables are shielded from the glaring Mediterranean sun by an overhead canopy made of thin cane reeds and long, billowy, white panels of drapery. The makeshift tented room creates a romantic mood particularly after dark when the tables are illuminated by the glow of candlelight. Guests are regularly joined by the Baronessa, a genteel woman with a gregarious manner, and time and again by her family and friends.

Kitchen preparation ordinarily consumes the better part of the day. It is an informally structured event presided over by the Baronessa supported by a high-spirited team of assistants, often including her sister and niece. They assemble within a medium-size kitchen where they are joined throughout the day by hungry guests lured by the aroma. Some guests merely engage in brief conversation and steal a sample; others offer to lend a hand.

The food is purely regional in flavor and prepared with ingredients grown on the estate. Neapolitan cuisine is dominated by a plethora of fresh vegetables that reach great heights in flavor during summer; at the forefront is the tomato—served raw, roasted, and stuffed or used to create outstanding sauces. Eggplant, sweet peppers, zucchini, and leafy greens are all used creatively and seasoned with subtlety, drawing on a

plentitude of dried herbs. Dry pasta, both long and short, appears in numerous ways. Fresh fruit—peaches, strawberries, nectarines, apricots, cherries, melons, table grapes, and figs—provide a refreshing conclusion to summer meals. They are presented in tempting fruit bowls, used in sweet pastries, or blended into gelato or sorbetto. Fine cheeses are produced from both buffalo milk and cow's milk. And fresh mozzarella, commonly known for its use with the ubiquitous Neapolitan pizza, is frequently melted over vegetables and pasta or added to salads, savory pies, and stuffings.

At Tenuta Seliano mozzarella di bufala appears one or more times during both lunch and dinner. The Baronessa always serves the mozzarella fresh, or unadorned, the day it is produced, most often at the start of a meal accompanied by sliced ripe tomatoes, a bowl of olives, crisp raw vegetables, or in the more traditional style, with a platter of prosciutto and *soppressata*, a type of dry sausage. She serves a delightful bread salad as a light luncheon dish; it is made with cubes of mozzarella and chunks of tomato dressed with olive oil produced from olives grown on the estate. She often serves fresh mozzarella at the end of the meal accompanied by a tossed garden salad and crusty bread. By the second day the Baronessa uses the mozzarella for cooking. As a warm antipasto, large squash blossoms are stuffed with mozzarella and anchovies, then breaded and fried until the cheese and anchovy have melted together and the crust is pleasingly crisp. A flaky pastry dough made with buffalo-milk butter is used for a savory Neapolitan pie called *pizza rustica*, which is filled with buffalo-milk ricotta, chunks of mozzarella, morsels of prosciutto, and a sprinkling of grated pecorino. Mozzarella also finds its way into a stuffed chicken breast that is served as a *secondo piatto,* or second course.

Whether spending an evening or several days at Tenuta Seliano, visitors will always come away enriched by the history and traditions of Paestum as well as the hospitality and warm-hearted friendship provided by the Baronessa.

The preparations for stuffed squash blossoms, BELOW. The Baronessa, at far left, with family members, taking a break from kitchen work, BOTTOM. The classic Neopolitan savory pie, Pizza Rustica, *OPPOSITE.*

Fiori di Zucca Ripieni

Squash Blossoms Stuffed with Mozzarella and Anchovies

At Tenuta Seliano large golden squash blossoms are filled with an anchovy filet and a square of mozzarella di bufala, *then breaded and fried.*

16 LARGE SQUASH BLOSSOMS

8 SALT-PACKED ANCHOVIES, FILLETED (SEE PAGE 12)

3 OUNCES (90 G) FRESH MOZZARELLA, CUT INTO 16 CUBES

3 LARGE EGGS, LIGHTLY BEATEN

1¼ CUPS (3½ OZ/100 G) FINE DRY BREAD CRUMBS

SUNFLOWER OIL, FOR FRYING

EXTRA VIRGIN OLIVE OIL, FOR FRYING

SEA SALT

1. Remove the stems and stamens from the squash blossoms. Rinse them under cold water and pat dry with paper towels. Stuff each blossom with an anchovy fillet and a cube of mozzarella. Twist the top of the blossom to seal it closed. Dip them into the beaten eggs, then coat with bread crumbs. Refrigerate for 30 minutes.

2. Heat 1 inch (2.5 cm) of oil, using equal amounts of sunflower oil and olive oil in a large heavy skillet with high sides over medium heat. When the oil is hot, add the squash blossoms, several at a time. Fry the blossoms until they are golden brown on all sides. Remove them with a slotted spoon and drain on paper towels. Sprinkle with salt. Fry the remaining blossoms in the same way. Serve immediately.

MAKES 6 TO 8 SERVINGS

Pizza Rustica

Savory Ricotta Pie

Pizza Rustica, *a classic Neopolitan savory pie on the order of a quiche, can be served in small wedges as an antipasto or in more substantial portions as a luncheon dish.*

For the Pastry Dough

2 CUPS (8 OZ/240 G) UNBLEACHED ALL-PURPOSE FLOUR

SEA SALT

8 TABLESPOONS (4 OZ/125 G) UNSALTED BUTTER, CHILLED

4 TABLESPOONS (2 OZ/60 G) SOLID VEGETABLE SHORTENING, CHILLED

6 TABLESPOONS (3 FL OZ/90 ML) COLD WATER

For the Filling

1¼ POUNDS (20 OZ/560 G) RICOTTA

6 OUNCES (180 G) FRESH MOZZARELLA, CUT INTO SMALL DICE

1½ OUNCES (45 G) IMPORTED ITALIAN PROSCIUTTO, CAPOCOLLO, OR DRY SALAMI, MINCED

¼ CUP (1 OZ/30 G) GRATED PECORINO ROMANO OR PARMIGIANO-REGGIANO

SEA SALT AND FRESHLY GROUND BLACK PEPPER

3 LARGE EGGS, LIGHTLY BEATEN

For the Egg Glaze

1 EGG YOLK, LIGHTLY BEATEN

1. To make the pastry dough, combine the flour and salt in a large bowl. Cut the butter and shortening into small pieces, the size of a large pea, and add to the flour. Working quickly, blend the fats with the flour, using your fingertips, until the mixture is the texture of cornmeal. Or use a pastry cutter. Make a well in the center of the bowl, add the water, and, using your hand, blend the water into the flour mixture, just until it is moistened. Turn the mixture out onto a pastry board or work surface. Gather it together to form a ball of dough. It does not have to be smooth, just hold together. Flatten the ball slightly, wrap in plastic wrap, and refrigerate for at least 2 hours. (The dough can be made a day ahead and refrigerated overnight.)

2. Preheat the oven to 350°F (175°C). Lightly butter a 9-inch (23-cm) springform pan.

3. To make the filling, place the ricotta in a large bowl. Add the mozzarella, prosciutto, and pecorino and combine. Season with salt and pepper to taste. Blend in the eggs.

4. Roll out two thirds of the dough on a lightly floured pastry board or work surface to a 14-inch (35-cm) round ⅛ inch (0.3 cm) thick. Line the springform pan with the round. Spoon in the filling and smooth the top with a rubber spatula. Trim off the excess dough, leaving a ½-inch (1.25 cm) border that extends above the level of the filling. Roll out the remaining dough into a sheet ⅛-inch (0.3-cm) thick. Cut the dough into 1½-inch (3.8-cm) wide strips using a fluted pastry wheel. Arrange the strips over the filling in a lattice pattern. Trim off the excess dough. Combine the egg yolk with 1 teaspoon water in a small bowl. Brush the lattice strips with the egg glaze. Bake for 75 to 80 minutes, or until puffed and golden. Cool the Pizza Rustica on a cooling rack for 15 minutes. Remove the outer ring of the springform pan and slide the pizza onto a flat serving platter. Serve warm or at room temperature.

MAKES 8 SERVINGS

Penne con Pomodoro al Gratin

Penne with Gratinéed Tomatoes

The region of Campania has been blessed with all of the proper elements for growing fruit and vegetables of unique quality—rich volcanic soil, a profusion of bright sunlight, and a gentle climate—and the diet of the region relies heavily on them. The goodness of Campania's San Marzano tomato, a thick-fleshed cooking tomato, is hailed around the world, and it has become a symbol of the region. The Baronessa tosses these gratinéed tomatoes with dry pasta. They can also be served as antipasto or as a contorno, *a side dish, with meat or poultry.*

⅔ CUP (4 OZ/120 G) SALT-PACKED CAPERS

2 MEDIUM CLOVES OF GARLIC, SLICED

⅓ CUP (½ OZ/15 G) BASIL LEAVES

16 LARGE PLUM TOMATOES, CORED, CUT IN HALF LENGTHWISE, AND SEEDED

½ CUP (4 FL OZ/125 ML) EXTRA VIRGIN OLIVE OIL

⅓ CUP (1 OZ/30 G) DRY BREAD CRUMBS

SEA SALT

1 POUND (900 G) PENNE

1. Preheat the oven to 350°F (175°C). Oil two 13 x 9-inch (33 x 23-cm) baking pans.

2. Soak the capers in 3 changes of cold water to remove the salt. Drain and dry them with paper towels.

3. Combine the capers, garlic, and basil leaves on a cutting board and finely chop them. Arrange the tomatoes, cut side up, in the pans. Sprinkle the chopped mixture over the tomatoes. Drizzle with olive oil and sprinkle with the bread crumbs. Roast the tomatoes for 1 hour and 15 minutes, or until they are very soft, but still hold their shape.

4. Fill a very large pot (at least 8 quarts/8 liters) with water and bring it to a boil. Add salt to taste and stir in the penne. Cover the pot, just until it returns to a boil. Uncover and boil the penne until al dente. Drain and transfer to a large serving bowl. Spoon the tomatoes on top of the penne and toss. Serve immediately.

MAKES 4 SERVINGS

Involtini di Pollo

Stuffed Boneless Chicken Breasts in White Wine

The Baronessa uses small cubes of mozzarella di bufala *along with a veal forcemeat in this stuffing for these boneless chicken breasts.*

For the Forcemeat

4 OUNCES (120 G) GROUND VEAL

2 LARGE EGGS, LIGHTLY BEATEN

1 MEDIUM CLOVE OF GARLIC, FINELY CHOPPED

1 TABLESPOON CHOPPED ITALIAN FLAT-LEAF PARSLEY LEAVES

⅓ CUP (1½ OZ/45 G) FRESHLY GRATED PARMIGIANO-REGGIANO

¼ CUP (¾ OZ/25 G) DRY BREAD CRUMBS

SEA SALT AND FRESHLY GROUND BLACK PEPPER

2 OUNCES (60 G) FRESH MOZZARELLA

1½ OUNCES (45 G) IMPORTED ITALIAN PROSCIUTTO, THINLY SLICED

6 WHOLE SKINLESS, BONELESS CHICKEN BREASTS, (3½ LBS/1.6 K), HALVED AND FLATTENED

⅓ CUP (3 FL OZ/80 ML) EXTRA VIRGIN OLIVE OIL

UNBLEACHED ALL-PURPOSE FLOUR, FOR DREDGING

1 CUP (8 FL OZ/250 ML) DRY WHITE WINE

1 CUP (8 FL OZ/250 ML) CHICKEN BROTH (FOR HOMEMADE, SEE PAGE 187)

SEA SALT AND FRESHLY GROUND BLACK PEPPER

1. To make the forcemeat, combine the ground veal, eggs, garlic, parsley, Parmigiano, and bread crumbs in a bowl. Add salt and pepper and blend thoroughly. To be sure the mixture is properly seasoned, pinch off a small piece and heat it in a nonstick skillet until cooked through. Taste and adjust the seasoning, if necessary.

2. Cut the mozzarella and prosciutto into 12 equal pieces each and set aside. Arrange the chicken breasts, skin side down, on a large work surface. Mound equal amounts of the veal mixture onto the center of each piece. Top with 1 piece each of mozzarella and prosciutto. Roll up the chicken, tuck in the ends to enclose the filling, and fasten with toothpicks or tie with butcher's twine.

3. Heat the olive oil in a heavy sauté pan large enough to hold the *involtini* in 1 layer over medium heat. When the oil is hot, lightly dredge half of the involtini in flour and add them to the pan. Brown on all sides, then transfer to a platter. Cook the remaining involtini in the same way and remove them from the pan. Pour the white wine into the pan and bring it to a boil. Cook the wine at a brisk simmer until it is reduced by half. Return the involtini to the pan along with any juice that has accumulated on the platter. Add the broth and season with salt and pepper to taste. Cover and simmer the involtini for 30 minutes, turning the pieces occasionally. Transfer the involtini to a serving platter and remove the toothpicks. If desired, the sauce can be reduced slightly to thicken it. Taste the sauce for additional seasoning and spoon it over the involtini. Serve immediately.

MAKES 6 SERVINGS

CLOCKWISE FROM LEFT, Ciambotta, *a Neopolitan version of ratatouille. A wagon loaded with hay for feeding the buffalo.* Penne con Pomodoro al Gratin. *Picking ladders in the orchard. The Baronessa lines a pan with pastry dough for her Pizza Rustica. Stuffed fried zucchini blossoms.*

Neapolitan cuisine is dominated by fresh vegetables that reach great heights in flavor.

Ciambotta
Vegetable Stew

A Neapolitan version of ratatouille, called ciambotta, *uses golden-fleshed potatoes in place of zucchini. The vegetable mélange is fragranced with dried oregano and fresh basil. Serve it as an antipasto or as a vegetable side dish.*

1 SMALL ONION, SLICED

1 MEDIUM CLOVE OF GARLIC, CRUSHED

¼ CUP (2 FL OZ/60 ML) EXTRA VIRGIN OLIVE OIL

¾ POUND (350 G) YUKON GOLD POTATOES, PEELED
    AND CUT INTO ¾-INCH (2-CM) CHUNKS

1 POUND (450 G) EGGPLANT, PEELED AND CUT INTO 1-INCH
    (2.5-CM) CHUNKS

1 RED BELL PEPPER, CORED, SEEDED, AND CUT INTO 1½-INCH
    (3.8-CM) PIECES

1 YELLOW BELL PEPPER, CORED, SEEDED, AND CUT INTO
    1½-INCH (3.8-CM) PIECES

3 LARGE PLUM TOMATOES, PEELED, CORED,
    AND COARSELY CHOPPED

½ TEASPOON DRIED OREGANO

3 MEDIUM BASIL LEAVES, TORN INTO SMALL PIECES

SEA SALT AND FRESHLY GROUND BLACK PEPPER

1. Sauté the onion and garlic in the olive oil in a large heavy sauté pan over medium heat. When the onion becomes translucent, add the potatoes, eggplant, and peppers. Increase the heat to high and cook the vegetables, tossing frequently, until the potatoes begin to brown. Stir in the tomatoes and oregano. Scatter the basil over the vegetables, toss, and season with salt and pepper to taste. Cover the pan and simmer for 45 to 50 minutes, stirring occasionally, or until the vegetables are tender. Serve hot or at room temperature.

MAKES 6 SERVINGS

Fagiolini con Prosciutto Cotto, *ABOVE.*
Peaches in Tenuta Seliano's orchard, *RIGHT.*

Fagiolini con Prosciutto Cotto
Sautéed Green Beans with Ham

The Baronessa sautés summer green beans with prosciutto cotto, *a mildly seasoned boneless ham produced near the city of Parma. Prosciutto cotto, which comes either roasted or steamed, can be found in Italian markets.*

1½ POUNDS (675 G) GREEN BEANS OR HARICOTS VERTS, TRIMMED

SEA SALT AND FRESHLY GROUND BLACK PEPPER

¼ CUP (2 FL OZ/60 ML) EXTRA VIRGIN OLIVE OIL

2 MEDIUM CLOVES OF GARLIC, THINLY SLICED

¼ POUND (125 G) IMPORTED ITALIAN PROSCIUTTO COTTO OR OTHER
    MILD COOKED HAM, SLICED ¼-INCH (0.6-CM) THICK AND CUT
    INTO ¼-INCH (0.6-CM) DICE

1. If the beans are very long, cut them in half. Fill a large pot (at least 6 quarts/6 liters) with water and bring it to a rapid boil. Add salt to taste. Stir in the beans and boil 4 to 6 minutes or just until tender. Drain in a colander, refresh under cold water, then drain again.

2. Heat the olive oil in a large skillet over medium heat. Add the garlic and sauté until golden. Add the ham and increase the heat to medium-high. Sauté, stirring constantly, for 2 minutes. Add the green beans, season with salt and pepper to taste, and toss just until they are heated through.

MAKES 6 SERVINGS

Crema Malakoff

Summer Trifle with Fresh Fruit

The many influences on the culture of Campania over the centuries, including Greek, Roman, French, Spanish, and Moorish, are reflected in the cuisine. Crema Malakoff is based on a classic French dessert called Charlotte Malakoff. *The French version is a towering molded creation made with ladyfingers, almond buttercream, and strawberries. The Neapolitan rendition takes the form of a trifle filled with fruit salad. The Baronessa uses summer fruit grown in her orchards; any mixture of seasonal fruit is suggested.*

For the Sponge Cake

 6 LARGE EGGS, SEPARATED

 ¾ CUP (5 OZ/150 G) SUGAR

 1¼ CUPS (5 OZ/150 G) UNBLEACHED ALL-PURPOSE FLOUR

For the Pastry Cream

 2 CUPS (16 FL OZ/500 ML) WHOLE MILK

 3 LARGE EGG YOLKS

 ½ CUP (3½ OZ/100 G) SUGAR

 ⅓ CUP (1½ OZ/45 G) UNBLEACHED ALL-PURPOSE FLOUR

 1 TABLESPOON DRY MARSALA WINE

For the Fruit Salad

 5 CUPS (2 LBS/900 G) MIXED SUMMER FRUIT, SUCH AS APRICOTS, BERRIES, CHERRIES, NECTARINES, PEACHES, AND STRAWBERRIES

 2 TABLESPOONS SUPERFINE SUGAR, OR TO TASTE

 2½ TABLESPOONS MARASCHINO LIQUEUR OR KIRSCH

To Assemble the Crema Malakoff

 1½ CUPS (12 FL OZ/375 ML) HEAVY CREAM

 3 TABLESPOONS SUPERFINE SUGAR

 1 TEASPOON VANILLA EXTRACT

 STRAWBERRIES, FOR GARNISH (OPTIONAL)

1. To make the sponge cake, preheat the oven to 350°F (175°C). Butter a 10-inch (25-cm) round cake pan and line the bottom with a round of parchment paper. Butter the paper and lightly dust the pan with flour.

2. Beat the egg yolks and sugar in a large bowl with an electric mixer at high speed until they are thick and lemony in color. Wash and dry the beaters. In another clean large bowl, beat the egg whites at medium speed until they are stiff but not dry. Using a large rubber spatula, fold both the egg whites and the flour into the egg yolk mixture, one third at a time, adding the flour through a sieve. Be careful not to overblend. Pour the batter into the cake pan and bake it on the center shelf of the oven for 30 to 35 minutes, or until the cake has pulled away from the sides of the pan and a toothpick inserted into the center comes out clean. Transfer the cake to a cooling rack for 15 minutes, then unmold onto the rack and cool completely. (The cake can be made the day before.)

3. To make the pastry cream, heat the milk in a large heavy saucepan over medium-low heat until scalded. While the milk is heating, whisk together the egg yolks and sugar in a large bowl. Add the flour and stir until it is completely dissolved. Slowly whisk one third of the scalded milk into the egg yolk mixture. Add the remaining milk all at once and blend thoroughly. Pour the mixture back into the saucepan and return it to the heat. Stir constantly until the pastry cream has thickened. Turn off the heat, stir in the Marsala wine and continue to stir for 1 minute. Pour the pastry cream into a bowl and smooth the top with a rubber spatula. Place a buttered round of wax paper on the surface to prevent a skin from forming. When cool, cover the bowl with plastic wrap, and refrigerate. (The pastry cream can be made the day before.)

4. To make the fruit salad, prepare the fruit by removing the stones from the apricots, nectarines and peaches. Cut them into ½-inch (1.25-cm) pieces. Halve and pit the cherries. Hull strawberries; leave very small ones whole, and cut larger ones in half or in wedges. Leave other berries whole. Place the fruit in a large bowl and toss with the sugar and maraschino liqueur or kirsch. Let stand for 30 minutes, tossing occasionally.

5. When ready to assemble the *Crema Malakoff*, slice the sponge cake into ⅜-inch-thick (1-cm-thick) slices, as you would slice a loaf of bread. Line the bottom and sides of a 2½-quart (2.5-liter) trifle bowl or serving bowl with three quarters of the cake slices. Drizzle the cake with juice from the fruit salad.

6. Beat the heavy cream with the sugar and vanilla until it is stiff. Fold ½ cup (2 oz/60 g) of the whipped cream into the pastry cream and refrigerate the remaining. Spoon two thirds of the lightened pastry cream into the trifle bowl and spread it to coat the sponge cake, leaving a hollow well in the center of the bowl. Using a slotted spoon, fill the well with the fruit salad, reserving the juice. Spread the remaining pastry cream over the top of the fruit salad, then cover with the remaining cake slices. Drizzle the cake with the reserved juice from the fruit salad.

7. Spread half of the remaining whipped cream over the cake and smooth it with a spatula. Prepare a pastry bag with a fluted decorating tip and fill the bag with the remaining whipped cream. Pipe decorative rosettes on the whipped cream and garnish with strawberries, if desired.

MAKES 12 SERVINGS

SERRA GAMBETTA

The sunny region of Apulia is distinctly reminiscent of Greece. It was once part of the ancient Greek settlements of Magna Graecia. The flat terrain framed by over four hundred miles of coastline forms the heel of the Italian boot. Apulia is virtually a boundless garden with olive trees, vineyards, wheat fields, almond trees, and extraordinarily flavorful vegetables and fruit.

Signora Perna Lanera and her son Domenico established a guesthouse on their farm in the countryside of Castellana-Grotte, a peaceful inland village in the Apulian province of Bari, just a short distance from their home in town. They converted a nineteenth-century country villa along with several smaller structures that once served as storage rooms and barns into small apartments and suites. Each apartment was outfitted with a small kitchen and provided with the necessary equipment for guests to do their own cooking. The Laneras call their agricultural retreat Serra Gambetta, a name the Signora's husband discovered on an old military map of the region. *Gambetta* is believed to be a kind of wild olive tree that once flourished in the area.

Apulia abounds with twisted old olive trees, ABOVE, that reach impressive proportions and shapes. The Signora's lemon cream, OPPOSITE, served with seasonal fruit from the orchards at Serra Gambetta.

Castellana-Grotte

The Signora is extremely passionate about Apulia and feels strongly that through food one can learn a lot about a culture—the people, the climate, the agriculture, and the economy. She would often instruct her guests (many were tourists from Switzerland, Germany, and Austria, or Italians from the northern or central regions) about *la cucina pugliese*. She would offer personal cooking tips, conduct cooking classes in their rooms, accompany them on trips to outdoor markets, even offer samples of local dishes she prepared at home. It should then come as no surprise that when the Signora was approached by a young family to provide them with meals during their stay, she enthusiastically agreed and has done so for others ever since.

Domenico built his mother a spacious kitchen in the villa and an outdoor wood-burning oven to bake bread and pizza in summer. Though the Signora's kitchen is equipped with a small gas stove, most of her cooking, regardless of the season, is done in a modest *caminetto,* or fireplace, constructed of limestone, a traditional means of cooking in Apulia. She often uses a terra-cotta casserole called a *tiella*. The Signora layers ingredients in the tiella—sometimes using fish, meat, or vegetables but always including yellow-fleshed potatoes—seasoning each layer and topping it with grated pecorino cheese or dry bread crumbs. The covered tiella is set over glowing embers in the caminetto and covered with a protective copper lid. Embers are then placed on the lid. The Signora calls this a *forno di campagna*, or country oven. Very often a tiella includes layers of rice, and some food historians believe that the tiella, which is also the name of the preparation, was introduced by the Spanish during their rule and that it is related to paella, a dish made with rice that is also composed in layers.

Another terra-cotta vessel the Signora often uses is a jug for cooking beans in the caminetto. Because it resembles a *pigna,* or pine cone, it is called a *pignata,* or *pignatello* if small. The Signora measures the beans by turning the pignata on its side, filling the pot-belly of the jug with a generous mound of beans. She then turns it upright and adds a clove of garlic, a small piece of celery, and a couple of cherry tomatoes, and water up to its neck. She covers the pignata with a tin lid and rests it beside a small pile of burning embers, where it simmers sluggishly for three or four hours until the beans have become soft and creamy. The Signora displays her pignata collection on a shelf above the caminetto.

The caminetto is also utilized for grilling fish, meat, and vegetables, as well as for deep-frying—a black iron skillet filled with olive oil is rested on a *trepiedi*, an iron tripod, over the burning fire. The Signora uses her outdoor oven for slow-roasting meats that have been raised on local farms.

Fish and seafood figure measurably in Apulia, but vegetables are the backbone of its cuisine. Summer vegetables lend themselves to countless cold or warm antipasto preparations. The Signora creates a saucy condiment with cherry tomatoes, snipped fresh herbs, and olive oil to serve with

crusty bread; she accompanies a mound of sheep's milk ricotta with chunks of tomatoes, cucumbers, and olives; she stuffs *crespelle*, or crepes, with vegetable fillings that change with the seasons; and she uses Swiss chard leaves, a common stand-in for spinach, as wrappers, stuffing them with a ricotta and chard filling.

When vegetables are served with pasta, the Signora precooks them and either sautés them with garlic, olive oil, and red chili pepper or simmers them in a light tomato-based sauce. She often prepares *cavatelli*, a typical Apulian pasta, to serve with her vegetable sauces. The pasta is made in a large wooden trough called a *tavoliere*. The Signora's tavoliere, which she also uses for making bread and pizza, dates back more than a century—handed down by her mother-in-law. The dough for the cavatelli is made inside the trough, then shaped and cut on a broad ledge that extends over one side.

Secondo piatto, the second course, could include vegetables combined with fish or meat, and vegetables are, of course, served as *contorni*, or side dishes. The Signora prepares a characteristic vegetarian Apulian dish made from puréed fava beans blended with wild bitter chicory. When she adds pan-seared sweet or hot frying peppers and cherry tomatoes it becomes a substantial secondo piatto. A bowl of black olives and sliced red onions are always served alongside. *Purè di Fave* can also be eaten as a warm antipasto, or as a *primo piatto*, before the meat, fish, or poultry course; or as a side dish, or *contorno*.

At times, crisp raw vegetables appear after the meal as a refreshing digestivo. When something sweet is desired, the magnificent summer orchard fruit at Serra Gambetta is difficult to resist—cherries, peaches, nectarines, and juicy sun-ripened apricots—for which the Signora frequently provides a lemon-infused crema, or custardy cream sauce, as an enrichment.

It is no wonder the Signora describes herself as a mother to her guests. Like a mother, she is always concerned that they are happy, comfortable, and above all, well fed.

Vegetables in Apulia are the backbone of the cuisine. Domenico supplies his mother with an unending collection from their fields. He grows a variety of leafy greens, BELOW, as well as fava beans, tomatoes, and peas, just to name a few. The long growing season in the south allows for several harvests, providing Italy with fresh vegetables through most of the year.

Almonds maturing on the branch, ABOVE. The Signora makes cavatelli in her wooden tavoliere, RIGHT. Ancient local structures of stacked stone called trulli, BELOW RIGHT, are found throughout the region. The Signora at a local market, BELOW.

Aperitivo di Limone

Lemon Aperitif

Guests at Serra Gambetta are often greeted at the table with an icy cold aperitivo prepared with white wine and freshly squeezed lemon juice to sip with antipasti.

1 BOTTLE (750 ML) DRY WHITE WINE

3 HEAPING TABLESPOONS SUPERFINE SUGAR

ZEST OF 2 LEMONS, EACH CUT IN ONE LONG STRIP

JUICE OF 2 LEMONS

1. Combine the white wine, sugar, lemon zest, and lemon juice in a large pitcher. Stir until the sugar is completely dissolved. Refrigerate for at least 4 hours.

2. Remove and discard the lemon zest. Fill the pitcher with 1½ cups ice and serve the *aperitivo* in chilled small wine glasses.

MAKES 8 SERVINGS

Salsa di Pomodorini

Cherry Tomato Sauce

Apulian cherry tomatoes, called pomodorini, are sweet and fleshy. The Signora combines the tomatoes with scallion, fresh herbs from the garden, and Apulian olive oil to make a condiment served with crusty bread or toasts.

1 PINT (20 OZ/600 G) CHERRY TOMATOES

1 SCALLION, WHITE AND LIGHT GREEN PART ONLY, TRIMMED

1 TABLESPOON FINELY CHOPPED MIXED FRESH HERB LEAVES, SUCH
  AS BASIL, MARJORAM, OREGANO, PARSLEY, AND THYME

3 TABLESPOONS EXTRA VIRGIN OLIVE OIL

SEA SALT

1. Cut the tomatoes in half crosswise and discard the seeds. Coarsely chop the tomatoes and transfer them to a small bowl.

2. Chop the scallion and add it to the tomatoes. Add the herbs and olive oil and season with salt to taste. Toss and let stand for 10 minutes before serving.

MAKES 1½ CUPS (12 FL OZ/375 ML)

Salsa di Pomodorini *can be served as antipasto or a light afternoon snack.*

Bietole Ripiene

Stuffed Swiss Chard

Vegetables serve as the foundation of the Apulian cuisine and there is no shortage of creative preparations. The Signora stuffs Swiss chard leaves with a ricotta filling made with additional leaves and the leftover stems. This dish can be prepared several hours ahead then baked just before serving.

1 POUND (450 G) SMALL SWISS CHARD LEAVES, TRIMMED AND
  WELL WASHED

SEA SALT AND FRESHLY GROUND BLACK PEPPER

1⅓ CUPS (10 OZ/300 G) RICOTTA

1 LARGE EGG, LIGHTLY BEATEN

⅓ CUP (1½ OZ/45 G) PLUS 2 TABLESPOONS GRATED PECORINO
  ROMANO

2 TABLESPOONS CHOPPED ITALIAN FLAT-LEAF PARSLEY LEAVES

1. Preheat the oven to 400°F (200°C). Butter a 13 x 9-inch (33 x 23-cm) baking pan.

2. Trim and reserve the stems from the 12 largest Swiss chard leaves. Fill a large pot (at least 6 quarts/6 liters) with water and bring it to a rapid boil. Add salt to taste and stir in the leaves. Boil for 3 minutes, or just until the leaves become flexible. Using a skimmer or slotted spoon, transfer the leaves to a colander, refresh under cold water, and drain. Keep the water boiling. Gently squeeze the Swiss chard to eliminate all of the water. Be careful not to tear the leaves. Dry them on paper towels and set aside.

3. Trim the stems from the remaining Swiss chard leaves. Cut all of the stems, including the reserved stems, into 2-inch (5-cm) lengths and cook them in the boiling water for 5 minutes. Add the leaves and cook for 2 minutes more. Drain the Swiss chard in a colander, refresh it under cold water, and drain again. Squeeze the Swiss

chard to eliminate all of the water, pat it dry with paper towels, and finely chop. Transfer to a large bowl and add the ricotta, egg, ⅓ cup (1½ oz/45 g) pecorino, parsley, and salt and pepper to taste.

4. Spread open the large Swiss chard leaves and arrange them on a work surface so that the flat side of the center rib is facing up. Mound equal amounts of the filling ½ inch (1.25 cm) from the tip end of each leaf. Fold the sides in to cover the filling. Roll the leaves toward the stem end. Arrange the stuffed swiss chard, seam side down, in the baking pan. Sprinkle with 2 tablespoons pecorino and freshly ground black pepper to taste. Bake for 25 to 30 minutes, or until puffed and lightly golden. Let stand for 10 minutes before serving.

MAKES 6 SERVINGS

Fagottini di Verdure

Crepes Stuffed with Zucchini and Squash Blossoms

Crepes, called crespelle *in Italian, are filled with all sorts of seasonal vegetable stuffings in Apulia. These plump little bundles, known as* fagottini, *are served as antipasto. The Signora cooks zucchini in a covered pot with a bit of onion, olive oil, and water for at least forty minutes. The result is pure essence of zucchini. As the Signora notes, "The most important ingredient in the kitchen is patience!"*

For the Crepes

- 2 LARGE EGGS
- ½ CUP (4 FL OZ/125 ML) WHOLE MILK
- ½ TEASPOON SEA SALT
- 1 CUP (4 OZ/120 G) UNBLEACHED ALL-PURPOSE FLOUR
- 3 TABLESPOONS (1½ FL OZ/45 ML) EXTRA VIRGIN OLIVE OIL PLUS ADDITIONAL FOR OILING THE PAN

For the Filling

- 1 LARGE ONION, THINLY SLICED
- 3 MEDIUM ZUCCHINI (9 OZ/250 G), TRIMMED AND CUT INTO ½-INCH (1.25-CM) DICE
- 2½ TABLESPOONS (1¼ FL OZ/40 ML) EXTRA VIRGIN OLIVE OIL
- SEA SALT
- 6 OUNCES (180 G) SQUASH BLOSSOMS
- ⅓ CUP (1½ OZ/45 G) PLUS 1½ TABLESPOONS GRATED PECORINO ROMANO
- 3 TABLESPOONS DRY BREAD CRUMBS
- 1 TABLESPOON CHOPPED ITALIAN FLAT-LEAF PARSLEY LEAVES

1. To make the crepes, whisk together the eggs, milk, and salt in a large bowl. Stir in the flour and beat until the mixture is smooth. Blend in ⅔ cup (5½ fl oz/165 ml) water and the olive oil. Let rest for 1 hour.

2. Use an 8-inch (20-cm) seasoned crepe pan or a nonstick skillet. If using a crepe pan, coat the bottom with a thin layer of olive oil. Heat over medium-low heat. When hot, remove the pan from the heat and let it cool. Wipe out the excess oil with a paper towel, leaving just a light film. It will not be necessary to oil the pan between each crepe. If using a nonstick skillet, just oil it lightly before making the first crepe.

3. Stir an additional ⅓ cup (3 fl oz/80 ml) water into the batter. Reheat the pan over medium-low heat. When hot, pour in a scant ¼ cup (2 fl oz/60 ml) of batter and rotate the pan to evenly coat the bottom. The crepe should be very lacy. When the bottom of the crepe is golden, flip it, using a long, thin metal spatula. Cook the underside, just until it is set. Transfer the crepe to a large plate and continue making crepes, using all of the batter. You should have 16 crepes. If not using immediately, stack the crepes on a plate with sheets of wax paper in between. Cover the plate with plastic wrap and refrigerate.

4. To make the filling, combine the onion, zucchini, 1½ tablespoons olive oil, and ⅓ cup (3 fl oz/80 ml) water. Season with salt to taste. Cover the pan and cook for 40 to 45 minutes, or until all of the liquid has cooked out and the zucchini is practically puréed. Remove the pan from the heat and let cool.

5. Remove the stems and stamens from the squash blossoms. Rinse the blossoms by dipping them in a bowl of cold water. Lift them out of the water to drain and transfer them to a small heavy saucepan with only the water that clings to them. Add the remaining 1 tablespoon olive oil and ¼ teaspoon salt. Cover the pan and cook the blossoms over low heat for 30 minutes. Uncover the pan and snip the blossoms with kitchen shears to coarsely chop them. Continue to cook the blossoms, uncovered, until all the liquid in the pan has evaporated. Remove the pan from the heat and let cool.

6. Combine the zucchini and blossoms in a large bowl. Mash with a fork to make a coarse purée. Add ⅓ cup (1½ oz/45 g) pecorino, the bread crumbs, and parsley. Blend the mixture and season to taste.

7. Preheat the oven to 400°F (200°C). Oil a 13 x 9-inch (33 x 23-cm) baking pan.

8. Arrange the crepes, browned side down, on a work surface. Spoon filling into the center of each, dividing evenly. Fold 2 opposite sides of each crepe toward the center to cover and completely encase the filling. Fold in the other 2 sides. Arrange the stuffed crepes, seam side down, in the baking pan. Sprinkle with the remaining 1½ tablespoons pecorino. Bake for 25 to 30 minutes, or until the crepes are heated through and the cheese is golden.

MAKES 6 SERVINGS

FOLLOWING PAGES, Fagottini di Verdure.

In Apulia, *crespelle* are filled with all sorts of vegetable stuffings.

Purè di Fave con Peperoni e Pomodorini

Fava Bean and Chicory Purée with Frying Peppers and Cherry Tomatoes

This purée of fava beans is perhaps the best loved dish of Apulia. The dried beans simmer slowly for more than four hours. Precooked chicory or dandelion greens are stirred into the purée along with small chunks of dried bread that act as a thickener. In summer the purée is served with pan-seared frying peppers and cherry tomatoes. Be sure to use split dried fava beans, which have already been skinned. They can be found at Italian or Middle Eastern markets.

1   POUND (450 G) DRIED SPLIT FAVA BEANS, SOAKED OVERNIGHT IN
    COLD WATER TO COVER BY 2 INCHES (5 CM)

SEA SALT

2   TABLESPOONS (1 FL OZ/30 ML) EXTRA VIRGIN OLIVE OIL

8   OUNCES (240 G) ITALIAN CHICORY OR DANDELION GREENS,
    TRIMMED AND WELL WASHED

1   SLICE SLIGHTLY DRY FIRM-TEXTURED, COUNTRY-STYLE BREAD
    (FOR PANE TOSCANO, SEE PAGE 78), TORN INTO SMALL PIECES

¾   POUND (375 G) RED OR GREEN SWEET FRYING PEPPERS

1   PINT (10 OZ/300 G) CHERRY TOMATOES

1. Drain the beans and transfer them to a large pot. Fill the pot with cold water to cover the beans by 2 inches (5 cm). Add 1 teaspoon salt and bring to a boil. Reduce the heat and simmer the beans, uncovered, for 4 hours, stirring occasionally. After the first 3 hours, add 1 tablespoon of the olive oil. As the mixture thickens, stir more frequently. If it becomes too thick and begins to stick to the bottom of the pot, add some water.

2. Fill a medium pot (at least 4 quarts/4 liters) with water and bring it to a boil. Add salt to taste and stir in the chicory. Boil just until tender, 3 to 5 minutes. Drain in a colander, refresh under cold water, and drain again. Squeeze the chicory to eliminate all of the water and coarsely chop.

3. After 4 hours of cooking, the fava beans will have the consistency of a coarse purée. Add the chicory and the bread. Stir over very low heat until the bread is blended smoothly into the purée. Season to taste.

4. Leave the peppers whole. Cut 2 parallel slashes across the middle of each pepper to prevent it from bursting as it cooks. Heat the remaining 1 tablespoon olive oil in a large skillet over high heat. Add the peppers and sear them on 1 side then turn with tongs and sear the other side. Season with salt to taste and transfer to a platter. Add

the cherry tomatoes to the skillet and sear them while rolling them in the pan. Season with salt and transfer to the platter with the peppers.

5. Spoon the purée into a large serving bowl and serve it with the peppers and cherry tomatoes.

MAKES 4 TO 6 SERVINGS

Note: Leftover *purè di fave* can be made into a large pancake. Slice a small onion and sauté it with 1 tablespoon olive oil in a medium nonstick skillet. When the onion is tender, add the leftover purée and flatten it with the back of a spatula into the shape of a pancake. Brown the pancake over low heat then flip it over and brown the other side. Serve immediately while hot.

Cavatelli con Fagiolini

Cavatelli with Green Beans and Tomatoes

The vegetable sauce the Signora serves with her handmade cavatelli requires a minimum of preparation. It begins with a simmering brew of tomatoes, olive oil, basil, and a dash of sea salt. Precooked green beans are tossed in close to the end. Nearly any vegetable can be used: zucchini, peas, cauliflower, or arugula.

When cutting and shaping the cavatelli *it is important to keep the pieces uniform. Take it slowly at the start, speed will come with practice. If time does not allow for a handmade pasta, a good quality imported dry pasta can be used with this sauce—orecchiette, also typical of Apulia, penne, or ziti.*

For the Pasta

6   CUPS (26 OZ/720 G) UNBLEACHED ALL-PURPOSE FLOUR

1½ CUPS (12 FL OZ/375 ML) WATER

For the Sauce

8   OUNCES (240 G) SLENDER GREEN BEANS OR HARICOTS VERTS,
    TRIMMED

2½ POUNDS (1.1 K) FRESH PLUM TOMATOES, PEELED, CORED,
    AND COARSELY CHOPPED

2   TABLESPOONS (1 FL OZ/30 ML) EXTRA VIRGIN OLIVE OIL

6   MEDIUM BASIL LEAVES, TORN INTO SMALL PIECES

SEA SALT

½   CUP (2 OZ/160 G) GRATED PARMIGIANO-REGGIANO PLUS
    ADDITIONAL FOR SERVING

1. To make the pasta dough for the *cavatelli*, use the flour and 1½ cups (12 fl oz/375 ml) water as directed on page 188, the section entitled Making the Dough. Knead the dough entirely by hand until it is smooth and very firm, about 15 minutes. It is not necessary to use all

Purè di fave, LEFT, served with pan-seared frying peppers and cherry tomatoes. Raw onions and olives are traditional accompaniments. BELOW, the Signora demonstrates her technique for shaping cavatelli.

of the flour. The remaining flour will be used when shaping the cavatelli. Flour the dough lightly, wrap it in a cotton kitchen towel and let it rest for 10 minutes.

2. Line 2 trays or baking sheets with cotton kitchen towels and lightly dust them with flour.

3. Cut off a small piece of the dough. Keep the unused portion wrapped in the towel. Roll the dough, by hand on the unfloured pastry board, into a rope ½ inch (1.25 cm) thick. Lightly flour the rope and cut it into small nuggets ½ inch (1.25 cm) long. Dust the nuggets with flour and toss. To shape the pasta into cavatelli, gently press each nugget with your thumb to flatten slightly and drag the pasta away from you. The dough should curl up around your thumb like a sea shell. Try to keep the cavatelli uniform in size and thickness so they cook evenly. Transfer the cavatelli to the towel-lined trays and dust with flour. Continue to make cavatelli using the remaining dough. Cover with cotton towels until they are ready to be cooked.

4. To prepare the sauce, cut the green beans into 2-inch (5-cm) pieces. Fill a large saucepan with water and bring it to a boil. Add salt to taste. Stir in the beans and boil for 4 to 6 minutes, or just until tender. Drain in a colander, refresh under cold water, and drain again.

5. Combine the tomatoes, olive oil, basil and ¼ teaspoon salt in a sauté pan large enough to hold all of the pasta. Simmer, uncovered, for 30 minutes. Add the green beans and cook just until heated through. Taste for seasoning.

6. Fill a very large pot (at least 8 quarts/8 liters) with water and bring it to a rapid boil. Add salt to taste. Stir in the cavatelli and cover the pot just until the water returns to a boil. Uncover and boil the cavatelli for 8 to 10 minutes, or until al dente. Drain, reserving some of the water. Transfer the cavatelli to the sauté pan and toss with the sauce over low heat. If the cavatelli seem dry, add some of the reserved cooking water. Sprinkle with ½ cup (2 oz/60 g) Parmigiano and toss just until melted. Transfer to a large serving bowl and serve immediately. Serve the cavatelli with a small bowl of Parmigiano for sprinkling.

MAKES 6 SERVINGS

Calamari in Tiella
Stuffed Squid Braised with Potatoes and Onions

A traditional Apulian layered casserole called a tiella combines potatoes with vegetables, meat, or fish in a covered terra-cotta cooking vessel that bears the same name. In this one the Signora stuffs squid with a piquant bread stuffing. As an alternative, use 1½ pounds of thick-fleshed fish, such as cod, cut into 1 inch-thick chunks. Sprinkle the top with dry bread crumbs instead of pecorino.

For the Stuffing
- 1½ CUPS (5 OZ/150 G) SLIGHTLY DRY FIRM-TEXTURED, COUNTRY-STYLE BREAD (FOR PANE TOSCANO, SEE PAGE 78), CRUSTS REMOVED, TORN INTO SMALL PIECES
- 2 LARGE EGGS, LIGHTLY BEATEN
- 1 SMALL CLOVE OF GARLIC, FINELY CHOPPED
- ⅓ CUP (1½ OZ/45 G) GRATED PECORINO ROMANO
- 1 TABLESPOON CHOPPED ITALIAN FLAT-LEAF PARSLEY LEAVES
- SMALL PINCH OF BAKING SODA
- SEA SALT AND FRESHLY GROUND BLACK PEPPER

- 12 MEDIUM SQUID (1½ TO 2 LBS/675 TO 900 G), 4 TO 5 INCHES (10 TO 13 CM) LONG, CLEANED, WITH TENTACLES
- 1 MEDIUM ONION, SLICED ¼ INCH (0.6 CM) THICK
- 1 MEDIUM CLOVE OF GARLIC UNPEELED
- 2 LARGE PLUM TOMATOES, CORED, SEEDED, AND COARSELY CHOPPED
- 1 TABLESPOON COARSELY CHOPPED ITALIAN FLAT-LEAF PARSLEY
- SEA SALT AND FRESHLY GROUND BLACK PEPPER
- 1 POUND (450 G) YUKON GOLD OR RUSSET POTATOES, PEELED AND SLICED ⅜ INCH (1 CM) THICK
- 1 SMALL HOT RED CHILI PEPPER, COARSELY CHOPPED
- ⅓ CUP (1½ OZ/45 G) GRATED PECORINO ROMANO
- 3 TABLESPOONS (1½ FL OZ/45 ML) EXTRA VIRGIN OLIVE OIL
- SPRIGS OF ITALIAN FLAT-LEAF PARSLEY, FOR GARNISH (OPTIONAL)

1. To make the stuffing, soak the bread in a small bowl of warm water for 5 minutes. Drain and squeeze dry. Blend the bread with the eggs, garlic, pecorino, parsley, and baking soda in a small bowl. Season with salt and black pepper.

2. Stuff the squid with the stuffing mixture. Fill them only halfway. The filling will expand when cooked. Seal the open end of the squid with toothpicks.

3. Arrange the onion, garlic, tomatoes, and parsley in a 3-quart (3-liter) round flameproof terra-cotta casserole at least 8½ inches (22 cm) in diameter or in an enameled cast-iron pot. Season with salt and pepper to taste. Pour 3 tablespoons of water into the casserole. Cover with the potato slices, slightly overlapping, and sprinkle with the chili pepper and additional salt and pepper. Arrange the stuffed squid and the tentacles on top. Sprinkle with pecorino and drizzle with olive oil. Cover and simmer slowly over low heat for 1 hour. Check the casserole occasionally to be sure it remains at a slow simmer. Garnish with sprigs of parsley, if desired, and serve immediately.

MAKES 4 SERVINGS

Note: If you do not have a flameproof terra-cotta casserole or an enamel-lined cast-iron pot, you can use any baking pan of the same capacity and dimensions. Bake, tightly covered, in a preheated 375°F (190°C) oven for 1 hour.

Crema di Latte
Lemon-infused Cream Sauce

The Signora serves fresh summer fruit with a custardy cream sauce that absorbs its flavor from the zest of a lemon. Any orchard fruit or berry would be appropriate in summer, poached pears or sliced oranges in fall or winter.

- 5 LARGE EGG YOLKS
- ¾ CUP (5 OZ/150 G) SUGAR
- ¾ CUP (3 OZ/90 G) UNBLEACHED ALL-PURPOSE FLOUR
- 1 QUART (1 LITER) WHOLE MILK
- ZEST OF 1 LEMON, CUT IN 1 LONG STRIP
- ⅛ TEASPOON GROUND CINNAMON

1. Pass the yolks through a sieve into a large heavy saucepan. Add the sugar and blend with a wire whisk. Add the flour and stir until it is completely dissolved. Slowly pour in the milk and stir vigorously until the mixture is smooth. Add the lemon zest and cook, stirring constantly, over low heat until the sauce has thickened, about 20 minutes.

2. Pour the sauce into a bowl. Remove the lemon zest and smooth the top with a rubber spatula. Place a buttered round of wax paper on the surface to prevent a skin from forming. When cool, cover the bowl with plastic wrap and refrigerate.

3. Remove the sauce from the refrigerator 15 minutes before serving. Pour it into a serving bowl or pitcher. Sprinkle with cinnamon and serve with fresh summer fruit and berries.

MAKES 5 CUPS (40 FL OZ/1200 ML)

Calamari in Tiella, *OPPOSITE.*

SANTA CATERINA

Chef Cuomo, ABOVE, grills fresh
fish at the open-air dining
room. The terraced lemon groves
of the Hotel Santa Caterina,
OPPOSITE, hug the side of the
cliff and are supported by
an intricate system of wooden
supports. Fruit, vegetables,
and herbs are interplanted with
the lemon trees.

The Amalfi coast in Italy's southern region of Campania is a continuous string of magnificent shorelines, picturesque fishing villages, and secluded inlets. Its beauty and splendor have captivated and lured artists, writers, and count-less romantics for centuries. The perilous twists and turns of the Amalfi drive, the road that hugs the shore, are infamous, and as the drive nears the compact resort city of Amalfi, the spectacle becomes even more dramatic. Jagged cliffs rise boldly from the shimmering azure waters and the village—clusters of white and ochre-toned buildings, arcades, and church towers—climbs up to the mountains and cascades down to the sea.

Gracefully crowning one of the precipitous cliffs is Amalfi's most esteemed hotel, the Santa Caterina. The original structure, built in 1880 by Giuseppe Gambardella, was redesigned and converted into a six-room guesthouse by his son, Crescenzo, shortly after the turn of the century. Nearly one hundred years later Hotel Santa Caterina remains a family-run establishment, presided over by Giuseppe's granddaughters, Giuseppina and Carmela Gambardella, who have elevated the hotel to grand luxury status, with seventy guestrooms, suites, and cottages.

The Santa Caterina is situated in an enviable position gazing across the Gulf of Salerno. Lush terraced gardens and lemon groves provide the restaurant kitchen with a profusion of sun-drenched ingredients, which are used to create dishes typical of Campania's coastal region. Olive trees flourish high in the cliffs among cherry, fig, and mandarin orange trees; tomato vines; cultivated and wild herbs; and plantings of eggplant, zucchini, green beans, potatoes, and lettuce. The kitchens of Amalfi have been blessed with great resources provided by these terraced gardens, by the plenitude of the sea, and by the fine dairy products produced in the nearby mountains and plains.

Chef Domenico Cuomo, honored for his skill and artistry, understands the food of the Amalfi coast well. He hails from Furore, a small village a mere five kilometers away. Each morning as the chef and his staff prepare for the day, the spacious well-equipped kitchen is a hub of activity. Provisions spill into the kitchen—baskets of fresh

Amalfi

vegetables and lemons are carried up from the gardens and the daily supply of fish and seafood is delivered—most of which was fished in local waters just hours before. Sous chefs and their assistants, attired in stiffly pressed whites, scurry about gathering ingredients and preparing for the day's tasks.

Chef Cuomo attends daily to the preparation of handmade pasta. Italy's *Mezzogiorno,* as the south is referred to, is known for its use of dry pasta made from hard durum wheat, or semolina, but each of the southern regions also has its traditional handmade pastas. Chef Cuomo's signature dishes reveal his proficiency as a pasta maker. He produces a handmade fusilli, small coils of pasta more familiar in the dry form, and *scialatiel-*

At Eolo, lunch is served at a table with a view of Amalfi's beachfront, ABOVE.

li, a fragrant stubby ribbon pasta, that is delicately flavored with specks of fresh basil and Parmigiano-Reggiano. Chef Cuomo blends the scialatielli in a large skillet with a rapidly cooked sauce made with diced eggplant sautéed until tender, chunks of tomatoes, more fresh basil, and a whisper of garlic. When steaming hot, he tosses in small bits of mozzarella and a sprinkling of Parmigiano.

Occupying a corner of the kitchen, pastry chef Michele Napoli spends early mornings grinding, whipping, and piping until he has filled his tall baker's rack with numerous *dolci,* or desserts, that will delight the hotel guests. Many of them are flavored with the large grapefruit-size lemon of Amalfi, called *sfusato amalfitano,* a sweet and juicy lemon with a concentrated flavor and thick mottled skin. The lemon orchards on the terraced cliffs of the Santa Caterina produce an abundant supply that appear in many of the savory offerings as well. There are *profiteroles al limone,* small cream puffs filled and coated with a delightfully tart lemon cream; lemon *crostata*; and hot lemon soufflé. Lemon marmelade is served at breakfast; fresh strands of pasta called *tagliolini* are presented in a lemon

cream sauce at dinner; and *limoncello,* a fragrant lemon liqueur, is offered icy cold as an after-dinner elixir.

During summer months lunch and banquet dinners are served in an open-air dining room. Guests glide down the side of the cliff in a glass-enclosed elevator that offers a glimpse of the terraced gardens and crystalline sea. Chef Cuomo and his staff reestablish themselves in a kitchen carved into the cliff. It opens onto a patio dining room, at sea level adjacent to the pool. Standing behind a large grill, the chef cooks a variety of vegetables, fish, and seafood over an open fire. Pizza, synonymous with the city of Naples, the capital of Campania, is baked in a wood-fired oven next to the grill, and is available with a variety of toppings.

Down the road from the Hotel Santa Caterina is a small restaurant, which shares the bounty of the hotel gardens. Caterina Gargano, the daughter of Giuseppina Gambardella, opened a small seaside restaurant that captures the flavors of Amalfi's past. Eolo, named for the ancient Greek god of the wind, is positioned near the entrance of the city at the bend of a cliff that benefits from a continuous flow of refreshing sea breezes. The blue waters below add to the decor at Eolo when the large arched windows are opened, creating an atmosphere of dining al fresco.

The menu reflects Caterina's research. Using ingredients that were once part of the cuisine of Amalfi, she creates dishes that reflect today's lighter attitude toward food. She leans heavily on the fine quality ingredients of the region, following the cycle of the seasons. She focuses on the abundance of fresh vegetables and fruit at the gardens of the Hotel Santa Caterina, on fish and seafood from local waters, and on grains and legumes that were at one time more important in the diet of the region. Caterina creates new menus every twenty days combining ingredients in simplistic and natural ways that emphasize their outstanding quality.

A basket of apricots and squash blossoms gathered from the gardens at Hotel Santa Caterina, LEFT, make a fine display in the dining room at Eolo. The village of Amalfi, which was one of the four great ancient maritime republics, clings to the cliffs above the harbor, RIGHT. The fishing nets are pulled in at the close of a long day at sea, BELOW.

Sauté di Frutti di Mare
Mixed Seafood Sauté

The local fish and seafood of Amalfi are intensely flavored with the sea, a taste that is unparalleled. Chef Cuomo combines several kinds of mollusks in this briny, soupy stew, which is served with toasted bread to soak up the broth. Depending on availability, he might use cannolicchi, *long thin razor clams;* tartufi di mare*, small clams believed to possess the qualities of an aphrodisiac;* datteri di mare*, mollusks that look like dates;* fasolari, *cockles;* vongole veraci, *flavorful baby clams symbolic of the region; and black-shelled* cozze, *mussels. Similar results can be obtained using a variety of domestic and imported mollusks.*

3 DOZEN MIXED MUSSELS, DEBEARDED AND SCRUBBED
3 DOZEN MIXED VERY SMALL CLAMS, SCRUBBED
2 TABLESPOONS FLOUR
12 SLICES SLIGHTLY DRY WHITE OR WHOLE-WHEAT FRENCH BREAD
¼ CUP (2 FL OZ/60 ML) EXTRA VIRGIN OLIVE OIL
3 MEDIUM CLOVES OF GARLIC, THINLY SLICED
3 MEDIUM PLUM TOMATOES, CORED AND COARSELY CHOPPED
2 TABLESPOONS SLIVERED ITALIAN FLAT-LEAF PARSLEY LEAVES
¾ CUP (12 FL OZ/375 ML) DRY WHITE WINE

1. Preheat the oven to 400°F (200°C).

2. Place the mussels and clams in a large bowl filled with cold water. Stir in the flour and soak for 15 minutes. Lift them out of the water and soak in clear water for 10 minutes. Drain. Keep refrigerated until ready to cook.

3. Arrange the bread slices in a single layer on a baking sheet and toast them in the preheated oven for 10 minutes. Turn the slices and toast them for 6 to 8 minutes more, or until lightly browned on each side. Transfer to a cooling rack to cool completely.

4. Heat the olive oil in a large sauté pan over medium heat. Add the garlic and cook until it is lightly golden. Add the tomatoes and 1 tablespoon parsley. Increase the heat to medium-high and cook, stirring constantly, for 1 minute. Pour in the white wine and simmer briskly until half the wine has evaporated. Add the mussels and clams, reduce the heat to medium, cover the pan, and cook until all the shells have opened, 10 to 15 minutes. Transfer the mixture to a large serving platter, sprinkle with the remaining parsley and arrange the toasted bread around the edge of the platter. Serve immediately.
MAKES 6 SERVINGS

Sauté di Frutti di Mare, *OPPOSITE.*

Conchiglie Gratinate
Gratinéed Mixed Seafood

This dish is served as primo piatto, *or first course, at Eolo but it would certainly suffice as a main course. Use an assortment of both firm-fleshed fish, such as swordfish, tuna, or mako shark, and flaky fish, like cod, scrod, or halibut. Clams should be as small as possible.*

7 SLICES SLIGHTLY DRY FIRM-TEXTURED WHITE BREAD
6 TABLESPOONS (3 FL OZ/90 ML) EXTRA VIRGIN OLIVE OIL
4 MEDIUM CLOVES OF GARLIC, FINELY CHOPPED
6 LARGE SHRIMP, PEELED AND DEVEINED
SEA SALT AND FRESHLY GROUND BLACK PEPPER
3 MEDIUM PLUM TOMATOES, CORED, SEEDED, AND CUT INTO ⅜-INCH (1-CM) DICE
1 TABLESPOON FINELY CHOPPED ITALIAN FLAT-LEAF PARSLEY LEAVES
1 POUND (450 G) ASSORTED WHITE-FLESHED FISH, SKINNED, BONED, AND CUT INTO 2 x ½-INCH (5 x 1.25-CM) CHUNKS
1 DOZEN SMALL MUSSELS, ON THE HALF SHELL, JUICE RESERVED
2 DOZEN SMALL CLAMS, ON THE HALF SHELL, JUICE RESERVED

1. Preheat the oven to 400°F (200°C). Oil 6 large individual baking shells or a gratin pan large enough to hold the fish and seafood in a single layer.

2. Discard the crusts from the bread and cut the bread into ⅜-inch (1-cm) dice for croutons. Heat 3 tablespoons (1½ fl oz/45 ml) olive oil in a large nonstick skillet over medium heat. Add half the garlic and stir. Add half the bread and brown lightly on all sides, tossing frequently. Transfer to a large bowl. Heat the remaining 3 tablespoons (1½ fl oz/45 ml) olive oil, add the remaining garlic and bread, and brown in the same way.

3. Butterfly the shrimps. Arrange them, outside down, on a work surface and flatten them slightly with a mallet. Season with salt and pepper. Spoon 1 teaspoon diced tomato onto the center of each shrimp and sprinkle with a pinch of the parsley. Roll the shrimp toward the tail end to enclose the filling.

4. Use half of the croutons to arrange a border around the edge of the baking shells. Place the fish, shrimp, and mollusks in a single layer within the border, dividing the mixture evenly among the shells. Season with salt and pepper. Add the remaining tomatoes and parsley to the croutons left in the bowl. Pour 2 tablespoons clam juice over the croutons and toss. Scatter this mixture over the fish and shellfish. Bake for 20 minutes, or just until cooked through.
MAKES 6 SERVINGS

The Hotel Santa Caterina is situated in an enviable position gazing across the Gulf of Salerno.

Insalata di Fagiolini Romani

Italian Flat Romano Bean Salad with Mint

Just harvested green and gold Italian flat Romano beans are delightful served cold—which means at room temperature in Italy.

For the Dressing

6 TABLESPOONS (3 FL OZ/90 ML) EXTRA VIRGIN OLIVE OIL
2 TABLESPOONS (1 FL OZ/30 ML) RED WINE VINEGAR
1 MEDIUM CLOVE OF GARLIC, SLICED
SEA SALT
2 TABLESPOONS COARSELY CHOPPED MINT LEAVES

SEA SALT
1½ POUNDS (675 G) GREEN AND GOLD ITALIAN FLAT ROMANO
BEANS, TRIMMED
1 SMALL TOMATO, CUT INTO WEDGES, FOR GARNISH (OPTIONAL)
SPRIGS OF MINT, FOR GARNISH (OPTIONAL)

1. To make the dressing, combine the olive oil, vinegar, garlic, and salt in a small bowl. Whisk together and let stand for 1 hour.

2. Fill a large pot (at least 6 quarts/6 liters) with water and bring it to a boil. Add salt to taste. Stir in the beans and boil for 5 to 10 minutes, or just until tender. Drain in a colander, refresh under cold water, then drain again. Transfer to a serving bowl. Stir the chopped mint into the dressing, pour it over the beans, and toss until thoroughly coated. Garnish with tomato wedges and sprigs of mint, if desired. Serve immediately.

MAKES 6 SERVINGS

Laganelle con Calamari e Ceci

Chickpea Pasta with Squid and Chickpeas

These wide handmade pasta ribbons, similar to fettuccine but slightly thicker, are used throughout southern Italy. At Eolo, Caterina combines white flour with chickpea flour in her version, tossed with squid, cherry tomatoes, and chickpeas.

For the Chickpea Pasta

1⅓ CUPS (6½ OZ/175 G) CHICKPEA FLOUR
4 CUPS (18 OZ/480 G) UNBLEACHED ALL-PURPOSE FLOUR
5 LARGE EGGS

For the Sauce

3 MEDIUM CLOVES OF GARLIC, SLICED
1 TO 2 SMALL HOT RED CHILI PEPPERS
½ CUP (4 FL OZ/60 ML) EXTRA VIRGIN OLIVE OIL
2 POUNDS (1.8 K) SMALL WHOLE SQUID, CLEANED AND CUT INTO
⅜-INCH-THICK (1-CM-THICK) RINGS, TENTACLES LEFT WHOLE
(1½ LBS/675 G CLEANED SQUID)
½ CUP (4 FL OZ/60 ML) DRY WHITE WINE
1 PINT (1 LB/450 G) CHERRY TOMATOES, CUT IN HALF
1½ CUPS (10 OZ/300 G) COOKED CHICKPEAS (CECI LESSATI PAGE 187)
¼ CUP (½ OZ/15 G) ITALIAN FLAT-LEAF PARSLEY LEAVES, COARSELY
CHOPPED
SEA SALT AND FRESHLY GROUND BLACK PEPPER

1. Sift together the chickpea flour and all-purpose flour, 3 times to blend thoroughly. To make the pasta dough, use the flour mixture and the eggs as directed on page 188, the section entitled Making the Dough. The dough will be kneaded and stretched in a manual pasta machine. Line 2 trays or baking sheets with cotton kitchen towels and dust lightly with the flour mixture.

2. Divide the dough into 6 equal portions and knead in the pasta machine as directed in the section entitled Kneading the Dough in a Pasta Machine. Stretch the dough as directed in the section entitled Stretching the Dough in a Pasta Machine, stopping 1 notch before reaching the last setting on the dial. Using a fluted pastry wheel, cut each sheet of pasta into 7-inch (18-cm) lengths and arrange them, side by side, on the towel-lined trays. Dry the pasta slightly, turning the sheets occasionally. The surface should be dry to the touch, but the pasta should remain flexible.

3. Attach the cutting blades to the pasta machine. Pass each sheet of dough through the wide cutting blade used for tagliatelle or fettuccine. If the dough cannot be inserted easily, flatten the edge with your fingertips. Transfer the *laganelle* to the towel-lined trays, dust with the flour mixture, and gently toss.

4. Fill a very large pot (at least 8 quarts/8 liters) with water and bring it to a rapid boil. Add salt to taste. Stir in the laganelle and cover the pot just until the water returns to a boil. Uncover and boil the laganelle 3 to 5 minutes, or just until tender.

5. While the pasta is cooking, make the sauce. Cook the garlic and chili pepper with the olive oil in a sauté pan large enough to hold the laganelle over medium heat until the garlic is golden. Add the squid and cook over medium-high heat just until it becomes firm, about 1 minute. Pour in the white wine and simmer briskly for 3 minutes. Add the tomatoes, chickpeas, and half of the parsley. Pour in ½ cup (4 fl oz/125 ml) of water from the pasta pot and simmer for 1 minute.

Season with salt and pepper to taste. To avoid tough rubbery squid do not cook more than 5 minutes.

6. Drain the laganelle, reserving some of the cooking water. Transfer to the sauté pan and toss with the sauce over low heat. If the mixture seems dry, add some of the reserved cooking water. Sprinkle with the remaining parsley and serve immediately.

MAKES 6 SERVINGS

Scialatielli con Melanzane, Pomodori, e Mozzarella

Handmade Basil Pasta with Eggplant, Tomatoes, and Mozzarella

This handmade pasta from the Hotel Santa Caterina is flavored with Parmigiano-Reggiano and fresh basil. Chef Cuomo often serves it with a seafood sauce, but in this version he uses a splendid summertime trio—tomatoes, eggplant, and fresh basil from the terraced gardens—combined with fresh mozzarella and Parmigiana-Reggiano. Dry pasta can also be used instead of fresh; penne would be a good choice.

For the Basil Pasta

    4   CUPS (18 OZ/480 G) UNBLEACHED ALL-PURPOSE FLOUR
    1   LARGE EGG
    1½ TEASPOONS FINELY CHOPPED FRESH BASIL LEAVES
    ¾   CUP (12 FL OZ/375 ML) WHOLE MILK
    PINCH OF SEA SALT
    ½   CUP (2 OZ/60 G) GRATED PARMIGIANO-REGGIANO

    1   MEDIUM EGGPLANT, SLICED ½ INCH (1.25 CM) THICK
    SEA SALT
    ⅓   CUP (3 FL OZ/80 ML) PLUS ¼ CUP (2 FL OZ/60 ML) EXTRA VIRGIN
        OLIVE OIL
    ⅓   CUP (1½ OZ/45 G) UNBLEACHED ALL-PURPOSE FLOUR
    3   MEDIUM CLOVES OF GARLIC, THINLY SLICED
    2   LARGE TOMATOES, CORED, AND CUT INTO ½-INCH (1.25-CM)
        CHUNKS
    6   MEDIUM BASIL LEAVES, SHREDDED
    8   OUNCES (240 G) FRESH MOZZARELLA, CUT INTO ⅜-INCH (1-CM)
        DICE
    1   CUP (4OZ/120 G) GRATED PARMIGIANO-REGGIANO

1. To make the pasta dough, use the flour, egg, basil, milk, salt, and Parmigiano-Reggiano as directed on page 188, the section entitled Making the Dough. The dough will be kneaded and stretched in a manual pasta machine. Line 2 trays or baking sheets with cotton kitchen towels and dust lightly with flour.

2. Divide the dough into 4 equal portions and knead in the pasta machine as directed in the section entitled Kneading the Dough in a Pasta Machine. Stretch the dough as directed in the section entitled Stretching the Dough in a Pasta Machine, stopping 1 notch before the last setting on the dial. Using a fluted pastry wheel, cut each sheet of pasta in half and arrange them, side by side, on the towel-lined trays. Dry the pasta slightly, turning the sheets occasionally. The surface should be dry to the touch, but the pasta should remain flexible.

3. Attach the cutting blades to the pasta machine. Pass each sheet of dough through the wide cutting blade used for tagliatelle or fettuccine. If the dough cannot be inserted easily, flatten the edge with your fingertips. Transfer the *scialatielli* to the towel-lined trays, dust with flour, and gently toss.

4. Layer the eggplant in a colander, salting each layer. Rest a heavy weight on the eggplant (use a large plate and fill it with 1 or 2 heavy cans). Let drain for 30 minutes. Rinse off the salt, then dry the eggplant with paper towels. Cut the eggplant into ½-inch (1.25-cm) dice. Heat ⅓ cup (3 fl oz/80 ml) of olive oil in a large skillet over medium-high heat. Dredge half of the diced eggplant in the flour and add it to the skillet. Cook the eggplant, tossing occasionally, until golden brown on all sides. Remove the eggplant with a slotted spoon to drain on paper towels. Dredge the remaining eggplant in flour and cook it in the same way.

5. Fill a very large pot (at least 8 quarts/8 liters) with water and bring it to a rapid boil. Add salt to taste.

6. Heat the remaining ¼ cup (2 oz/60 g) olive oil in a heavy sauté pan large enough to hold the pasta over medium heat. Add the garlic and cook until it is lightly golden. Increase the heat to high and add the tomatoes, basil, eggplant, and ½ cup (4 fl oz/125 ml) of water from the pasta pot. Simmer briskly just until the tomatoes soften and the mixture thickens slightly. Season with salt to taste.

7. Lower the scialatielli into the boiling water and cover the pot until it returns to a boil. Uncover and boil the scialatielli 1 or 2 minutes, or until al dente. Drain the scialatielli in a large colander reserving some of the water. Transfer to the sauté pan, sprinkle with mozzarella and Parmigiano, and toss over low heat just until the cheeses melt. If the scialatielli seem dry, add some of the reserved cooking water. Serve immediately.

MAKES 6 SERVINGS

CLOCKWISE STARTING TOP LEFT,
Eolo's Pesce Serra ai Fiori di Zucca, *bundles of fish wrapped in zucchini blossoms. Chef Cuomo hand rolling fusilli around a thin metal rod. At Hotel Santa Caterina* Fusilli Divina Costiera *is prepared with wild arugula gathered from the gardens surrounding the hotel.* Pesce alla Griglia, *a whole grilled fish with fresh mint sauce as served in the open-air dining room at Hotel Santa Caterina. Eolo's cantaloupe sorbet.*

Fusilli Divina Costiera

Handmade Fusilli with Tomatoes, Clams, and Arugula

La divina costiera, *the divine coast, is how Longfellow referred to the splendor of Amalfi, which was once his home. Chef Cuomo reflects the flavors of Amalfi's land and sea in* Fusilli Divina Costiera, *made with his handmade pasta. Tiny clams, called* vongole veraci, *simmer with garlic, tomatoes, capers, and parsley. Fresh arugula is wilted in the sauce before tossing with the fusilli.*

Shaping and curling each strand of fusilli takes time and patience. If you are short on either one, serve the sauce with dry fusilli. Use the smallest clams you can find—New Zealand cockles, if available, are most suitable.

For the Fusilli

3½ CUPS (16 OZ/420 G) UNBLEACHED ALL-PURPOSE FLOUR
SEA SALT

For the Sauce

2 POUNDS (1.8 K) SMALL CLAMS, PREFERABLY NEW ZEALAND COCKLES, SCRUBBED

1 TABLESPOON UNBLEACHED ALL-PURPOSE FLOUR

2 TABLESPOONS SALT-PACKED CAPERS

2 MEDIUM CLOVES OF GARLIC, SLICED

SEA SALT

½ CUP (4 FL OZ/125 ML) EXTRA VIRGIN OLIVE OIL

¾ POUND (675 G) PLUM TOMATOES, CORED, SEEDED, AND CUT INTO ¾-INCH (2-CM) CHUNKS

2 TABLESPOONS CHOPPED ITALIAN FLAT-LEAF PARSLEY LEAVES

8 OUNCES (225 G) ARUGULA, TRIMMED, WELL WASHED, AND DRIED

1. To make the pasta, use the flour, a pinch of salt, and 1 cup (8 fl oz/250 ml) of water as directed on page 188, the section entitled Making the Dough. Knead the dough entirely by hand until it is smooth and very firm, about 15 minutes. It is not necessary to use all of the flour. The remaining flour will be used when shaping the fusilli. Dust the dough with flour and wrap it in a cotton kitchen towel. Let the dough rest for 30 minutes.

2. Line 2 trays or baking sheets with cotton kitchen towels and dust lightly with flour.

3. Cut off a small piece of the dough about the size of a grape. Keep the unused portion wrapped in the towel. Roll the dough by hand on a pastry board or work surface, into a ¼-inch-thick (0.6-cm-thick) rope. Cut the rope into 2-inch pieces. To make the spiral shape, dust each piece of the dough with flour and curl one end around a ⅛-inch-thick (0.3-cm-thick) bamboo skewer or thin metal rod. Hold it in place and rest the skewer on the board. Roll it away from you. The pasta will wrap itself around the skewer like a coil. To thin the coil, hold it in place with 2 hands and roll the skewer back and forth while gently stretching the coil outward. The finished fusilli will be about 2 inches long. The length of the fusilli can vary slightly, but all pieces should be the same thickness in order to cook evenly. This will take some practice. Shape the remaining pieces of dough into fusilli. Continue until all of the dough has been used. Transfer the fusilli to the towel-lined trays, dust lightly with flour and let the fusilli dry slightly. (The fusilli can be made a day ahead and covered with a clean towel.)

4. To make the sauce, place the clams in a large bowl filled with cold water. Stir in the flour and soak for 15 minutes. Lift them out of the water and soak in clear water for 10 minutes. Drain the clams.

5. Soak the capers in 3 changes of cold water to remove the salt. Drain and dry them with paper towels. If the capers are very large, coarsely chop them.

6. Fill a very large pot (at least 8 quarts/8 liters) with water and bring it to a rapid boil. Add salt to taste. Stir in the fusilli and cover the pot until it returns to the boil. Uncover and boil the fusilli for about 3 to 5 minutes, or until al dente.

7. Meanwhile, sauté the garlic with the olive oil in a sauté pan large enough to hold the fusilli over medium heat until the garlic is golden. Stir in the tomatoes, parsley, and capers. Increase the heat to high and add the clams and 1 cup (8 fl oz/250 ml) of water from the pasta pot. Cook briskly just until all of the clams have opened. Reserve a small handful of the arugula for garnish and add the rest to the pan. Stir until the arugula has wilted. Add salt to taste. Remove the sauce from the heat until the pasta is done.

8. Drain the fusilli in a large colander, reserving some of the cooking water. Transfer the fusilli to the sauté pan and toss with the sauce over low heat. If the mixture seems dry, add some of the reserved cooking water. Transfer to a large serving bowl and garnish with the reserved arugula.

MAKES 6 SERVINGS

Pesce alla Griglia con Salsa di Menta

Grilled Fish with Mint Sauce

Chef Cuomo grills spigola, *a type of sea bass, or* pezzogna, *a fish similar to red snapper, and serves it with a sauce redolent with garlic and fresh mint.*

For the Mint Sauce
¾ CUP (6 FL OZ/185 ML) EXTRA VIRGIN OLIVE OIL
1 SMALL CLOVE OF GARLIC, FINELY CHOPPED
2 TABLESPOONS (1 FL OZ/30 ML) WHITE WINE VINEGAR
3 TABLESPOONS (1½ FL OZ/45 ML) LEMON JUICE
SEA SALT
½ CUP (1 OZ/30 G) CHOPPED MINT LEAVES

1 WHOLE STRIPED BASS, RED SNAPPER, OR SEA BASS, SCALED AND GUTTED (2½ TO 3 POUNDS/1.2 TO 1.4 K)
SEA SALT
1 MEDIUM CLOVE OF GARLIC, CHOPPED
1 TEASPOON CHOPPED ITALIAN FLAT-LEAF PARSLEY LEAVES
1 TEASPOON CHOPPED MINT LEAVES
3 TEASPOONS EXTRA VIRGIN OLIVE OIL
2 TEASPOONS UNBLEACHED ALL-PURPOSE FLOUR

1. To make the mint sauce, combine the olive oil, garlic, vinegar, lemon juice, and salt to taste in a medium size bowl. Blend with a whisk and stir in the mint. Make the sauce at least 1 hour ahead.

2. Preheat the broiler or light a grill at least 15 minutes ahead. If broiling, use an oiled broiler pan or oil a rack and place it in a baking pan. If grilling, adjust the grill rack 4 to 5 inches from the heat source.

3. Rinse the fish in cold water and dry it with paper towels. Season the cavity with salt. Combine the garlic, parsley, and mint. Rub the mixture into the cavity, then drizzle the cavity with 1 teaspoon of the olive oil. If broiling, arrange the fish on the rack of the broiler pan. Season the top surface of the fish with salt, dust with 1 teaspoon of the flour through a small sieve, and drizzle with 1 teaspoon olive oil. Place the fish under the broiler, 4 to 5 inches (10 to 13 cm) from the heat source, for 8 to 10 minutes, or until the top of the fish is cooked through. To test for doneness, insert a small paring knife into the fleshiest part of the fish. It should be flaky and opaque. Turn the fish using a large metal spatula. Sprinkle the top with salt, dust with the remaining 1 teaspoon flour, and drizzle with the remaining 1 teaspoon olive oil. Broil for 8 to 10 minutes more, or until thoroughly cooked.

If grilling, salt, dust with flour, and drizzle olive oil over 1 side of the fish, then place it on the grill, floured side down. Grill for 8 to 10 minutes. Before turning the fish, sprinkle the top surface with salt, dust with flour, and drizzle with olive oil. Slide a very large metal spatula under the fish to lift it from the grill and carefully turn it. Grill the fish 8 to 10 minutes more, or until it is thoroughly cooked. Transfer to a large serving platter and serve with the mint sauce.
MAKES 4 SERVINGS

Pesce Serra ai Fiori di Zucca

Fish Wrapped in Squash Blossoms

*The sweet flavor of an under-appreciated local fish—*pesce serra—*inspired Caterina to unite it with squash blossoms and summer zucchini. A firm-textured fish like mako shark, swordfish, or tuna would work as well.*

8 MEDIUM ZUCCHINI (1½ LBS/675 G), TRIMMED
SEA SALT AND FRESHLY GROUND BLACK PEPPER
¼ CUP (4 FL OZ/125 ML) EXTRA VIRGIN OLIVE OIL
2 MEDIUM CLOVES OF GARLIC, FINELY CHOPPED
⅔ CUP (5½ FL OZ/165 ML) DRY WHITE WINE
1½ POUNDS (675 G) FIRM-FLESHED FISH, SUCH AS MAKO SHARK, YELLOWFIN TUNA, OR SWORDFISH, 1 INCH (2.5 CM) THICK, SKIN REMOVED
24 SQUASH BLOSSOMS, STEMS REMOVED
1 LARGE EGG, LIGHTLY BEATEN

1. Slice four of the zucchini lengthwise ¹⁄₁₆ inch (0.2 cm) thick using a large chef's knife or mandoline. You should have 24 slices. Fill a large pot (at least 6 quarts) with water and bring it to a boil. Add salt to taste. Blanch the zucchini in the boiling water for 2 minutes, or just until flexible. Shred the remaining 4 zucchini. Heat the olive oil in a large sauté pan over medium-high heat. Add the shredded zucchini and the garlic. Sauté for 2 minutes, stirring frequently. Pour in the wine and boil briskly for 2 minutes. Season with salt and black pepper to taste.

2. Cut the fish into 24 pieces, about 2½ inches (6 cm) long and ½ inch (1.25 cm) wide. Season with salt and pepper to taste.

3. Cut the squash blossoms open and remove the stamens. Rinse them under cold water and pat dry with paper towels. Brush the inside of each with the beaten egg and wrap it lengthwise around a piece of fish. Wrap a slice of blanched zucchini around the center of each piece and arrange the packets on top of the shredded zucchini in the pan. Cover and simmer for 7 to 10 minutes, or until the fish is cooked.
MAKES 6 SERVINGS

Profiteroles al Limone
Cream Puffs Filled with Lemon Cream

Lemons straight from the orchards of the Hotel Santa Caterina are used in pastry chef Michele Napoli's Profiteroles al Limone. *The puffs are mounded high and garnished with slivers of lemon zest.*

For the Lemon Pastry Cream
- 1½ CUPS (12 FL OZ/375 ML) WHOLE MILK
- ½ VANILLA BEAN
- 3 LARGE EGG YOLKS
- ½ CUP (4 OZ/125 G) SUGAR
- 6 TABLESPOONS (1½ OZ/45 G) UNBLEACHED ALL-PURPOSE FLOUR
- GRATED ZEST OF 1 LEMON

For the Cream Puffs
- 1 CUP (8 FL OZ/250 ML) COLD WATER
- 8 TABLESPOONS (4 OZ/120 G) UNSALTED BUTTER, CUT INTO PIECES
- 1 TEASPOON SUGAR
- SEA SALT
- 1 CUP (4 OZ/120 G) UNBLEACHED ALL-PURPOSE FLOUR
- 4 LARGE EGGS

- 1 CUP (8 FL OZ/250 ML) HEAVY CREAM
- ZEST OF 1 LEMON, CUT INTO JULIENNE STRIPS, FOR GARNISH

1. To make the pastry cream combine the milk and the vanilla bean in a medium-size heavy saucepan. Heat over medium-low heat until scalded. While the milk is heating, whisk together the egg yolks and sugar in a large bowl. Add the flour and stir until it is completely dissolved. Slowly whisk one third of the scalded milk into the egg yolk mixture. Add the remaining milk all at once and blend thoroughly. Pour the mixture back into the saucepan and return it to the heat. Stir constantly until the pastry cream has thickened. Turn off the heat, add the grated lemon zest, and continue to stir for 1 minute. Remove the vanilla bean and pour into a bowl. Smooth the top with a rubber spatula and place a buttered round of wax paper on the surface to prevent a skin from forming. When cool, cover the bowl with plastic wrap and refrigerate. (The pastry cream can be made the day before.)

2. Preheat the oven to 425°F (215°C) and adjust 2 racks in the center of the oven. Butter 2 large baking sheets.

3. To make the cream puffs, combine the cold water, butter, sugar,

OPPOSITE, Profiteroles al Limone.

and a pinch of salt in a medium-size heavy saucepan over medium-low heat. Bring to a boil and melt the butter. As soon as the water reaches a boil, remove the pan from the heat. Add the flour all at once and stir with a wooden spoon. When the flour is thoroughly blended, return the pan to the flame. Stir vigorously for 1 to 2 minutes, or until the mixture pulls away from the sides of the saucepan forming a ball of dough. Remove the pan from the heat and rest it on a damp towel. Beat in the eggs, one at a time. Incorporate each egg thoroughly before adding the next.

4. Scrape the cream puff paste into a pastry bag, fitted with a ½-inch (1.25-cm) round tip. Pipe out 24 small mounds of dough 1½ inches (3.8 cm) in diameter and spaced 2 inches (5 cm) apart onto the 2 baking sheets. Moisten your index finger with water and gently flatten the pointed peaks. Place the baking sheets in the oven, staggered so that they are not one on top of the other. Bake for 20 to 25 minutes, or until puffed and golden. Reverse the positions of the baking sheets after 15 minutes so they bake evenly. Turn off the heat and cool the puffs thoroughly in the oven with the door slightly ajar.

5. Beat the heavy cream until it is stiff. Stir 1 tablespoonful of the whipped cream into the pastry cream then fold in the rest. Spoon about one quarter of the mixture into a pastry bag fitted with a ¼-inch (0.6-cm) plain tip. Make a small slit on the side of each puff and fill with the lightened pastry cream. Stack the puffs on a large platter and spoon the remaining cream over them. Sprinkle with the lemon zest and serve immediately.

MAKES 12 SERVINGS

Sorbetto di Melone
Melon Sorbet

This icy, refreshing melon sorbet served at Eolo is made from ripe cantaloupe. Any sweet melon can be used.

- 2 CANTALOUPES
- ⅓ TO ⅔ CUP (2½ TO 5 OZ/75 TO 150 G) SUPERFINE SUGAR

1. Cut the cantaloupes in half and scoop out the seeds. Cut the halves into wedges, remove the skin, and cut the flesh into 1-inch (2.5-cm) chunks. Purée the cantaloupe in a food processor until smooth. Add sugar to taste, starting with ⅓ cup (2½ oz/75 g). Chill the purée in the refrigerator for at least 2 hours.

2. Freeze the purée in an electric ice-cream maker according to the manufacturer's instructions. Store the *sorbetto* in the freezer until ready to serve. Scoop into frozen wine glasses or dessert bowls.

MAKES 6 SERVINGS

Albicocche Ripiene
Stuffed Apricots

In early summer, the orchards at the Hotel Santa Caterina provide Eolo with fresh apricots which Caterina stuffs with amaretti cookies and poaches in amaretto liqueur. Be sure to use apricots that are fully ripe yet firm.

- 10 LARGE, FIRM APRICOTS (2½ LBS/1.25 K)
- 2 TABLESPOONS UNSALTED BUTTER
- 3 TABLESPOONS SUGAR
- ⅔ CUP (5½ FL OZ/165 ML) AMARETTO LIQUER
- 12 AMARETTI COOKIES, CRUSHED
- PINE NUTS, FOR GARNISH (OPTIONAL)

1. Peel the apricots with a vegetable peeler, cut them in half, and remove the stones. Cut two of the halves into large chunks and set aside. Slightly enlarge the hollows in the remaining halves, using a melon-ball cutter.

2. Melt the butter in a large nonstick skillet. Add the sugar and cook over medium heat, stirring constantly until the sugar dissolves and becomes light caramel in color. Pour in the amaretto liqueur and simmer, stirring, for 2 minutes. The syrup will sputter when the amaretto is added. Be sure to wear oven mitts to prevent burns. Add half of the apricots to the syrup and poach them at a slow simmer, turning them from side to side to cook evenly, until almost tender, about 5 to 10 minutes. Test for tenderness by piercing with a small paring knife. Remove them with a slotted spoon and drain, inverted on a shallow platter. Cook the remaining apricots in the same way.

3. Add the crumbled amaretti cookies to the syrup that remains in the skillet. Cook over low heat, crushing the cookies with the back of a wooden spoon until they have melted into a coarse purée. Scrape the contents of the skillet into a food processor, add the reserved apricot chunks, and process until the mixture is smooth.

4. Return the mixture to the skillet and simmer slowly, stirring constantly, until it is as thick as molasses and dark brown in color. Cool the mixture in the skillet for 5 minutes. Spoon equal amounts of the filling into the hollows of the apricots. Garnish the top of each apricot with pine nuts, if desired. Serve the stuffed apricots warm or at room temperature.

MAKES 6 SERVINGS

Caprese
Chocolate Almond Cake

Pastry chef Michele Napoli at Hotel Santa Caterina uses the finest almonds he can find in his version of Caprese, a classic Neapolitan chocolate almond cake.

- 4 OUNCES (125 G) SEMISWEET CHOCOLATE, CHOPPED
- 8 TABLESPOONS (4 OZ/125 G) UNSALTED BUTTER, SOFTENED
- ½ CUP (4 OZ/125 G) SUGAR
- 4 LARGE EGGS, SEPARATED
- 1 CUP (6 OZ/180 G) SLIVERED ALMONDS, GROUND
- ⅓ CUP (1½ OZ/45 G) PLUS 2 TABLESPOONS UNBLEACHED ALL-PURPOSE FLOUR

For Garnish (optional)

- 1 CUP (8 FL OZ/250 ML) HEAVY CREAM
- 2 TABLESPOONS SUPERFINE SUGAR
- 1 TEASPOON VANILLA EXTRACT
- CONFECTIONERS' SUGAR, FOR DUSTING

1. Preheat the oven to 350°F (175°C). Butter an 8-inch (20-cm) round cake pan and line the bottom with a round of parchment paper. Butter the paper and lightly coat the pan with flour.

2. Melt the chocolate in a double boiler over barely simmering water and let it cool to room temperature.

3. Beat the butter and sugar in a large bowl with an electric mixer at high speed until it is light and fluffy. Beat in the egg yolks, one at a time. Combine the almonds with the melted chocolate and blend the mixture into the batter. Add the flour and mix on low speed until it is completely dissolved. Wash and dry the beaters. In another clean large bowl, beat the egg whites at medium speed until they are stiff but not dry. Using a large rubber spatula, stir one quarter of the egg whites into the chocolate mixture. Gently fold in the remaining egg whites, being careful not to overblend. Pour the batter into the cake pan and bake for 40 minutes, or until a toothpick inserted into the center comes out clean. Transfer the cake to a cooling rack for 10 minutes. Unmold onto the rack and cool completely.

4. If desired, make whipped cream to serve as a garnish. Combine the heavy cream, superfine sugar, and vanilla in a large bowl. Beat with an electric mixer at high speed until the cream is stiff.

5. Dust the cake with confectioners' sugar and transfer it to a large cake plate. Serve with a dollop of whipped cream, if desired.

MAKES 8 SERVINGS

Il Brodo di Carne
Homemade Meat Broth

This broth can be made with any combination of meats and poultry. Try it with chicken, turkey, veal, or beef. The broth should be delicately flavored so that it does not intrude upon other ingredients when it is used in sauces, soups, or risotto.

6 POUNDS (2.6 K) MEAT AND BONES
1 LEEK, TRIMMED AND WELL WASHED
1 LARGE CELERY STALK, HALVED
2 SPRIGS OF ITALIAN FLAT-LEAF
   PARSLEY
1 LARGE ONION, ROOT END TRIMMED
2 LARGE CARROTS, SCRUBBED
1 LARGE TOMATO (OPTIONAL)
1 TEASPOON SEA SALT
8 BLACK PEPPERCORNS

1. Combine the meat and bones in a large stockpot. Add 5 quarts (5 liters) cold water and place the pot over medium heat. Simmer, uncovered, for 20 minutes, skimming off the foam that rises to the top.

2. Fold the leek in half. Tie it together with the celery and parsley and place it in the stockpot. Add the onion, carrots, tomato, if using, salt, and peppercorns. Simmer uncovered for 3 hours.

3. Discard the solids and strain the broth through a fine sieve. Let it cool, uncovered. Refrigerate and skim off the solidified fat. Store the broth in the refrigerator for up to 3 days or in the freezer for up to 2 months.

MAKES 4 QUARTS/4 LITERS

Il Brodo di Verdure
Homemade Vegetable Broth

2 LARGE ONIONS, HALVED
3 LARGE CARROTS, SCRUBBED AND
   COARSELY CHOPPED
2 LARGE CELERY STALKS, COARSELY
   CHOPPED
2 LARGE LEEKS, TRIMMED, WELL
   WASHED, AND COARSELY CHOPPED
1 LARGE TOMATO
2 MEDIUM YUKON GOLD POTATOES,
   SCRUBBED
1 SMALL TURNIP, SCRUBBED AND
   COARSELY CHOPPED
6 SCALLIONS, TRIMMED AND
   COARSELY CHOPPED
1 LARGE CLOVE OF GARLIC,
   UNPEELED
3 SPRIGS OF ITALIAN FLAT-LEAF
   PARSLEY
1 POUND (450 G) SWISS CHARD,
   TRIMMED, WELL-WASHED AND
   COARSELY CHOPPED
1 ZUCCHINI, TRIMMED, AND
   COARSELY CHOPPED
1 TEASPOON SEA SALT
8 BLACK PEPPERCORNS

1. Combine all the ingredients in a large stockpot. Add 5 quarts (5 liters) cold water and place the pot over medium heat. Simmer, uncovered, for 2 hours.

2. Allow the broth to cool. Strain the broth through a fine sieve, discard the solids, and cool completely. Refrigerate the broth for 4 to 5 days or store it in the freezer for up to 2 months.

MAKES 3 QUARTS/3 LITERS

Ceci Lessati
Cooked Chickpeas

1 POUND (450 G) DRIED CHICKPEAS
2 CLOVES OF GARLIC, UNPEELED
1 CELERY STALK, HALVED
2 TABLESPOONS (1 FL OZ/30 ML)
   EXTRA VIRGIN OLIVE OIL
SEA SALT

1. The night before cooking the chickpeas, place them in a large colander, toss, and remove any small stones. Rinse the chickpeas and transfer them to a large bowl. Fill the bowl with cold water to cover by 2 inches (5 cm) and soak overnight.

2. The following day, drain the chickpeas and transfer them to a large heavy pot. Fill the pot with cold water to cover the chickpeas by 2 inches (5 cm). Add the garlic, celery, olive oil, and a pinch of salt. Simmer, partially covered, for 1 to 2 hours, or until tender. Cooking time varies greatly, depending on the age and dryness of the chickpeas. Add salt to taste and simmer for 5 minutes more.

MAKES 1⅛ QUART /1⅛ LITER

Fagioli Stufati
Tuscan-style Cannellini Beans

The Tuscans, who have been tagged *mangiafagioli*, bean-eaters, often serve these hearty beans as a *contorno*, or side dish, with grilled, roasted, or stewed meat, poultry, and game. Pass a cruet of extra virgin olive oil to drizzle over the top. These beans can also be added to soups, used as the base for a bean salad, or transformed into *fagioli all'uccelleto* (page 88), cannellini beans cooked with tomatoes and sage.

1 POUND (450 G) DRIED
   CANNELLINI BEANS
2 CLOVES OF UNPEELED GARLIC
6 FRESH OR DRIED SAGE LEAVES
   OR ½ TEASPOON DRIED
   CRUSHED SAGE
¼ CUP (2 FL OZ/60 ML) EXTRA
   VIRGIN OLIVE OIL
1 THIN SLICE PANCETTA OR
   IMPORTED ITALIAN PROSCIUTTO
SEA SALT
10 WHOLE BLACK PEPPERCORNS

1. The night before cooking the beans, place them in a large colander, toss, and remove any small stones. Rinse the beans and transfer them to a large bowl. Fill the bowl with cold water to cover by 2 inches (5 cm) and soak overnight.

2. The following day, drain the beans and transfer them to a large heavy pot. Fill the pot with cold water to cover the beans by 2 inches (5 cm). Add the garlic, sage, olive oil, prosciutto, a pinch of salt, and the black peppercorns. Simmer, partially covered, for 1 to 2 hours, or until tender. Cooking time varies greatly, depending on the age and dryness of the beans. Add salt to taste and simmer for 5 minutes more.

MAKES 1⅛ QUART /1⅛ LITER

MAKING PASTA

Handmade fresh pasta is a delicacy worthy of holidays, special occasions, or whenever you want to eat well. The technique is not difficult—after all fresh pasta has been made at home for centuries—but it does require patience and practice. Organization is my best advice—have all of your ingredients and equipment ready before you begin. A large pastry board is helpful for making the dough, kneading, cutting, and rolling out, but a clean smooth counter will work as well. If your recipe calls for a manual pasta machine, I recommend only one brand, Imperia,

imported from Italy and available at Williams-Sonoma stores. You will need a fork, drum sieve or strainer, and a pastry scraper. A fluted pastry wheel for cutting the dough is required in only some of the recipes. Have several clean cotton kitchen towels handy and trays or baking sheets for drying the dough.

Before you begin, I would like to offer one more word of advice, be frugal with flour—pasta dough that is slightly moist and sticky can easily be remedied by kneading additional flour into the dough; over-floured dough will produce a less than satisfactory pasta.

Making the Dough

Mound the flour on a large wooden pastry board or work surface. Make a well in the center. Add the remaining ingredients to the well. Beat the ingredients in the well with a fork to blend thoroughly. Be careful not to let the well collapse. While stirring, gradually draw in flour from the inner rim of the well (see photo right) just until the mixture becomes very thick and unmanageable. Scrape the dough off the fork. Use your hands and a pastry scraper to gather the mixture together forming a very soft mass of dough. Gently knead the mass incorporating just enough flour to form a soft ball of dough. Flour the dough and set it aside. Use a pastry scraper to scrape up the flour and dough stuck to the board. Sift it through a drum sieve or strainer. Discard the small bits of dough left in the sieve. Reserve the sifted flour to further knead and stretch the dough. Whenever the board becomes encrusted with dough, scrape it up and resift. Dried bits blended into the dough can later cause it to tear.

Flour the board with some of the reserved flour. Knead the dough,

gradually incorporating flour, until it is firm but still slightly sticky. If the dough is to be kneaded and stretched through a manual pasta machine, flour the dough, wrap it in plastic wrap, and go to the section entitled Assembling a Manual Pasta Machine. If it is to be kneaded and stretched entirely by hand, follow the directions in the recipe.

Assembling a Manual Pasta Machine

Clamp the machine to a sturdy tabletop or countertop. Insert the handle into the slot on the side of

the machine. Set the rotating dial, which adjusts the position of the rollers, to the first setting. In this position, the rollers are widest apart. This setting is used for kneading the dough. Do not attach the cutting blades.

Kneading the Dough in a Pasta Machine

Divide the dough into smaller portions as indicated in the individual pasta recipes. Use 1 piece of dough at a time. Flour the unused portions and keep them tightly wrapped in plastic wrap until you are ready to use them. Flatten the dough, flour

it, and feed it through the rollers. After the dough has passed through the rollers the first time, flour only 1 side then fold it into thirds, like a business letter floured side out.

Flour lightly in order to control the amount of flour absorbed by the dough. Excess flour will result in a dough that is tough and dry. Using your fingertips or knuckles, press the dough to seal the layers (see photo center). Feed the dough into the machine, open end first. Repeat this procedure of flouring, folding, and feeding into the machine, 8 to 10 times, or until the dough is very smooth and no longer sticky.

Stretching the Dough in a Pasta Machine

Turn the dial to the next position to bring the rollers closer together. Lightly flour both sides of the dough. Do not fold. Pass the dough through the rollers only once. As the dough passes through the rollers it will be thinned and stretched (see photo bottom). Turn the dial to the next setting and repeat the procedure. Continue to thin and stretch the dough, turning the dial 1 setting at a time, until the desired thinness is reached as indicated in the recipe. Cut and dry the sheet of dough as instructed in the recipe. Knead and stretch the remaining pieces of dough in the same way.

TRAVEL RESOURCES

Al Buon Padre
Azienda Agricola Giovanni Viberti
Frazione Vergne-Via delle Viole, 2
12060 Barolo (CN) ITALY
Tel/Fax 0173/56192

La Luna e i Falò
Localita Aie 37
14053 Canelli (AT) ITALY
Tel 0141/831643

La Viranda
Localita Corte, 64
14050 San Marzano Oliveto (AT) ITALY
Tel 0141/856571
Fax 0141/75735

Borgo Spante
Localita Ospedaletto
05010 San Venanzo (TR) ITALY
Tel 075/8709134
Fax 075/8709201

Janet Hansen
c/o La Cucina Focolare
P. O. Box 54
Boulder, CO 80306 USA
800-988-2851

Fattoria di Montagliari
Via di Montagliari, 29
50020 Panzano in Chianti (FI) ITALY
Tel 055/852014
Tel./Fax 0173/56192

Hotel Relais La Suvera
53030 Pievescola di Casole d'Elsa (SI)
ITALY
Tel 0577/960300
Fax 0577/960220

Ristorante Baffo
Via Stelvio
23030 Chiuro (SO) ITALY
Tel 0342/482337

Cascina La Pomera
Frazione San Lorenzo
15049 Vignale Monferrato (AL) ITALY
Tel 0142/933378

Castello Il Corno
Via Malafrasca, 64
50026 San Casciano in Val di Pesa (FI)
ITALY
Tel 055/8248009
Fax 055/8248035

Dré Casté
Azienda Agricola il Mongetto
Via Piave 2
15049 Vignale Monferrato (AL) ITALY
Tel 0142/933442
Tel/Fax 0142/933469

Serra Gambetta
Azienda Agrituristica Serra Gambetta di
Domenico Lanera
Via per Conversano, 204
70013 Castellana-Grotte (BA) ITALY
Tel 080/4962181

Tenuta Seliano
Azienda Agrituristica Seliano
84063 Paestum (SA) ITALY
Tel 0828/723634
Fax 0828/724343

Hotel Santa Caterina
S.S.Amalfitana 9
84011 Amalfi (SA) ITALY
Tel 089/871012
Fax 089/770093

Eolo Ristorante
Via P. Comite, 3
84011 Amalfi (SA) ITALY
089/871241

MAIL ORDER SOURCES

The following suppliers are good sources for many of the products used in this book. The publisher and the authors of *The Four Seasons of Italian Cooking* are not responsible for the products sold by these companies, and it is not our intention to promote any of these purveyors.

Agata & Valentina
1505 First Avenue
New York, New York 10021
212-452-0690
Olive oils, vinegars, dry pastas, salt-packed anchovies, salted capers, San Marzano tomatoes, dried herbs from Greece, rice.

Balducci's Mail Order
42-26 12th Street
Long Island City, New York 11101
800-BALDUCCI
Web site: www.balducci.com
Olive oils, vinegars, dry pasta, polenta, cheese, cured meats, San Marzano tomatoes, honeys, rice, truffles.

Citarella
2135 Broadway or 1313 Third Avenue
New York, New York
800-588-0383
E-mail: Citarela@aol.com
Meat, fish, cured meats, cheeses, olive oils, salted capers, polenta, porcini mushrooms in olive oil, truffles, rice.

Kenyon Cornmeal Company
Usquepaugh, Rhode Island 02892
800-7-KENYON
Cornmeal for polenta, rye flour.

King Arthur Flour
P.O. Box 876
Norwich, Vermont 05055-0876
800-827-6836
All-purpose flour, stone-ground whole-wheat flour.

Marché aux Delices
120 Imlay Street
Brooklyn, New York 11231
888-547-5471
Web site: www.auxdelices.com
Wild and cultivated mushrooms, dried porcini mushrooms, truffles, sea salt, farro.

Phipps Country Store & Farm
P.O.Box 349
Pescadero, California 94060
800-279-0889
Dried beans, lentils, buckwheat flour.

Zingerman's Mail Order
422 Detroit Street
Ann Arbor, Michigan 48104
888-636-8162
E-mail: Zing@Chamber.Ann-Arbor.Mi.US
Olive oils, vinegars, sea salt, honeys, dry pasta, salted capers, rice, cheeses.

There were many who contributed generously throughout the development of this book. The authors wish to extend their sincere appreciation to Gisella Isidori, Larry Frascella, Michael Feldman, René Lavergneau, Nora Negron, and Janis Donnaud. We are also grateful for the advice provided by Charlie Balducci, Gino Roselli, René González, Sergio Stefani, Deborah Mintcheff, Margaret Happel, Giuseppe Grappolini, Angela Zambelli, Alán Hurtado, Linda Rivero, Doug Turshen, Betty Alfenito, Anne Disrude, Anna Teresa Callen, and Marya Dalrymple. Our deepest gratitude goes to Alessandra Mortola, Amy Lord, Jee Levin, Laura Smyth, and to Teresa Graham and the staff at Time-Life Custom Publishing. A special thank you to Gianluca Viberti for his knowledge and generosity.